# PROPHETIC
# & PUBLIC

# PROPHETIC & PUBLIC

## The Social Witness of U.S. Catholicism

Kristin E. Heyer

Georgetown University Press/Washington, D.C.

As of January 1, 2007, 13-digit ISBN numbers will replace the current 10-digit system.
Paperback: 978-1-58901-082-6

Georgetown University Press, Washington, D.C.

An earlier version of chapter 3 appeared as "Bridging the Divide in Contemporary
U.S. Catholic Social Ethics," in *Theological Studies* 66 June 2005: 401–40, and is used
by permission.


Library of Congress Cataloging-in-Publication Data

Heyer, Kristin E., 1974–
    Prophetic and public : the social witness of U.S. Catholicism / Kristin E. Heyer.
        p. cm. — (Moral traditions series)
    Includes bibliographical references and index.
ISBN-13: 978-1-58901-082-6 (pbk. : alk. paper)
    1. Christian sociology—Catholic Church. 2. Church and social problems—United
States. 3. Church and social problems—Catholic Church. I. Title. II. Series.
BX1753.H52 2006
261.8088'28273—dc22                         2005027235

This book is printed on acid-free paper meeting
the requirements of the American National Standard
for Permanence in Paper for Printed Library Materials.

13   12   11   10   09   08   07   06        9   8   7   6   5   4   3   2
First printing

Printed in the United States of America

For my parents,

Robert J. Heyer and Jean Marie Hiesberger

*To be both prophetic and public, a countersign to much of the culture, but also a light and leaven for all of it, is the delicate balance to which we are called.*

—Joseph Cardinal Bernardin

*Democracy serves what is true and right when it safeguards the dignity of every human person, when it respects inviolable and inalienable human rights, when it makes the common good the end and criterion regulating all public and social life.*

—Pope John Paul II

# Contents

# Acknowledgments

Although writing a book can be a solitary endeavor, I owe a debt of gratitude to many people for its completion. I am particularly grateful to David Hollenbach, S.J., Tom Massaro, S.J., and Mary Jo Bane for their valuable guidance of this project at its initial stage and for their own exemplary commitment to the active role of the church in the world. I am indebted to Lisa Sowle Cahill for her support throughout my doctoral work; her own method has informed my attempts to bring together divergent perspectives in this book. I am grateful for the conversations and debates with friends in graduate school at Boston College that have influenced my conclusions on Christian engagement here.

Thanks to my colleagues in the Department of Theological Studies at Loyola Marymount University for their friendship and willingness to help with valuable references and advice. I am grateful to my department chair, Jeff Siker, for encouraging the book's publication. Tom Rausch, S.J., and Jim Walter graciously read an earlier version of chapter 3 and provided insightful feedback. My ethics colleague and good friend Jon Rothchild served as a helpful sounding board along the way. Thanks to Jeremy Cruz and Brian Geremia for their assistance preparing the manuscript for publication and for our lively conversations about Christianity and politics.

Many thanks are due to Jim Keenan, S.J., and Richard Brown at Georgetown University Press for this opportunity to give my ideas a public voice. Jim has long welcomed junior scholars "into his peerage," and I very much appreciate his encouragement along the way. I am grateful for the comments of the press's two anonymous reviewers. An earlier version of chapter 3 appeared as "Bridging the Divide in Contemporary U.S. Catholic Social Ethics," *Theological Studies* 66 (June 2005): 401–40. I remain indebted to those whom I interviewed for this project for their candid and thoughtful reflections, as well as for their tireless work for justice and peace in our nation and world.

Special gratitude goes to my husband, Mark Potter, whose support, humor, and insights sustained me throughout every stage of this project. His lived witness to Christian solidarity and his passion for life remind me daily of what truly matters. The arrival of Owen Xavier provided a great deal of joy and perspective during the book's final stages. I dedicate this book to my parents, Robert Heyer and Jean Marie Hiesberger, who served as my first models of living out the Catholic faith. They gave me the foundations and courage to pursue this vocation, and their continued lives of dedicated, prophetic service to the church and world humble and inspire me.

# Abbreviations and Acronyms

| | |
|---|---|
| ACLU | American Civil Liberties Union |
| AFL-CIO | American Federation of Labor and Congress of Industrial Organizations |
| CAFTA | Central American Free Trade Agreement |
| CDF | Congregation for the Doctrine of Faith |
| FMLA | Family and Medical Leave Act |
| FTA | Free Trade Agreement |
| NAACP | National Association for the Advancement of Colored People |
| NCCB | National Council of Catholic Bishops |
| NCC | National Council of Churches |
| NCWC | National Catholic Welfare Council (1919–22) National Catholic Welfare Conference (1922–66) |
| NGO | nongovernmental organization |
| NOW | National Organization for Women |
| OGL | Office of Government Liaison (United States Conference of Catholic Bishops [USCCB]) |
| PAC | political action committee |
| PCUSA | Pax Christi USA |
| SDWP | Social Development and World Peace (Office of) |
| SMART | Sensible, Multilateral American Response to Terrorism |
| TANF | Temporary Assistance to Needy Families |
| USCC | United States Catholic Conference |
| USCCB | United States Conference of Catholic Bishops |
| WIC | Women, Infants and Children Nutrition Program |

# Introduction

In a nation founded on religious tolerance that has become one of the most religiously diverse and religiously observant liberal democracies in the world, it is no surprise that the proper relationship between religion and public life has remained an open question. An even longer history of debate surrounds church-society and church-world questions from a Christian perspective. From the early Christian communities onward, believers have struggled with what Jerusalem has to say to Athens, as well as how, when, and under what circumstances. Today the question remains no less relevant, and in the U.S. context it has taken on renewed urgency. Debate has arisen in recent years regarding the appropriate public role for religion in light of the reemergence of the Christian right as a political force in the 1990s and the charitable choice provisions of 1996 Welfare Law encouraging states to involve faith-based organizations as providers of government-funded support services to low-income families. President George W. Bush's "Faith-Based Initiative" raised concerns from all sides about the potential dangers of an expanded role for religion in public life. Most recently, the increasing prevalence of moral values as electoral and legislative considerations and explicit expressions of religiosity in politics have raised the stakes even further. From stem cell research to preemptive war to same-sex unions, many contemporary political issues reflect religious commitments. Now, more than ever, policies cast in theological language have global implications.

In the U.S. Catholic context in particular, these questions have taken on new relevance. For example, the clergy sexual abuse scandal that came to light in January 2003 raised doubts about the credibility of Catholic social advocacy. Many Americans inside and outside the church believed that the U.S. bishops should have turned their energies and resources toward internal reform rather than public policy work. Several bishops' threats to deny Communion to John Kerry and other Catholic politicians who support abortion rights gained widespread media attention during the 2004 presidential campaign. The sanctions generated extensive debate over the precise obligations of Catholic politicians and voters, the appropriate role of the church vis-à-vis politics, and the relative significance of different political issues with moral dimensions. On the one hand, in the contemporary U.S. context, some secularists remain unconvinced that most forms of public religion pose no threat to democratic values; on the other hand, many Christians remain ambivalent about whether and how religion should attempt to influence or contribute to the nation's public life.[1]

Many Americans remain nervous about public theology due to the perception that religion "belongs in the sacristy," or due to their apprehensions about the co-optation of Christian rhetoric for partisan ends. Nevertheless, religious imagery and language have been used authentically and to powerful effect in American public life, in some cases to unassailable ends by those who would restrict its use (Martin Luther King Jr. in the civil rights movement, for example). Religious claims have bolstered campaigns ranging across the ideological spectrum in recent U.S. history, from the Vietnam-era antiwar movement to the antiabortion crusade. Social scientific literature has documented vast and diverse forms of political participation by U.S. churches—which largely manage to respect democratic values—such as the activity of religious lobbying groups. This book aims to bring a normative perspective to what have heretofore been chiefly descriptive efforts to analyze Christian involvement in political life. By putting theological and ethical sources into conversation with the concrete practices of Catholic advocacy organizations, this study analyzes the appropriate possibilities for and limits to public religious engagement.

Public theology, broadly conceived, considers these questions of public morality and religiopolitical engagement. Public theology connects religious faith, concepts, and practices to their public relevance for wider society and culture. It entails efforts to specify the church's self-understanding and strategy as it confronts the contemporary world and its social questions. Although, in principle, public theology can be employed in any setting, in practice, its use has been confined primarily to the United States and its particular cultural and political characteristics.[2] This inclusive sense of public theology describes well the scope of this volume.[3]

Theology can go public in ways respectful of others' freedoms and in ways that preserve its particular identity amid a pluralistic democracy. Indeed, there exist a number of forms of public theology, at local to national to international levels; from the direct provision of human services to academic discourse on religious dimensions of public issues; from preaching to teaching; from taking countercultural stances on an individual or familial level to grassroots organizing. Thus, Roman Catholic political advocacy on the national level exhibits only one instance of taking theology public, but as a case study it provides useful examples of church members and leaders relating theological principles to social issues at the national level in attempts to directly influence policy and culture. The three organizations profiled here—the United States Conference of Catholic Bishops (USCCB), NETWORK Social Justice Lobby, and Pax Christi USA—do not comprehensively account for the full spectrum of Catholic advocacy, but they represent a range of constituencies and leadership models, and they exemplify the tensions exhibited in Catholic social ethics explored herein.[4] It was important to select explicitly Catholic advocacy groups rather than ecumenical lobbies or think tanks to adhere to this study's parameters, although the lobbies and think tanks claim significant Catholic membership and influence in the contemporary U.S. context. Finally, each of the organizations selected addresses a reasonable range of issues, and does not serve as a single-issue lobby. This is a significant characteristic for the sake of comparative analysis.[5]

Religious advocacy organizations that shed light on public theology in the U.S. context are, of course, not limited to those tied to the Roman Catholic Church. Nevertheless, I restricted the case studies to Catholic organizations, due to the ecclesial distinctiveness of the Catholic lobby. The ways in which Catholic groups approach public life are shaped significantly by the fact that theirs is uniquely a world church, a truly international institution. The Catholic Church has a tightly organized hierarchy with clearly defined official church teachings (yet with some degree of pluralism amid believers, certainly in the U.S. context). Social and political issues taken up by Catholic lobbyists generally tend to defy strictly partisan boundaries, often serving as a bridge between liberal Protestant and evangelical approaches to social issues, due, in part, to Catholic positions on poverty and welfare, on the one hand, and abortion and education policy on the other. Finally, Catholic lobbies benefit from institutional strength (hospitals, schools, charities, universities, the Church itself), and the Catholic tradition has a rich history of intellectually and socially engaging political issues. In his recent article, "What Is a Public Religion?" sociologist José Casanova calls post–Vatican II public Catholicism an exemplar of the type of public religion called for in contemporary U.S. society.[6] My hope is that the findings of this study will have worthwhile implications relevant beyond the U.S. Catholic context alone.

Ernst Troeltsch notes that the genius of the Catholic Church is the way it incorporates both church and sect types, co-opting the sectarian impulse into religious orders as a sect within the wider church.[7] Today, however, those embodying sect within the Catholic landscape are not limited to clergy or religious, but also include laity living in the world who believe that the mainstream church model is insufficiently countercultural or attentive to Gospel mandates. Within its broader aim of determining possibilities for and limits to Catholic public theology in the contemporary U.S. context, this book focuses on these two strands or types that persist within the Catholic landscape. In critically examining these more public and radicalist stances as represented by the contemporary work of J. Bryan Hehir and Michael Baxter, C.S.C., I attempt to move discussions of public theology beyond rigid typologies toward a more creative and dynamic tension between each model's distinct emphases, rather than the destructive tension that sometimes prevails.

In the course of bridging this methodological divide and more broadly exploring the normative contours of Catholic public theology, the book's first three chapters take up theoretical considerations of religiopolitical engagement. Chapter 1 addresses the permissibility of public religious engagement from a philosophical perspective, and then considers the promise that public theology holds for helping to improve public discourse, generate social capital, and build civic skills from a sociological perspective. From chapter 2 onward, I move into theological considerations of public theology and political advocacy from a Roman Catholic perspective. Chapter 2 demonstrates that insights from Vatican II, Catholic social teaching, and the work of Pope John Paul II have yielded a Catholic stance that is institutionally depoliticized, yet socially and politically active in service of protecting human life and dignity and pursuing the common good. That said, significant tensions persist within this overall social mandate, illustrating the complexities inherent in relating the fullness of the tradition to social and political problems between the times. I explore the tensions between different theological emphases and sources as well as those involved in relating religious vision to moral principles and policy orientations. These tensions come into even greater relief in chapter 3's analyses of two classic representations of different methodologies as represented Hehir and Baxter. In my comparative analysis of their approaches, I move beyond their mere coexistence and argue that proper discernment of context constitutes a particularly important practice for public theology, regardless of one's basic stance.

In chapter 4, my analysis turns to the concrete case studies of three U.S. Catholic advocacy groups—USCCB, NETWORK, and Pax Christi USA. In analyzing the various ways that the organizations' Catholic identities impact their social and political efforts, I show how these case studies present significant challenges to standard typological distinctions, underscoring the inadequacy of any one theoretical approach on its own. Chapter 5 explores the norms that result from the cumulative insights and liabilities of each model, endorsing a fully theological and fully public approach that actively engages the fullness of the tradition with the signs of the times. Moreover, the mutual clarification of theory by praxis reveals several directives in particular that should guide public theology and political advocacy: Catholic public engagement should both embody and advocate the values it advances. It should be dialogical and discerning in its method, in order to avoid distortion both from within and without. Finally, Catholic political engagement should be guided by a commitment to addressing a comprehensive range of social issues. In the end, I urge prophetic, critical engagement that models gospel values and engages the wider world on issues that touch human life and dignity.

Michael Himes and Kenneth Himes, whose approach reflects the fully theological and fully public approach for which the book's conclusions call, state well the imperative of our task at hand in their own volume on public theology:

> The Catholic Christian has always appreciated the vocation of those who go to the desert or the mountaintop, so long as their motive is love of the city. But the one who retreats from the cares and concerns of his brothers and sisters because those concerns seem a distraction from God simply does not know what the word "God" means in Christian discourse. And so we cannot abandon politics, in its classical meaning, the attempt to construct a society which makes the good life (however we may understand that) possible for human beings. We cannot attempt to become that strangely American oxymoron, a "private citizen."[8]

## NOTES

1. Jeffrey Stout's most recent book attempts to overcome this impasse between secular liberalism and theological traditionalism, arguing that democracy itself is a tradition that inculcates habits and virtues. Jeffrey Stout, *Democracy and Tradition* (Princeton, NJ: Princeton University Press, 2004).

2. In the U.S. context, the predominant themes of public theology discourse include "the role of religion in a democratic polity, the relationship of the Christian social vision to political liberalism, the status, function and strategic significance of church-sponsored social institutions in the modern welfare state, and the relationship of biblical and theological resources to the reality of a global capitalist economy" (J. Bryan Hehir, "Public Theology in Contemporary America: Editor's Forum," *Religion and American Culture* 10, no. 1 (Winter 2000): 1–27 at 20). For a comprehensive overview of the meaning(s) of public theology particularly compared with civil religion, political theology, public religion, and public philosophy, see E. Harold Breitenberg, Jr., "To Tell the Truth: Will the Real Public Theology Please Stand Up?" *Journal of the Society of Christian Ethics* 23, no. 2 (Fall/Winter 2003): 55–96.

3. It is in this broad sense of public theology that this study encompasses the approaches of J. Bryan Hehir and Michael Baxter, C.S.C., both of whom have raised different objections to a more narrow sense of public theology per se. Social ethics will be used in a similar way to this broad sense of public theology. More specifically, social ethics refers to "normative ethical reflection upon social structures,

processes, and communities," such as government, politics, and economic life. See Joseph L. Allen, "Social Ethics," in James F. Childress and John Macquarrie, eds., *The Westminster Dictionary of Christian Ethics* (Philadelphia: Westminster Press, 1986), 592–93 at 592. Furthermore, in a more specific sense than outlined above for the book's scope, the term public theology within the text refers to more theoretical efforts to discover and communicate the socially significant meanings of religious symbols, language, and traditions. See David Hollenbach, S.J., "Editor's Conclusion" in Hollenbach, ed., "Theology and Philosophy in Public," *Theological Studies* 40 (1979): 700–715 at 714.

4. In the interest of full disclosure, I was a member of NETWORK Social Justice Lobby before beginning the book's research, and am still a member. Membership entails sending money annually and receiving written materials and e-mail action alerts.

5. The case studies I have chosen are intended to be representative of such advocacy; they do not constitute an exhaustive survey. Certainly, direct service organizations such as Catholic Charities USA and institutional organizations such as the Catholic Health Association are engaged in implicit and explicit advocacy, as well.

6. Cf. José Casanova, "What Is a Public Religion?" in Hugh Heclo and Wilfred M. McClay, *Religion Returns to the Public Square: Faith and Policy in America* (Washington, D.C.: Woodrow Wilson Center Press, 2003), 111–40.

7. Ernst Troeltsch, *The Social Teaching of the Christian Churches*, 2 vols. (New York: Harper Torchbooks, 1960. Orig., 1912, first trans., 1931).Troeltsch describes the church type, on the one hand, as universal in its calling, responsible for collaborating with institutions of wider society, and able in some part to adjust itself to the world due to its endowment with objective grace and redemption. His sect type, on the other hand, constitutes a more stringent voluntary society that lives apart from the world and is less interested in collaboration with social institutions than in witnessing to a way of life in contrast to the wider society.

8. Michael J. Himes and Kenneth R. Himes, O.F.M., *Fullness of Faith: The Public Significance of Theology* (New York/Mahwah, NJ: Paulist Press, 1993), 186.

# CHAPTER ONE

# Public Theology in Contemporary U.S. Civil Society

Given the origins of the United States and the religious diversity that continues to characterize the nation, it is no surprise that the proper relationship between religion and public life in the United States has remained an open question. Despite evidence of the involvement of religion in public life and recent theological and sociological literature on public theology, many Americans oppose any attempts to integrate religion into the public square. Thus, the legitimacy of public theology, or the effort to discover and communicate the socially significant meanings of religious symbols, language, and traditions, is often called into question by believers and unbelievers.[1]

In their discomfort with public theology, some simply find it antithetical to the perceived tradition of complete separation between church and state, engendered by the oft-cited "wall of separation" metaphor.[2] Others perceive faith as an eminently private affair. To them the idea of public religious engagement is nonsensical. Still others point to how divisive and violent religiously motivated speech and action have been in history, often emphasizing the wars of religion in the sixteenth and seventeenth centuries as the very impetus to liberal democratic institutions and Enlightenment thinking. From a more religious perspective, many worry that public religious involvement risks diminishing religious purity or particularity. Finally, others throw the whole debate into question with antifoundationalist charges that we are unable to communicate beyond our particular communities even if we try, or that all talk of principles for guiding public discourse is merely political through and through, and will necessarily privilege some religions at the expense of others.

In the course of probing the possibilities for and limits to taking theology public in a pluralistic democracy, we begin with exploration of the legitimacy of public theology on nontheological grounds, engaging a variety of secular challenges to public religious engagement. A survey of the philosophical debate over the use of religious language in public discourse and sociological evidence regarding believers' participation in American public life suggests auspicious potential for religious engagement that respects democratic values and contributes to the public good.

## PHILOSOPHICAL PERSPECTIVES ON RELIGION AS A LEGITIMATE AND POSITIVE FORCE IN PUBLIC LIFE

In order to ascertain the legitimacy of public theology, we first must explore some of these prevalent misgivings, such as an opposition to public religious engagement arising out of particular interpretations of the First Amendment, the tradition of political liberalism, and postmodernism. We probe each of these objections below in the context of a range of philosophical perspectives on the relation of religion to public life in order to introduce the promise of public theology in contemporary U.S. society.

### The First Amendment and Public Theology

Many Americans' understanding of the relationship of religion to public life is influenced by the image of an impenetrable wall of separation between church and state. Such an attitude assumes that any form of public religious engagement necessarily transgresses that boundary and endangers tolerance of difference amid pluralism. While the institutional separation of church and state is a hallmark of American democracy, the First Amendment guarantees of free exercise and free speech protect religious participation in public life. In fact, the text of the First Amendment itself holds simply that religious institutions should encounter neither discrimination nor favoritism. The only element of separation at play applies strictly to the institutional aspects of religious bodies and the state.[3] Although church-state separation has often been understood more broadly as the separation of church and society, the state makes up only a limited part of society.[4]

The First Amendment's institutional differentiation and protection was "never intended to separate the church from wider society or religion from culture," however.[5] The challenge has been and continues to be to distinguish the religious and political spheres without conflating them on the one hand, or absolutely dividing them on the other.[6] For the purposes of theological engagement, the setting of public deliberation relevant here is more broad than the church-state sphere governed by the First Amendment.[7]

Nevertheless, modern liberal theory often conceives of the public arena in more narrow and institutional terms, leading to rules restricting public engagement. "By limiting the notion of public to policy decisions made within governmental institutions, modern liberal theory radically truncates the sphere of *res publica*, the sphere which in classical political theory refers to civil society as a whole." In reality, associational life is political and public, in the sense that it engages citizens' interests and issues of the polis, broadly conceived.[8] The wider civil society refers to a sense of public as contrasted to the state per se, and involves citizens reflecting and deliberating together on matters of common concern.[9] It is in this realm—the public arena more broadly conceived—that the public theology and political advocacy explored here take place.

Many have argued for the importance of civil society generally in fostering civic virtue in American society and around the globe.[10] Theologian David Hollenbach, S.J., summarizes the domain and function of civil society in this way: "Civil society is the more encompassing reality [than the state or market], composed of numerous communities of small or intermediate size such as families, neighborhoods, churches, labor unions, corporations, professional associations, credit unions, cooperatives, universities, and a host of other associations. Note that though these communities are not political in the sense of being part of the government, they are not private either. They are the social realities that form the rich fabric of the body politic."[11] In this manner, we can begin to see that public theology can appropriately participate on this civil societal level and contribute to the important task of civic deliberation about the public good. The First Amendment protects public theology as politics of persuasion, not coercion, and religious activity within the wider society need not infringe on church-state limits.[12] Finally, from a theological perspective, the First Amendment does not render the truth claims of a particular religion relative or meaningless; rather, it is political and therefore neutral on the proportionate value of religious doctrines. As Catholic theologian John Courtney Murray, S.J., puts it, the First Amendment's guarantees of free exercise and against establishment are "articles of peace, not articles of faith."[13] Such civil liberties do not compromise religious beliefs, therefore, and public theology need not compromise civil liberties.

## Persistent Concerns about Public Religion

Even given the proper differentiation between state and society, however, some Americans believe that, given the reality of religious pluralism in the United States, religious beliefs and arguments should remain private. Particularly in a society that prizes tolerance, such as the United States, many conceive of religion as a necessarily private affair that should not be imposed on others or that should not enter into political discourse. Others fear that religiously motivated speech and action are inherently coercive and divisive, if not potentially violent. For these reasons, bringing religious reasoning into public debate amid pluralism risks stirring up passion and endangering social stability.[14]

Since the seventeenth and eighteenth centuries, when the political tradition of liberalism developed in response to emergent moral and religious pluralism, and the institutions of liberal democracy developed in the wake of religious wars throughout Western Europe, the specter of religious divisiveness and violence often hovers over debates concerning public discourse, even centuries later. Certainly, the important advances in human rights and the juridical separation of church and state institutions remain important achievements of the liberal democratic tradition and offer preferable alternatives to violent intolerance. Yet, as many have pointed out, in our own day religious wars threaten Americans far less than a public discourse that is too eviscerated to address questions of the public good.[15] These reservations about the potentially divisive and violent nature of public religion or calls for religion's privatization amid pluralism lie at the heart of dominant philosophical positions on the proper role of religion in public life.

## Range of Philosophical Positions

Many Americans worry that religious traditions may advance a conception of the good life that other citizens do not share, and thus they favor the privatization of such conceptions of the good, exalt values of toleration and freedom, and propose that citizens only use rational, reasonable arguments in public debate. In contemporary American society, for the most part, the tradition of political liberalism continues to carry the day. Political liberalism assumes a multiplicity of goods in a society that is neutral among those goods, and therefore holds that a liberal political community must protect each individual's right to choose his or her good.[16] This position is often referred to as prioritizing the right to the good, because it holds that principles of justice that constrain an individual's pursuit of the good from infringing on another individual's pursuit of the good must be established.[17]

John Rawls famously portrays this dominant framework in his book, *Political Liberalism*.[18] In this influential work, Rawls examines whether and how religion and other comprehensive doctrines may be compatible with the basic institutions of a liberal democracy. He correctly identifies the deep disagreements about the good life among members of our society. In Rawls's view, these disputes mean that it is necessary to avoid basic questions about the comprehensive good of human life if we have any chance of achieving consensus. As Rawls asserts, "we simply apply the principle of tolerance to philosophy itself" when deliberating our political and economic institutions.[19]

During his career, however, Rawls somewhat shifted his stance on the use of religious argument in public discourse. He moved from bracketing and excluding religious arguments (or other arguments based on a comprehensive doctrine) from public discourse, to allowing their use as long as public reasons are also provided in due course. Rawls relies on the idea of public reason in his latest works, arguing that because politics relates to the public good, political arguments should be made in terms of public reason, or in terms accessible to all reasonable citizens. In this effort, he seeks to replace comprehensive doctrines about truth and goodness with the idea of the politically reasonable. He does so in an attempt to achieve overlapping consensus on basic questions of justice from adherents to different and conflicting comprehensive doctrines.

To this end, Rawls establishes rules for public discourse such as his proviso, which allows one to argue from within one's comprehensive doctrine (for our purposes, to engage religion in public) provided that in due course public reasons are added.[20]

Another feature of the family of (permissible) political conceptions is reciprocity, which sheds light on what Rawls means by public reason. Reciprocity is the limiting feature of a family of political conceptions of justice that constitute public reason. Political power is properly exercised only when we sincerely believe that the reasons we would offer for our political actions—were we to state them as government officials—are sufficient, and we also think that other citizens might reasonably accept our rationale. Although Rawls moves away from a liberalism that sharply contrasts and separates church and state, and his own concessions to Martin Luther King Jr. suggest a more inclusive public discourse than his other writings affirm, Rawls's works remain the standard for the politically liberal position that prioritizes the reasonable nature of public arguments.[21]

Many agree with Rawls that pluralism, democracy's principles of respect and toleration, and the historic separation of church and state in the United States all require that religious reasoning be excluded from public discourse. Others, however, call for the engagement of all voices, religious voices included, in public debate. They hold a more deliberative concept of respect whereby citizens respect one another's religious and moral convictions by engaging them, rather than by privatizing or bypassing them. This communitarian critique of political liberalism is advanced by Michael Sandel, among others, who summarizes the effects of political liberalism on religion in this way:

> In one respect, the liberal tradition seeks to secure for religion the most favorable conditions; given its emphasis on toleration and respect for conscience, liberal political theory promises the fullest religious liberty for each consistent with a similar liberty for all. In another respect, however, liberalism limits the reach of religion;

its insistence that government be neutral among competing moral and theological visions, that political authority be justified without reference to religious sanction, would seem to confine religion to private life and resist a public role.[22]

Sandel and others protest that it is not always reasonable to bracket religious claims, especially on grave moral issues. Sandel claims that the fact of reasonable pluralism that liberals take as their starting point also characterizes concepts of justice. He concludes that public reason's requirements are unduly restrictive, exclude significant aspects of public deliberation, and therefore impoverish public discourse.[23]

There coexist along a spectrum a number of philosophical positions on the proper role and scope of religious language and symbols in public discourse and political life, within and beyond these brief liberal and communitarian sketches. Kent Greenawalt has characterized the differences as exclusive and inclusive in his recent article about the proper role of religion in political debate.[24] He characterizes the overall debate as divided into two basic positions.

On the one hand, he states that there is an exclusive position held by those who challenge any introduction of religion into politics. Usually for reasons of fairness and political stability, adherents to this view assert that decisions in democracies should be based on democracy's shared premises and forms of public justification accessible to all citizens, religious or not. Similar to Rawls, exclusivists may deem religious beliefs and practices acceptable for individuals or religious communities, yet they insist that in lawmaking when "citizens are coerced, the state acts unfairly unless it has reasons that have force for all citizens. Religious reasons do not qualify."[25] Summarizing the stance of the exclusive position, Greenawalt writes that "people should refrain from making religious arguments because these arguments do not fit with how liberal democracies should work."[26]

One proponent of this "exclusive" position is Robert Audi. Audi holds that government should be neutral toward religion and that religion and politics should remain separate at both the church-state level and in the political conduct of individuals. He writes that civic virtue requires political activity to be bound by principles of secular rationale and secular motivation. That is, not only should citizens advocate laws or policies strictly in terms of publicly accessible secular reasons, but they also must be motivated primarily by these secular reasons, even if there are other available reasons for such a stance. He adds that religious ethicists should find common ground between secular and religious reasons—that is, that they should find theo-ethical equilibrium—and refrain from advocating positions that are not backed by secular reason. Audi does not find these requirements overly burdensome for believers; he asserts that Western theism entails belief in an omniscient, omnipotent, and omnibenevolent God, and therefore believers should be able to, and should, find secular equivalents to religious reasons.[27]

On the other hand, Greenawalt outlines what he terms an inclusive position. According to this view, rules regarding the type of reasoning that citizens may use (particularly those rules that exclude religious language) are unduly restrictive. Adherents to this position assert that both citizens and officials should be permitted to rely on any sources of understanding that they find most convincing and trustworthy, because it poses an undue burden to citizens to separate their political stances from their deepest sources of insight.[28] Proponents of this view believe that religious and other comprehensive doctrine-grounded reasons should be permitted in public, allowing citizens to use whatever reasons they find appropriate, because it is impossible to escape our more situated (religious) perspectives or to find such a thing as an adequate independent source, anyway. Furthermore, in many cases religious reasons or foundations are already operative, but remain implicit and unexamined. In this case, it is preferable to have them out in the open and debatable. As Martin Marty suggests, "a republic would be better off if everyone brought into the open whatever motivates and impels the citizens to decide and to act."[29] According to this view, offering our motives and rationales for our public contributions with integrity and without maneuvering to translate or filter will promote a more honest civil discourse and healthy democratic life.

Similar to many adherents to the communitarian stance outlined above, adherents to the inclusive position often deem the shared premises or overlapping consensus that others rely on to be insufficient for resolving many political issues. Rather than judging religious or other moral arguments as inaccessible and therefore unfair outright, this position holds that fairness demands we all rely on whatever we find most convincing and that only a "full airing of all those views will enrich everyone's understanding."[30] In a book coauthored with Audi, Nicholas Woltersdorff counters Audi's exclusive stance, insisting that government need only be impartial toward the plurality of religions, and that religion and politics should not be separated at either the institutional or individual level.[31] He believes that liberal epistemological constraints violate religious convictions and personal integrity (claiming that religious and sociopolitical existence are inseparable); infringe upon free exercise by trivializing religious convictions; and demean the particularity of believers' traditions and identities.[32] Inclusivists concede that not every ground will qualify, because some justifications (e.g., racism) may be contrary to liberal democracy's premises. Yet inclusivists oppose the view that religion is incompatible with underpinnings of the North American political order.[33] Nevertheless, as Mary Jo Bane persuasively claims, religiously based arguments are subject to debate once they are offered in the public square, and they are just as open to criticism as are their secular counterparts.[34] Thus there

exists a range of philosophical positions regarding the role of religion in public discourse that provide the context for the potential legitimacy of public
theology.

## Possibilities and Limits of Public Theology

Having explored the shape of the debate regarding public theological engagement, we turn now to an explication of how public theology can play a positive role in civil society in ways that are respectful of the differences that
characterize U.S. pluralism. Many inclusivists make a compelling case for permitting citizens to introduce untranslated religious arguments into public discourse in the realm of civil society, but some exclusivists' legitimate concerns
suggest that limits may restrict religious-based claims at the state or juridical
levels.[35] A hybrid of the strictly inclusive and exclusive approaches articulated
above, or an inclusive approach that accounts for some standards of engagement, emerges as most compelling. Only such a combination will adequately
attend to both the legitimacy and promise of religious engagement and the demands of life amid pluralist democracy.[36]

Although we have begun to explore some of the possibilities for public
theology at the civil societal level, it is also appropriate, given our pluralist,
democratic context, to circumscribe some limits to public theology and religious engagement. As we have already seen, the First Amendment imposes institutional limits on the interactions of church and state, and so our first limit
entails the restriction of such engagement to the civil societal level. Beyond
this, it is necessary to provide some guidelines for communicating across comprehensive doctrines in respectful and accessible ways in order to facilitate
interaction that engages our genuine differences.

For some, liberal conceptions of the reasonable need not be about secularization or exclusion, but rather about helping provide guidelines for genuine dialogue.[37] Audian rules of secular rationale and motivation unduly restrict the contributions of religious citizens. Without some effort to find
common terms of engagement, however, the genuine give-and-take of public
conversation cannot fruitfully ensue. Without any eventual effort to communicate in ways accessible to others of different backgrounds or worldviews,
discourse will devolve into chaos or tyranny—people talking at rather than
with one another. An inclusive public sphere serves best that allows both religious arguments and arguments that make efforts to be transtraditionally
accessible.[38]

Even inclusivists, who want to permit citizens to use whatever reasons
they find appropriate, acknowledge the need for restraints or virtues governing the manner of discussion. Many name civility, lawful conduct, and respect
for the freedom and equality of others, which entails genuine listening and a

willingness to change one's mind.[39] According to theologian Ronald Thiemann, "the important thing is not whether an argument appeals to a religious warrant; the issue is whether the warrant, religious or not, is compatible with the basic values of our constitutional democracy."[40] Thiemann appropriately opposes blanket threshold requirements for entrance into public discussion, and instead favors the cultivation of virtues of citizenship for all participants—believers and unbelievers alike. Among the guidelines or virtues Thiemann suggests are (1) public accessibility (encouraged, not demanded, intended to promote better mutual understanding); (2) mutual respect; and (3) moral integrity (including consistency of speech, consistency between speech, and integrity of principle).[41]

Thiemann also includes the right to dissent (both religiously and politically), referring to Michael Walzer's idea of the connected critic as an appropriate role for religious participants in political life: "Connected critics are those who are fully engaged in the very enterprise they criticize. Because they care so deeply about the values inherent in the democratic enterprise, their critique serves to call a community back to its better nature. . . . This dialectic between commitment and critique is the identifying feature that distinguishes acts of dissent that display genuine moral integrity from those that represent mere expediency or self-interest."[42] Thus, religious participation in public life, in ways that respect democratic values, need not imply full assent to particular political organizations or reigning policy positions of the day. These guidelines or virtues for discourse articulated by Thiemann serve well as our limits to public theological engagement amid an overall inclusivist approach.

One final set of virtues particularly relevant to religious contributions in public discourse entails an epistemological humility and openness appropriate to genuine exchange amid pluralism. It is important for religious voices to bear in mind the difference between the absolute nature of their horizon or the claims that their faith makes on them, and the relative nature of their understandings and expressions of the broader (public) implications of such claims. One of the most influential public theologians of the twentieth century, Reinhold Niebuhr, articulates the need for such virtues in any approach to solving the conflict between secular universalism and religious particularity. He calls for each group to "proclaim its highest insights while yet preserving a humble and contrite recognition of the fact that all actual expressions of religious faith are subject to historical contingency and relativity. Such a recognition creates a spirit of tolerance and makes any religious or cultural movement hesitant to claim official validity for its form of religion or to demand an official monopoly for its cult.[43]

Hollenbach has referred to the virtue required for sustaining public dialogue about the common good amid pluralism as intellectual solidarity. Here he preserves the importance of tolerance in a liberal democracy and moves beyond it to propose a form of engagement key to sustaining a viable public theology. As he puts it, intellectual solidarity entails "a willingness to take other persons seriously enough to engage them in conversation and debate about what they think makes life worth living, including what they think will make for the good of the polis . . . the spirit of solidarity is similar to tolerance in that it recognizes and respects differences [in beliefs and lifestyles]. It does not seek to eliminate pluralism through coercion. But it differs radically from pure tolerance by seeking not avoidance but positive engagement with the other through both listening and speaking . . . in an atmosphere of genuine freedom. . . . Where such a conversation about the good life begins and develops, a community of freedom begins to exist."[44] Hence, a public theology modeled on this concept of intellectual solidarity engages others toward better understandings and achievement of the public good in a spirit of humility and respect, without coercion.

Thiemann's standards of accessibility, respect, and integrity; the virtues of humility and openness; Walzer's concept of the connected critic; and Hollenbach's idea of intellectual solidarity together provide valuable guidelines for public theological engagement in the U.S. context. An inclusivist approach tempered by these virtues or standards of engagement most adequately accounts for the integrity of believer-citizens, the realities of pluralism, and the potential contributions of public theological engagement. Before we turn to an exploration of the ways in which such religious engagement can concretely serve the public good, one final challenge to public theology warrants mention: Postmodern challenges probe deeper than a mere exclusive position and raise objections to any standards of engagement, such as those outlined here.

## Postmodern Challenges

In one sense, postmodern critiques in recent decades have shown that even liberal rules that exclude religion in favor of secular discourse based on independent sources are tradition dependent and historically situated. It would appear that the postmodern lesson that one can never argue from foundations that are somehow above a specific context would support public theology: It seems unjust to prohibit such discourse because religious beliefs are tradition dependent. A radically historicist version of this critique, however, underscores the imperative of relegating religion to private life and the impossibility of making any common comprehensive claims about the common or public good. Richard Rorty's philosophical position on this matter illustrates lines of critique that surpass even strictly exclusivist claims and show how deep runs the radically historicist challenge.

Philosophers such as Rorty question whether any foundations exist across communities.[45] In Rorty's view, morality is simply "what we do" and immorality is "what we do not do."[46] From his perspective, appeals to morality are simply appeals to a sense of identity that is shared with others who make up the "we" of a particular community; it has no other basis. As he writes, "ideas like religious freedom and tolerance are affirmed by those of us who are heirs of the Western tradition of constitutional democracy simply because this tradition has made us the kind of people who in fact affirm such things."[47]

Rorty refers to this as the priority of democracy to philosophy, because this tradition of democracy is more important than are philosophical or theological disputes about human nature and morality to heirs of the Enlightenment in the West.[48] Hence, according to this view, deliberation about such questions should remain private, helping make all people more pragmatic and liberal. Going beyond a Rawlsian position that holds that for the sake of respecting pluralism of comprehensive views we relegate or translate such views, Rorty doubts their reference to any objective reality and privatizes them to advance the liberalness and pragmatism of citizens generally (because, in his view, such comprehensive questions and answers are a bit arbitrary).[49] We begin to see how radical historicism poses a challenge to public theology.

Similar to Rorty, some philosophers and postliberal theologians assume that the particular, contextual origin of norms or practices or beliefs requires that they also remain local in application and private in meaning.[50] Others, such as Catholic theologian David Tracy, take a different course beyond radically historicist challenges by "shift[ing] the major focus of the debate from 'origins' to 'effects.'"[51] Tracy seeks ways to bridge the divide between the particular origins of (religiously grounded) claims and the universal implications of (religious) arguments about the human person or human good through his models of the classic and conversation. According to Tracy, particularism may actually help attempts to use religious resources such as biblical symbols amid postmodern challenges to public dialogue.[52] The classic texts and symbols of religious traditions evoke the fundamental issues and limit questions that every human confronts in his or her life.[53] In his view, amid a pluralism of particular religious and philosophical commitments, there exist experiences we share as humans. Tracy argues that religious symbols have disclosing and transforming power in the public realm, even for those outside the particular source's belief system (e.g., as evidenced by the phenomenon of "atheists for Niebuhr"). As such, theological language and religious symbols are more universally accessible than the rules against their public use imply, and they disclose meaning in a manner not reducible to the structure of argument.

It follows, then, that not all philosophers and theologians are convinced that the radically historicist challenge thoroughly undermines efforts to engage religious traditions in dialogue about the public good. For some, in fact, postmodern historicism demonstrates that rules purporting to be neutral that prohibit religion from the public square no longer hold water. In Thiemann's view, "the point is that we cannot by philosophical or political fiat decide in advance which arguments we will accept in the public square. Rather, we must learn to understand and evaluate all arguments that seek a public hearing."[54] His view is postmodern in its attention to the impossibility of ahistorical, deductive rationality but more optimistic about the possibilities for an inclusive public conversation that may achieve results. In response to Rorty's suggestion that we make it seem bad taste to bring religion into public policy discussions by privatizing religion, Michael Perry recommends we instead "make it seem bad taste to sneer when people bring their religious convictions to bear in public discussions of controversial moral/political issues."[55] Such postmodern critiques—along with related objections that any standards for public discourse will inevitably be "political all the way down" or will unduly burden more orthodox approaches that remain more suspicious of reason or natural law—relate to broader theological questions of the relationship of reason to revelation and nature to grace.[56] It is important to note that within the Roman Catholic tradition, reason and revelation are generally considered complementary, not contradictory. Yet, as we shall see, Michael Baxter's theological stance reflects comparable concerns about the inherent bias of standards for discourse and the inability of rule-based engagement to adequately challenge the dominant paradigm.

Having explored the legitimacy and promise of public theology on the civil societal level, we now turn to evidence that, rather than serving as a threat to democratic values, public religion may serve the common good in positive ways. At its best, public theology involves religious engagement in articulating and achieving the public good, not simply jockeying to promote each denomination's own private interests.[57]

## SOCIOLOGICAL PERSPECTIVES ON RELIGION AS A LEGITIMATE AND POSITIVE FORCE IN PUBLIC LIFE

Theologian Robin Lovin notes that theories such as those that seek to eliminate religious influence from public discourse are curiously abstract and do not accurately characterize the actual role that faith plays in many citizens' lives. In the real world beyond the domain of academic theorizing, citizens regularly engage their understandings in public of the good life and right action—including religious understandings.[58] This book's overall task entails putting theories such as those we have just examined—and, for the most part, theological theories—into conversation with how religion actually plays out in public life and how believers participate in that life. Martin Marty suggests several potential public roles for religion in a democracy, maintaining, like Lovin, that religion is already active in the public arena. Marty lists the following roles among the civic roles that public theology can perform: providing discourse with needed resources (themes of prophecy and religiously based social critique, in particular); helping diminish political fanaticisms (by appeals to an absolute and transcendent loyalty); combating apathy; providing a voice for the voiceless; and providing stamina for enduring societal crises.[59] Believers can draw upon overlooked resources in a place where secular rationality reigns.

### Revitalization of American Public Discourse

In recent decades, secular and religious thinkers alike have bemoaned the state of public discourse in the United States and called for a revitalization of civil society. Some have characterized the current atmosphere as one entrenched in culture wars.[60] Others counter that Americans, in fact, do agree on much and that they, above all, tolerate others' views about questions of value.[61] Still others retort that mere tolerance is insufficient for the types of genuine engagement today's problems demand.[62] Concerns about incommensurability in public discourse and the insufficiency of tolerance as the chief public virtue point to a common problem of the lack of common resources—symbols, language, values—that extend beyond the rationalistic criteria of political liberalism and with which Americans can address issues of public policy and concern. Public theology and religiopolitical engagement are well poised to help enlarge and enrich public discourse about the common good.

Because of exclusivist efforts to safeguard accessible discourse, many argue that secular public discourse has become "chaste, sober, and thin," lacking the ability to "stir human hearts and minds to sacrifice, service, and deep love of the community."[63] Many in the United States largely agree to disagree, and deal with pluralism by privatizing questions of the good. The integration of theological resources holds promise for helping to foster the robust public deliberation necessary to test competing conceptions of the good. Public theology can provide resources for evoking the loyalties and imagination required for the genuine consideration of public mission, policies, and identity crucial to addressing the questions posed by advancing technology, globalization, and unprecedented economic growth.

Public religious engagement can complement this dominant political liberalism that has contributed to the nakedness of the American public forum, serving as an important antidote to the country's presently impoverished discourse. In *Habits of the Heart*, Robert Bellah and his colleagues lament the enervated nature of American public discourse due, in their view, to its confinement to only one of the nation's three moral traditions. They find that the legacy of individualism is alive and well in the public square, but that the other two moral languages—civic republicanism and biblical religion—retain little influence.[64] The legacy for the United States of the eighteenth century American Enlightenment consists of the dominance of interest and utility rather than of the freedom within the context of interdependence and community.[65] Broadly understood, with the rising criticism of utilitarianism (beginning in the late eighteenth century and more forcefully in the nineteenth and twentieth centuries), freedom was defined as freedom to pursue self-interest unencumbered. Furthermore, interest came to dominate as the chief category for the analysis and evaluation of human motives, to the point where it replaced virtue and conscience in the nation's moral vocabulary.

Lovin contrasts the contract model of the Enlightenment to the covenant theology of the nation's founders, and he calls for a retrieval of the covenant context and the emphases to reform the dominant Enlightenment legacies. He notes that a theological understanding of our human interconnectedness that yields moral obligations and a sense of the common good can counter the prevailing sense that we are thrown together at random or by choice, without any sense of mutual obligation or shared good.[66] Lovin writes, "A view of public life that begins with an understanding of human nature informed by religious traditions would thus recapture much of the sense of mutual accountability and commitment to a common project that characterized the ideal of a covenant society in Puritanism. . . . For a public covenant exists to the extent that people in discussion measure the goals and performances of public policy against a normative idea of human nature and to the extent that they hold themselves open and accountable to the same scrutiny."[67]

In line with this articulation, Marty maintains that religious themes such as "community, tradition, memory, intuition, affection, and hope" can complement the resources of secular rationality.[68] As Bellah and Lovin suggest, therefore, theological resources can serve to complement the prevailing American ethos by balancing conceptions of freedom as unfettered self-assertion with conceptions of freedom as conditional and achieved in community.

According to Lovin, "a public theology that builds on the moral aspiration for a covenanted community clearly does not seek to impose alien or sectarian norms on our national life."[69] Rather, as theologians Michael Himes and Kenneth Himes put it, "public theology makes clear the theological foundations of much of our constitutional system."[70] Moreover, as noted, public theology must be advanced in a charitable and humble manner—because religious contributions may be as contingent and relative as philosophical or empirical ones, given human finitude and sin.

Accordingly, a model of public discourse inclusive of theological contributions holds promise for enlivening the impoverished civil discourse in the United States. Inclusion of theology in the public forum helps to enable the public deliberation necessary to test competing conceptions of the good and better respect the fact of reasonable pluralism than does a restriction to reasonable language or public philosophy.[71] Such integration of *both* theologically explicit language and symbols in public debate *and* philosophical or empirical arguments will help to ensure that public theology is thick enough to evoke the loyalties, imagination, and other resources required to address the contemporary American cultural inadequacies (e.g., lack of community, identity, purpose) but also retains resources to address public issues amid pluralism in accessible ways when it is necessary or prudent to do so. Such dialogue must be marked not only by fully theological entry and engagement, but also by the virtues of tolerance and humility, given the fact of pluralism. Efforts to use public theology to enlarge and invigorate public discourse may explicitly draw on particular symbols and rituals while remaining modest and open to genuine dialogue. Thus, "public theology becomes truly public when it becomes also civil discourse."[72]

## Social Capital and Civic Skills

In recent years, scholars have repeatedly asserted that the renewal of civil society and an increase in social capital are indispensable for reconnecting individuals and revitalizing our society.[73] Robert Putnam describes social capital as the value conferred by social networks, asserting "social contacts affect the productivity of individuals and groups" in ways analogous to physical or human capital. He asserts that social capital highlights the fact that dense networks of reciprocal social relations strengthen civic virtues.[74] He has named churches as important loci for generating such capital, and has argued that even the economic health of communities "may depend on underlying social networks of friends, cooperators and neighbors who espouse and embody reciprocity, trust, solidarity, and engagement."[75]

Two-thirds of all small groups in the United States are directly connected with churches and synagogues or meet in their spaces, and two-thirds of those active in U.S. social movements claim that their involvement is religiously motivated.[76] In his national study of student volunteers in the United States, sociologist Robert Wuthnow concludes that "churches and synagogues remain the primary place where instruction is given about the spiritual dimension of caring."[77] Several recent studies have shown that the social capital that religious institutions generate can increase the civic involvement and democratic potential in American society.[78] For example, a 2001 survey completed by the

John F. Kennedy School of Government at Harvard University, the "Social Capital Community Benchmark Survey," confirms that religiously active persons are more likely than persons who are not religiously active to vote, give blood, be active in their communities, know and trust other people, be perceived as good citizens, and have a more diverse group of friends.[79] Sociologist John Coleman, S.J., confirms that "the sociological evidence linking religion to social capital seems overwhelming."[80]

The findings of Sidney Verba, Kay Lehman Schlozman, and Henry Brady in their sociological study, *Voice and Equality: Civic Voluntarism in American Politics*, point to the significant role that religious institutions play in facilitating political participation in the United States.[81] They find that churches outperform their two main competitors, the workplace and nonpolitical civic associations, in providing social capital and civic skills and in providing transferable civic skills to the more disenfranchised.[82] Verba and his colleagues name several factors that influence political involvement: the motivation and the capacity to become politically active, and access to networks of recruitment through which requests for political activity are mediated.[83] Their study found churches and synagogues to be important sites for the cultivation of each of these factors, providing not only religious motivation and encouragement for civil involvement, but also the skills and networks otherwise unavailable to some. Other arenas such as the workplace and nonpolitical civic groups tend to reward only those who already possess human capital (generally those in the middle class or above).[84] Verba, Schlozman, and Brady conclude, "[Religious institutions] play an unusual role in the American participatory system by providing opportunities for the development of civic skills to those who would otherwise be resource-poor."[85]

Their study finds that the opportunities for developing civic skills—such as organizational and communication skills—are available on a more equal basis by way of church membership than by way of family ties, occupation, or socioeconomic status. Among the authors' conclusions is the idea that "the domain of equal access to opportunities to learn civic skills is the church."[86] Coleman suggests that the findings in the study by Verba and his colleagues indicate that even secularists might prefer a more public role for religion based on the secular goods churches provide: "greater volunteering; greater contributions to public civic organizations and charities; greater voting behavior."[87] Certainly, this study shows how churches help provide concrete civic skills— even beyond the more readily apparent motivations for civil involvement that religious communities might offer—particularly to those who would be otherwise less enfranchised.

Coleman finds it unsurprising that churches are significant sites for developing social capital: "Few other organizations so think of themselves explicitly as communities. Few so insistently raise up norms of reciprocity—

'neighbor love and care.' It is almost the expected *ethos* of a church that it will have wider outreach to the needy."[88] Studies show, however, that it is membership in religious communities that generates social capital and predicts civic engagement, rather than simply any individual's spirituality in and of itself, cut off from a church or congregation.[89] Whether they are particular congregations or parachurch organizations, these religious groups provide the communal context for facilitating such civic skills. Coleman has been conducting a study of various parachurch outreach organizations that are independent from particular denominations and congregations (e.g., Habitat for Humanity, Bread for the World) and some paracongregational organizations (e.g., Salvation Army and Catholic Charities USA). His initial findings show that such special purpose religious groups further develop the social capital originally fostered in participants by their particular congregations. Such service agencies and community organizing groups are able to build on that original social capital and multiply it into larger entities that cut across race, class, and geography to advance civic goals, such as building low-income housing, securing greater neighborhood police protection, and reducing classroom size in schools.[90]

Coleman has found that participants in such groups closely connect (if not conflate) their sense of discipleship and citizenship.[91] He writes, "At best, religious social capital remains a potent source to join up with other civic organizations' social thrust for the renewal of an American sense of mutual trust, community, and solidarity."[92] Hence, religious congregations as well as parachurch organizations can serve to generate, invest, multiply and spend social capital. Although raising awareness and encouraging political activism are certainly not the primary aims of religious communities, the motivation and skills they provide in these more civic areas point to the revitalizing effects religion can have on public life. The case studies of Catholic political advocacy organizations in chapter 4 will shed further light on the links between religion and civic participation.

We have now begun to establish not only the legitimacy of public theology in a liberal democracy, but also its actual and potential contributions to renewing public discourse and improving the overall health of our democracy. As Perry puts it, "Given the influential role that some religiously grounded moral beliefs play in our politics, it is important that we test such beliefs in public political argument. Moreover, our political culture cannot be truly deliberative unless we let ourselves be tested by religiously grounded moral beliefs. It is important, therefore, that we 'public-ize' religion, not privatize it."[93] If, in fact, religion already contributes to public life both in cultivating civic skills and social capital and in more direct ways that we shall explore, it is even more urgent that we foster an inclusive public discourse with religious reasons and motivations freely voiced.

## NOTES

1. See David Hollenbach, S.J., "Editor's Conclusion," in Hollenbach, ed., "Theology and Philosophy in Public," *Theological Studies* 40 (1979): 700–715 at 714.

2. The "wall of separation" phrase traces back to letters written by Roger Williams (1635) and then Thomas Jefferson (1802). The phrase became more common constitutional parlance, however, through Justice Hugo Black's decision in 1947 (Hugo Black, *Everson v. Board of Education of the Township of Ewing et al.*, U.S. 330, 15, 16). See Ronald F. Thiemann, *Religion in Public Life: A Dilemma for Democracy* (Washington, DC: Georgetown University Press, 1996) 42, 67, for the text and citations for all three references.

3. Richard McBrien, *Caesar's Coin: Religion and Politics in America* (New York: Macmillan Publishing Co., 1987), 39.

4. Ibid., 42.

5. Joseph Cardinal Bernardin, "Religion and Politics: The Future Agenda," *Origins* 14 no. 21 (November 8, 1984), 321–28 at 323.

6. McBrien, *Caesar's Coin*, 39.

7. Michael J. Himes and Kenneth R. Himes, O.F.M., *Fullness of Faith: The Public Significance of Theology* (Mahwah, NJ: Paulist Press, 1993), 19.

8. Thiemann, *Religion in Public Life*, 152.

9. Robert N. Bellah, Richard Madsen, William M. Sullivan, Ann Swidler, Stephen M. Tipton, *The Good Society* (New York: Knopf, 1991), 179.

10. See, for example, Alan Wolfe, *Whose Keeper? Social Science and Moral Obligation* (Berkeley and Los Angeles: University of California Press, 1989), on the need for civil society to complete the project of modernity to counterbalance forces of the state and the market. See David Hollenbach, S.J., "The Contexts of the Political Role of Religion: Civil Society and Culture," 30 *The University of San Diego Law Review* (Fall 1993): 877–901, on the potential role for religious communities in civil societies in the U.S. and the Eastern and Central Europe contexts. See also recent work in this area by Robert D. Putnam: Putnam, *Bowling Alone: The Collapse and Revival of American Community* (New York: Simon & Schuster, 2000); and Putnam with Robert Leonardi, and Raffaella Y. Nanetti, *Making Democracy Work: Civic Traditions in Modern Italy* (Princeton, NJ: Princeton University Press, 1993).

11. David Hollenbach, S.J., "Civil Society: Beyond the Public-Private Dichotomy," *The Responsive Community* 5, no. 1 (Winter 1994–95): 15–23 at 19.

12. Himes and Himes, *Fullness of Faith*, 19–20.

13. John Courtney Murray, S.J., *We Hold These Truths: Catholic Reflections on the American Proposition* (Kansas City, MO: Sheed & Ward, 1960, 1988) 56. Murray made significant contributions to the Catholic Church's own understanding and acceptance of this differentiation between state and society in his writings on religious liberty that contributed to the Second Vatican Council document, *Dignitatis humanae*. We shall return to theological perspectives on public engagement in chapter 2.

14. Robert Audi and Nicholas Woltersdorff, *Religion in the Public Square: The Place of Religious Convictions in Political Debate* (Lanham, MD: Rowman & Littlefield Publishers, Inc., 1997), 78.

15. I would argue that this generalization holds, even post–September 11th. Although the world may face violent threats and unrest related to intractable religious differences or religious mandates, within the United States the threat is not one abetted by open discussion of religious and moral positions at the very least. For an examination of the role of religion in deadly conflict and religious actors in peace building and reconciliation efforts, see R. Scott Appleby, *The Ambivalence of the Sacred: Religion, Violence and Reconciliation* (Lanham, MD: Rowman & Littlefield Publishers, Inc., 2000).

16. The presumed secular nature of U.S. culture is shifting somewhat, with the increasing use of explicitly Christian language and imagery by Evangelical Protestants in elected office and the wider public square. It remains to be seen how this shift will affect standard philosophical assumptions and long-term practices regarding religion and public discourse.

17. Michael Sandel, "Freedom of Conscience or Freedom of Choice?," in Terry Eastland, ed., *Religious Liberty in the Supreme Court: The Cases that Define the Debate over Church and State*, published in conjunction with the Ethics and Public Policy Center, Washington, D.C. (Grand Rapids, MI: William B. Eerdmans, 1993), 483–96 at 484. Sandel's article originally appeared in James Davison Hunter and Os Guinness, eds., *Articles of Faith, Articles of Peace* (Washington, D.C.: Brookings Institute, 1990), 74–92. Significantly, Rawls notes that the principles themselves should not refer to any one conception of the good life.

18. John Rawls, *Political Liberalism* (New York: Columbia University Press, 1993).

19. John Rawls, "The Idea of an Overlapping Consensus," 7 *Oxford Journal of Legal Studies* (1987): 1–25 at 13.

20. The implications of Rawlsian rules such as the proviso turn on one's interpretation of its "in due course" clause, however. On a narrow interpretation of in due course—that one must give properly public reasons in order to be taken seriously in political discussion—Rawls remains open to communitarian critiques that his ideal of public reason remains too thin to make politics work (we shall examine such critiques below). Evidence also exists, however, for a more broad interpretation of "in due course"—that citizens give public reasons in political discourse only at the point at which votes are cast or judicial decisions are made—in which case Rawls approaches a more inclusive vision of political discourse. If people must introduce public reasons in order to be taken at all seriously in any political activity, the rule is unduly restrictive. On a more narrow interpretation that would require the introduction of public reasons only at points of political transactions, however, the rules would not affect the background culture of civil society and would simply indicate a way of introducing accessible means for determining matters with coercive effects (laws). Some language shifts in "The Idea of Public Reason Revisited" from a focus on ideals of science and common sense to those of civility and reciprocity imply that the more narrow interpretation is plausible.

21. See Ian S. Maclean, "Religion in American Politics: Liberalism and Religion in Question," *Religious Studies Review* 28, no. 1 (January 2002): 33–39 at 33. The writings and speeches of Martin Luther King Jr. have remained a sticking point for Rawls. Rawls allows King's use of religious arguments because the outcome of the movement he headed—the increase of political justice—was an improved one

for public reason. But this is problematic, because Rawls makes an exception to his criteria retrospectively and in an outcome-based manner. See Rawls, *Political Liberalism*, 250–51.

22. Sandel, "Freedom of Conscience or Freedom of Choice?" 483.

23. Sandel, "A Response to Rawls' Political Liberalism," in Sandel, *Liberalism and the Limits of Justice*, 2nd ed., (Cambridge: Cambridge University Press, 1988), 184–218.

24. Kent Greenawalt, "Religion and American Political Judgments," 36 *Wake Forest Law Review* 219 (Summer 2001): 401–22 at 404.

25. Ibid., 405.

26. Ibid., 406.

27. Audi and Woltersdorff, *Religion in the Public Square*, 9–37.

28. Greenawalt, "Religion and American Political Judgments," 406.

29. Martin Marty, *Politics, Religion and the Common Good: Advancing a Distinctly American Conversation about Religion's Role in Our Shared Life*, (San Francisco: Jossey-Bass Publishers, 2000), 47.

30. Ibid., 406–7.

31. Audi and Woltersdorff, *Religion in the Public Square*.

32. Ibid., 77, 105.

33. Greenawalt, "Religion and American Political Judgments," 407.

34. Mary Jo Bane, Professor of Public Policy and Management, Kennedy School of Government, Harvard University (and former assistant secretary of U.S. Health and Human Services), speaking on the role of religious organizations in the welfare reauthorization debates of 1996. Plenary address, Annual Meeting of the Society of Christian Ethics, Chicago, IL (January 5, 2001). Bane adds that there exists no real threat of any one religion dominating the debate in the contemporary U.S. context.

35. Nevertheless, such religious involvement may have secondary effects that reach beyond society in the symbiosis that occurs between background culture and the state apparati. Rawls insists that his idea of public reason applies only to debates of political questions in the public political forum (discourses of judges, top government officials, and candidates), not to the background culture that may have full open discussion. Hollenbach argues that background culture is also properly public, and that Rawls overlooks the symbiosis between the two. See David Hollenbach, S.J., "Public Reason/Private Religion? A Response to Paul J. Weithman," *Journal of Religious Ethics* 22 (Spring 1994): 39–46 at 45. I agree with Hollenbach that there exists such a symbiosis, and that by permitting religious argument in this background culture—whether it is called civil society, public, political, or nonpublic—the effects will filter up to the more (appropriately) restricted areas of judicial decision making or transactions on the Senate floor. As Michael Perry puts it, "It is quixotic, in any event, to attempt to construct an airtight barrier between religiously grounded moral discourse in public culture—which discourse is not merely legitimate but important—and such discourse in public political argument." See Perry, "Why Political Reliance on Religiously Grounded Morality is not Illegitimate in a Liberal Democracy," 36 *Wake Forest Law Review* (Summer 2001): 217–51 at 240–41.

36. It is also appropriate to consider the permissibility of religious engagement in public life in terms of a spectrum, making some distinctions among the

appropriate behavior of judges, legislators, and citizens. With Greenawalt, I would hold that judges and legislators should give greater weight to reasons that are generally accessible than to reasons that are generally less available. Nevertheless, "some reliance on religious reasons is appropriate, especially since the generally available reasons are radically indecisive about some crucial social problems." Citizens, on the other hand, "should regard themselves as free to connect religious convictions to political positions." Greenawalt adds that religious leaders entangled with partisan politics "risk alienating those with opposed religious views, polarizing politics on religious grounds, and making religion too political." See Greenawalt, "Religion and American Political Judgments," 411, 413. For example, the teaching of the U.S. bishops that nonviolence is an option for individuals but states have the right, in fact an obligation, to defend their citizens, by force if necessary, illustrates these important distinctions.

37. It is debatable whether exclusivist liberals such as Rawls conceive of the term *reasonable* in this more dialogical or accessible sense rather than in a rationalistic sense. In adapting his position following the publication of *A Theory of Justice*, Rawls's rules of public reason become less about favoring secularism and making public life rationalistic than about ensuring accessible reasoning regarding matters of basic justice that affect all, regardless of comprehensive doctrine.

38. I shall similarly advocate the inclusion of both theological contributions and natural law or philosophical mediations of theological values and principles in chapter 5.

39. See, for example, Audi and Woltersdorff, *Religion in the Public Square*, 112–13.

40. Thiemann, *Religion in Public Life*, 156. In proposing such norms or virtues for inclusive public engagement, Thiemann relies on the least objectionable threshold requirements proposed by Amy Gutmann and Dennis Thompson in their article, "Moral Conflict and Political Consensus," in R. Bruce Douglass, Gerald M. Mara, and Henry S. Richardson, eds., *Liberalism and the Good*, (New York and London: Routledge, 1992), 125–47.

41. Here Thiemann suggests that "self-critical communities seeking to forge some sense of common aims and purposes from the diverse interests of their citizens . . . will inevitably assign high value to the broad accessibility of public arguments" understood as "arguments whose premises are open to public examination and scrutiny." See Thiemann, *Religion in Public Life*, 135–38; Gutmann and Thompson, "Moral Conflict and Political Consensus," 134–47.

42. Thiemann, *Religion in Public Life*, 140. Michael Walzer develops his notion of the connected critic in his *Interpretation and Social Criticism* (Cambridge: Harvard University Press, 1987); and *The Company of Critics: Social Criticism and Political Commitment in the Twentieth Century* (New York: Basic Books, 1988).

43. Reinhold Niebuhr, *Children of Light and Children of Darkness* (New York: Charles Scribner's Sons, 1944), 134–35, 138.

44. Hollenbach, "Contexts of the Political Role of Religion," 892. For more on Hollenbach's intellectual solidarity, see his "Afterword, a Community of Freedom," in R. Bruce Douglass and Hollenbach, *Catholicism and Liberalism* (Cambridge: Cambridge University Press, 1994); "Is Tolerance Enough? The Catholic University and the Common Good," in *Conversations on Jesuit Higher Education* 13 (Spring 1998): 5–15; and *The Common Good and Christian Ethics* (Cambridge: Cambridge University Press, 2002).

45. Richard Rorty's position has been characterized in different ways, from radically secularist to antifoundationalist to radically historicist. In his recent exchange with Rorty, Woltersdorff refers to Rorty as a Darwinian pragmatist. See Nicholas Woltersdorff, "An Engagement with Rorty," and Rorty, "Religion in the Public Square: A Reconsideration," *Journal of Religious Ethics* 31 (2003): 141–49 and 129–39. For our purposes here, Rorty's position simply serves to represent contemporary philosophical challenges to the existence of universal foundations for public discourse.

46. David Hollenbach's description of Rorty's position is in "Religion and Political Life," *Theological Studies* 52 (1991) 87–106 at 92. See Richard Rorty, "The Priority of Democracy to Philosophy," in Merrill D. Peterson and Robert C. Vaughan, eds., *The Virginia Statute of Religious Freedom: Its Evolution and Consequences in American History* (Cambridge/New York: Cambridge University Press, 1988), 259.

47. See Rorty, "Priority of Democracy to Philosophy" 259, 263.

48. Ibid., 263.

49. As Hollenbach puts it, "For Rorty, the exclusion of religious and philosophical understandings of the good life from the public domain is desirable in itself, not just a necessary consequence of the fact of pluralism." See Hollenbach, "Contexts of the Political Role of Religion," 890.

50. See, for example, George Lindbeck, *The Nature of Doctrine: Religion and Theology in a Postliberal Age* (Philadelphia: Westminster Press, 1984).

51. David Tracy, "Particular Classics, Public Religion, and the American Tradition," in Robin Lovin, ed., *Religion and American Public Life* (New York: Paulist Press, 1986), 118.

52. See David Tracy, *The Analogical Imagination: Christian Theology and the Culture of Pluralism* (New York: Crossroad, 1986) for more on his concept of the classic. He writes that a classic is a bearer of a claim "that transcends any context from my preunderstanding that I try to impose upon it, a claim that can shock me with the insight into my finitude as finitude, a claim that will interpret me even as I struggle to interpret it. I cannot control the experience, however practiced I am in techniques of manipulation. It happens, it demands, it provokes." A religious classic also displays this structure, but its particular content involves "a claim to the truth as the event of a disclosure-concealment of the whole of reality *by the power of the whole*—as, in some sense, a radical and finally gracious mystery." That is, the religious classic elicits the trust that how we ought to live and the inherent nature of reality are finally one. See Tracy, *Analogical Imagination*, 119, 163–64.

53. Tracy names questions provoked by our radical contingency and mortality, by human suffering and oppression; why we feel responsibility to live an ethical life; the meaning in the love, joy, trust, and inexplicable hope we experience. See Tracy, *Plurality and Ambiguity: Hermeneutics, Religion, Hope* (San Francisco: Harper & Row, 1987), 86–87.

54. Thiemann, *Religion in Public Life*, 156.

55. See Richard Rorty, "Religion as a Conversation-Stopper," in *Common Knowledge* 3, no. 1 (1994): 1–6; Perry, "Political Reliance on Religiously Grounded Morality," 240.

56. These dimensions will be taken up in detail from a theological perspective in chapters 2 and 3. For a discussion of philosophical objections to any stan-

dards for public discourse as necessarily privileging certain religious traditions, see Ashley Woodiwiss, "Ecclesial Profiling," 36 *Wake Forest Law Review* (Summer 2001): 557–70; Stanley Fish, *The Trouble with Principle* (Cambridge, MA: Harvard University Press, 1999); Stephen Macedo, "Liberal Civic Education and Religious Fundamentalism: The Case of God v. John Rawls," 105 *Ethics* 468 (1995): 468–96; and David M. Smolin, "Regulating Religious and Cultural Conflict in a Postmodern America: A Response to Professor Perry," 76 *Iowa Law Review* (1991): 1067–1104.

57. In this vein, Hollenbach likens Perry's inclusivist stance to Benjamin Barber's view of democratic politics: rather than individuals asserting "I want x," instead suggesting "X would be good for community to which I belong." See Hollenbach, "Religion and Political Life," 100, citing Benjamin Barber, *Strong Democracy: Participatory Politics for a New Age* (Berkeley: University of California, 4th printing, with new preface, 1990), 171.

58. Lovin, "Perry, Naturalism and Religion in Public," 63 *Tulane Law Review* (1989), 1517–39 at 1518–19.

59. Marty names as the voiceless the "fetus, the comatose, the mentally limited, [and] the defenseless." See Marty, *Politics, Religion and the Common Good*, 51 and 48–58.

60. See James Davison Hunter, *Culture Wars: The Struggle to Define America* (New York: BasicBooks, 1991).

61. See Alan Wolfe, *One Nation After All: What Americans Really Think About God, Country, Family, Racism, Welfare, Immigration, Homosexuality, Work, The Right, The Left and Each Other* (New York: Viking Penguin, 1998).

62. See Hollenbach, "Afterword, a Community of Freedom"; and "Is Tolerance Enough?"

63. John A. Coleman, S.J., "A Possible Role for Biblical Religion in Public Life," in Hollenbach, ed., "Theology and Philosophy in Public," 706.

64. See Robert N. Bellah, Richard Madsen, William M. Sullivan, Ann Swidler, and Steven M. Tipton, *Habits of the Heart: Individualism and Commitment in American Life* (New York: Harper & Row, 1985). For an explication of the nature these distinct strands within U.S. history, see Bellah, *The Broken Covenant: American Civil Religion in Time of Trial* (New York: Seabury Press, 1975) and John A. Coleman, *An American Strategic Theology*, (New York/Ramsey, NJ: Paulist Press, 1982) especially chapter 9, "American Culture and Religious Ethics," 184–99.

65. Although the Enlightenment legacy is directly antithetical to Puritan covenant theology, the Enlightenment tradition actually co-opts the language and symbols of the foundational religious traditions—both traditions use law of nature, notions of equality, and balance as harmony within an individual or polity. See Coleman, *American Strategic Theology*, 189–90.

66. See Lovin, "Social Contract or Public Covenant?" in Lovin, ed., *Religion and American Public Life* (New York: Paulist Press, 1986), at 135.

67. Ibid., 142–43.

68. Marty, *Politics, Religion and the Common Good*, 51.

69. Lovin, "Resources for a Public Theology," in Hollenbach, ed., "Theology and Philosophy in Public," *Theological Studies* 40 (1979): 700–715 at 707.

70. Himes and Himes, *Fullness of Faith*, 14. When considering different religious resources in our cultural patrimony, it is important to distinguish public theology

from civil religion. Civil religion refers to a set of shared symbols, beliefs, and rituals that express religious aspects of national identity and purpose. Public theology, as we have seen, is the effort to discover and communicate the socially significant meanings of Christian symbols and traditions, unpacking the social consequences of one's faith. Whereas civil religion makes explicit the underlying beliefs and symbols behind a society's public identity and mission (and may similarly serve in some of the ways we are suggesting here that public theology can temper the individualist strand in American public life), public theology begins with the beliefs and symbols of a particular tradition and attempts to relate them to public issues. See Himes and Himes, *Fullness of Faith*, 20–21, for a discussion of the similarities and differences between public theology and civil religion. See Robert N. Bellah, "Civil Religion in America," *Daedalus* 96 (1967): 1–21; and Bellah, "Afterword: Religion and the Legitimation of the American Republic," in *The Broken Covenant: American Civil Religion in the Time of Trial*, 2nd ed. (Chicago: University of Chicago Press, 1992), 164–88 for more on the phenomenon of civil religion.

71. See Sandel, "A Response to Rawls' Political Liberalism," 184–218.

72. Coleman, *An American Strategic Theology*, 215.

73. Maclean, "Religion in American Politics," 37. See, e.g., Putnam, *Bowling Alone*, and Putnam, with Robert Leonardi and Raffaella Y. Nanetti, *Making Democracy Work*. See also Peter Berkowitz, *Virtue and the Making of Modern Liberalism* (Princeton, NJ: Princeton University Press, 1999), and Christopher Beem, *The Necessity of Politics: Reclaiming American Public Life* (Chicago: University of Chicago Press, 1999).

74. Putnam, *Bowling Alone*, 18–19.

75. Coleman, "Public Religion and Religion in Public," 36 *Wake Forest Law Review* 219 (Summer 2001): 279–304 at 287; Putnam and colleagues, *Making Democracy Work*, 152–62.

76. Robert Wuthnow, *Sharing the Journey: Support Groups and the Quest for a New Community* (New York: Free Press, 1994), 56–57; Hilary Cunningham, *God and Caesar at the Rio Grande: Sanctuary and the Politics of Religion* (Minneapolis, MN: University of Minnesota Press, 1995), 97.

77. Robert Wuthnow, *Learning to Care: Elementary Kindness in an Age of Indifference* (New York: Oxford University Press, 1995), 9.

78. Coleman, "Public Religion and Religion in Public," 284.

79. The survey included a sample of 3,000 respondents nationally and 29,400 respondents in forty selected U.S. communities across twenty-nine states. It found that 71 percent reported that they trust people at their house of worship as compared with 52 percent who trust their co-workers and 31 percent who trust members of their own race. For survey results, see www.cfsv.org/communitysurvey/index.html (accessed May 27, 2005).

80. Coleman, "Public Religion and Religion in Public," 282.

81. Sidney Verba, Kay Lehman Schlozman, and Henry Brady, *Voice and Equality: Civic Voluntarism in American Politics*, (Cambridge: Harvard University Press, 1995), 9.

82. Ibid., 17–19.

83. Ibid., 3.

84. Ibid., 17–19.

85. Ibid., 18. Their study identified the particular strength of black churches in generating social capital, but show that even non-black churches offer congregants civic skills and society a more egalitarian, communitarian, and participatory ethos. See 328–30 and 381–84.

86. Ibid., 320.

87. Coleman, "Public Religion and Religion in Public," 284–85.

88. Ibid., 285.

89. See Wuthnow, *Sharing the Journey*, 326.

90. Coleman, "Public Religion and Religion in Public," 291.

91. See Coleman, "Under the Cross and Flag: Reflections on Discipleship and Citizenship in America," *America* (May 11, 1996): 6–14.

92. Coleman, "Public Religion and Religion in Public," 292.

93. Perry, "Political Reliance on Religiously Grounded Morality," 240.

# CHAPTER TWO

# Catholic Foundations of Public Theology and Political Participation

We have encountered an array of objections to public religious engagement on various secular grounds—yet secularists are not alone in avoiding public religious engagement. Many Christians protest that such engagement risks diminishing religious purity, and that the church's primary task is to preach the gospel, not to become entangled in politics. The fact that political power can serve as a force for manipulation and violent coercion leads such Christians to question whether gospel ideals can ever be compatible with participation in public policy-related activities. Yet others believe that social action and public engagement—even on a political level—are constitutive of the gospel's call for all Christians.[1] For these, the broader culture provides the arena where the Good News for the world must be communicated and made incarnate.[2] They believe that if creation and incarnation reveal the intrinsic relationship between God and the world, and if God's grace touches all areas of life, as most Christians claim, then it is implausible to entirely isolate or separate politics from the religious sphere of life.[3]

If the public engagement of religion in civil society is in fact viable and potentially beneficial, then what are the possibilities for and limits to public theology and religiopolitical engagement from a theological perspective?[4] The Catholic position is predominantly characterized by mutual understanding and exchange between gospel and culture; it holds that the church can and should cooperate with other citizens of goodwill toward achieving the public good. Catholic foundations for such collaboration deepen a sense of the theological possibilities for engagement, yet the tradition also functions in such a way as to set some limits as well, guarding against politicization and co-optation of the church, for example. Different models of Christian public theology and political engagement have expressed themselves in the American context as elsewhere, ranging from open embrace of culture, to complete withdrawal from the world to preserve gospel values. A range of approaches and attitudes may be found among and within the various Christian churches as well as within the Roman Catholic Church. A brief overview of Ernst Troeltsch's classic formulations of the major differences broadly conceived sets the stage for theological foundations of engagement within the Catholic tradition.

## TROELTSCHIAN TYPES AND THEOLOGICAL TENSIONS

In his seminal two-volume work on *The Social Teaching of the Christian Churches*, Ernst Troeltsch traces the ways in which Christian churches have engaged social questions (and their church-state, church-society, church-world dimensions) during the past two millennia.[5] In examining how churches have conceived of their relationship to the world, he categorizes the tendencies in three ways: church, sect, and mysticism types. Troeltsch describes the church type as universal in its calling, responsible for collaborating with institutions of wider society, and able in some part to adjust itself to the world due to its endowment with objective grace and redemption. His sect type, by contrast, constitutes a more stringent voluntary society that lives apart from the world and is less interested in collaboration with social institutions than in witnessing to a way of life by contrast to the wider society.[6] When Troeltsch drew his distinctions in the early twentieth century, the church-sect division was largely a Catholic-Protestant split (although Lutheranism and Calvinism fit with the church model). As Catholicism has evolved in the twentieth century, however, this church-sect debate has come to characterize intra-Catholic debates, as well.[7]

In fact, Troeltsch thought the genius of the Catholic Church was that it solved the problem by incorporating both church and sect, co-opting the sectarian impulse into religious orders as a sect within the wider church. Today, however, those embodying sect within the Catholic landscape are not limited to clergy or religious, but include laity living in the world who believe that the mainstream church model is insufficiently countercultural or attentive to Gospel mandates.[8] This more evangelical or prophetic "sect" approach seeks conversion rather than teaching or persuasion. We shall analyze these sectarian or prophetic challenges to the church type or collaborative majority within Catholicism in the U.S. context in greater detail in the chapters that follow. Categories of church and sect do not, of course, exhaust the modes of U.S. public Catholicism; for example, ethnic Catholicism, in particular, has confounded the distinctions these typologies imply.[9] Moreover, mapping living religions or scholars' approaches onto any pure typology inevitably falls short. Nevertheless, categories such as these will help us to discern, critique, and perhaps transcend tendencies within the contemporary landscape.

In the early 1950s, John Courtney Murray, S.J., framed these differences that persist in contemporary Catholicism in terms of the relationship of grace to nature in ways that remain relevant. Murray delineates two different orientations that American Catholics adopted in response to the question of Christian humanism. The first is an eschatological humanism that is scripturally based and that emphasizes the permanence of sin and the discontinuities between grace and human effort. This stance focuses on the Cross's inversion of human values as Christianity's central truth, thereby prescribing spiritual withdrawal. Murray calls the second orientation an incarnational humanism. This stance emphasizes the catholicity of the church's redemptive scope, the fact that (although transcendent), grace perfects nature, and that human nature, although sinful, is not corrupt. Murray notes that the two models are not mutually exclusive, and that both are integral to the Gospel, complementary, and that each run inherent risks (either of surrendering this world to the unregenerate or of leading to inner self-despoilment).[10]

Thus, Murray's orientations reveal some ways in which proponents of different models of public theology inevitably draw on different strands of the tradition to justify their particular approaches; we might find an emphasis on God as universal creator and redeemer within the church type, and an emphasis on Jesus as Lord or Jesus as Lawgiver in the sect type. The fullness of the scriptural and theological tradition is ambivalent with respect to the social role of the church, reflecting tensions inherent in Christians' status as being in the world but not of it. Not only do questions about social engagement arise from a set of circumstances that are today distinct from those of the early Christian communities reflected in the epistles, but we also find dissimilar passages and themes in scripture that are not easily reconcilable, regarding the proper relationship between Christianity and state or society.[11] Scripture does provide foundations on which to build and directives for action in analogous ways. The task of public theology includes putting scriptural mandates—such as love of neighbor, care for the vulnerable, and liberation and justice for the oppressed—into practice in the complex world in which we live.[12] These distinctive scriptural directives point to the importance of context for discerning the appropriate response and to the ambivalence inherent in the Christian tradition with respect to social witness.

Broadly understood, Catholic social thought and action are generally based on Catholic beliefs about the fundamental goodness of creation, the mediation of the divine through the human (incarnation, sacramental principle), and the Catholic insistence on the universality of God's concern.[13] Whereas these theological foundations ground the church's social mission and direct it toward engagement with the world overall, as we shall see, other theological emphases temper that public mandate and lead to differences in how the social mission plays out. Discontinuities between this world and the next, the pervasiveness of sin, and the gospel call to peacemaking all mitigate against an unequivocal embrace of the world and, for some, against any cooperation with non-Christians in temporal justice efforts.

Individuals and groups therefore necessarily choose a canon within the canon amid the fullness of what the tradition as a whole imparts (incarnation *and* crucifixion, mercy *and* rigor, justice *and* faith). For example, as Murray's distinctions suggest, taking the cross or the incarnation as one's primary lens significantly affects one's public theological stance: The former leads to emphases on conversion as new birth, the distinctiveness of Christian community and its values over and against worldly values; the latter stresses the universality of grace, sin, and salvation, the goodness of created nature, and a consequently more world-affirming model of engagement. In one sense, the tensions exhibited by divergent scriptural themes and theological emphases must remain as constitutive of life between the times.

Given the tensions between our identities as believers and citizens borne out in this brief overview of Christian approaches and theological themes, how exactly are Christians called to live, being at once members of the City of God and the earthly city? As we have begun to see, different attitudes have expressed themselves in the American context as elsewhere, ranging from active engagement with society to ecclesiastically focused witness. Within the Roman Catholic theological and social traditions, particularly post–Second Vatican Council (Vatican II), however, a general tendency toward a more church-type engagement model of public theology has prevailed. The Catholic stance essentially holds that in spite of the risks and tensions that exist for a pilgrim people, discipleship requires faithful citizenship.[14] That said, despite this overall embrace of an engagement model, the tensions highlighted above yield an ambivalence within even the Catholic social tradition itself. As a result, various expressions of public Catholicism emphasize a range of attitudes toward secular society and modes of civic involvement. For example, the U.S. bishops' peace pastoral at once enumerates policy recommendations for a just defense policy rooted in universalistic principles and calls disciples to share in Jesus' cross amid a world estranged from Christian values, expecting persecution, even martyrdom.[15]

In order to probe this Catholic posture and the tensions within it, we turn first to an overview of magisterial teaching on public engagement (and political participation in particular), by exploring the legacy of Vatican II, papal and episcopal teachings on the matter, and the leadership of Pope John Paul II. Taken together, these sources reveal the extent to which it is permissible on Christian grounds to participate in political life, broadly understood, and the principal values that should guide such engagement. Building on the established distinction between church-state and church-society levels of religious engagement, the Catholic social tradition instructs that the church should remain depoliticized, but that the gospel call and exigencies of the world require the public engagement of the institutional church and her members. This social mandate includes roles for Christians at civil-societal levels that have political impact and implications. We finally treat the tensions within this social mandate, as embodied in the writings and actions of John Paul II and revealed in the methodology of Catholic social teaching. These examples illustrate the complexities inherent in how we relate the fullness of the tradition to social and political problems, given eschatological tensions and pluralism within the tradition.

## THE LEGACY OF VATICAN II FOR THE CHURCH'S SOCIAL MISSION

The Second Vatican Council inaugurates a watershed shift in the institutional church's self-understanding as it confronts the wider world. An exploration of two of major conciliar documents, *Gaudium et spes* and *Dignitatis humanae*, reveals the Council's legacy for the church's social mission to be one of de-politicized engagement with the world. Post–Vatican II episcopal statements further underscore the significant relationship between Catholic faith and political responsibility, calling disciples to active witness guided by Catholic social principles.

### *Gaudium et spes*

At the Second Vatican Council, the Catholic Church experienced a shift away from conceiving of church and world in opposition to one another and away from the traditional split between the sacred and secular.[16] The Council marked a move toward perceiving an element of the sacred within temporal and political realms and toward a commitment to engagement with and service to the world.[17] The Council's *Gaudium et spes* exemplifies this shift, calling for dialogue with the world and an examination of social, cultural, and political realities in light of the gospel. The document makes this new relationship to the world clear from the beginning: "The Council can provide no more eloquent proof of its solidarity with the entire human family with which it is bound up, as well as its respect and love for that family, than by engaging with it in conversation about these various problems."[18] Here the church's social teaching was bolstered with ecclesiological grounding; no longer was the social teaching considered only as a narrow category within moral theology, but rather it came to be understood as a means of fulfilling the church's very mission.[19]

*Gaudium et spes* also speaks to how church-world, church-society, and church-state relationships should be structured. The document presents the human person as the bond between the church and the world, and the task of the church as safeguarding the dignity of the person (no. 76). It also connects an "affirmation of the church's transcendence with an equally strong assertion that the eschatological ministry of the church includes work in history to protect human dignity, promote human rights, foster the unity of society, and provide a sense of meaning to all areas of societal life."[20] In *Gaudium et spes*, the Council urges Christians, as "citizens of two cities," to attend to temporal duties in light of the spirit of the Gospel. They condemn an attitude of otherworldliness that deemphasizes earthly duties on the view that our only abiding city is that which is to come.

Although the text of *Gaudium et spes* warns about particular temptations of a worldly focus, it does so within a framework that emphasizes the link between religious and earthly duties. For example, in reference to Romans 12:2, "Be not conformed to this world," the council states, "By the world here is meant that spirit of vanity and malice which transforms into an instrument of sin those energies intended for the service of God and man" (no. 37). They follow this distinction with a warning about abandoning concern for building up this earth in this life: "Therefore, while we are warned that it profits a man nothing if he gain the whole world and lose himself, the expectation of a new earth must not weaken but rather stimulate our concern for cultivating this one. . . . [Earthly progress] can contribute to the better offering of human society, it is of vital concern to the Kingdom of God."[21] *Gaudium et spes* thus identifies the ambivalent nature of worldly concerns, yet warns against total rejection of worldly activity as a substitute for discernment and selective engagement.[22]

The document also directly addresses the proper role of the church in terms of political participation. The Council states that although the church is not tied to any particular political or economic system or any form of human culture, its moral role in proclaiming the dignity of the human person can "anchor the dignity of human nature against all tides of opinion."[23] The foundation of transcendent human dignity also grounds the limits of political participation: "The role and competence of the church being what it is, she must in no way be confused with the political community, not bound to any political system. For she is at once a sign and safeguard of the transcendence of the person."[24] The Council, however, also affirms the church's duty to protect human dignity and promote human rights, cultivate the unity of the human family, and offer a sense of meaning to all aspects of human activity in concrete ways in our shared social life.[25] The church is called to political engagement in order to protect human dignity without conflating the Catholic faith with particular or partisan political systems.

Hence, the church does not have a specifically political charism, yet it falls within its competence to address the moral and religious dimensions of social and political problems. Hehir concludes that, although this indirect role for the church's engagement in the political order entails endless distinctions and decisions, "the effort must be made precisely because the alternatives to an indirect engagement are equally unacceptable: a politicized church or a church in retreat from human affairs. The first erodes the transcendence of the gospel; the second betrays the incarnational dimension of Christian faith."[26] Furthermore, *Gaudium et spes* explicitly connects the role and purpose of the government to the common good; this connection has implications for Christians' collaboration with government structures in promoting human fulfillment.[27] This influential council document marks a significant development in the church's understanding of its relationship to the world, its social ministry, and the implications for Christians' political responsibility.

### Dignitatis humanae

Another major Council document, *Dignitatis humanae*, further sustains a public role for the church and its members. The *Declaration on Religious Liberty* represents a landmark development in church teaching on religious liberty in terms of the differentiation and proper relationship between church and state. Beyond that legacy, however, it also affirms that within the meaning of religious liberty lies the freedom for religious groups to make explicit the human and social implications of theological doctrine. The document indicates that religious freedom also means that "religious bodies should not be prohibited from freely undertaking to show the special value of their doctrine in what concerns the organization of society and the inspiration of the whole of human activity."[28]

Murray, among those chiefly responsible for the document's development of doctrine and conclusions on religious liberty, notes, "Implicitly rejected here is the outmoded notion that 'religion is a purely private affair' or that 'the Church belongs in the sacristy.' Religion is relevant to the life and action of society. Therefore religious freedom includes the right to point out this social relevance of religious belief."[29] In one respect, the impact of *Dignitatis humanae* has been the depoliticization of church-state relationships and the impact of *Gaudium et spes* has been the legitimation of social ministry. Taken together, their legacy has been, as Hehir puts it, "to plunge the Church more deeply into the political arena precisely because the protection of human dignity and the promotion of human rights in fact happen in a political context."[30] The legacy of Vatican II regarding the church's social mission is one of freedom, transcendence, and independence for the church from political systems but also one of legitimate engagement with the world.[31] Whereas the particular challenges of negotiating how and when the church should involve itself while remaining independent are ongoing ones, the post–Vatican II church has joined her personal and sacramental ministry to a social and public presence, thereby legitimizing a public church, on the whole.

## Catholic Social Teaching and Faithful Citizenship

In addition to these Council documents, the body of Catholic social encyclicals during the past century and U.S. Catholic bishops' statements in recent decades encourage social and political participation and outline key principles that should guide such advocacy. This body of documents that compose Catholic social teaching affirms the link between faith and civic responsibility, the moral function of government, and its connection to the common good. The council's ecclesiological grounding of social ministry was solidified in the 1971 and 1974 synodal documents, *Justitia in mundo* and *Evangelii nuntiandi*.[32] For example, *Justitia in mundo*, resulting from the 1971 Synod of Bishops, famously states, "Action on behalf of justice and participation in the transformation of the world fully appear to us as a constitutive dimension of preaching the gospel, or, in other words, of the church's mission for the redemption of the human race and its liberation from every oppressive structure."[33] This makes clear the inherent connection between social engagement and the church's very mission.[34] Although *Evangelii nuntiandi* focuses more on the church's mission to evangelize all peoples, it also emphasizes the profound connections between evangelization and human development and liberation.[35]

On November 24, 2002, the Congregation for the Doctrine of Faith issued a doctrinal note affirming the obligation of all Catholics to participate in social, economic, and political life based on the values of their faith. The document affirms the institutional church's role in raising the moral dimensions of public issues and articulating a moral judgment "on temporal matters when this is required by faith and moral law." It reminds lay Catholics that by fulfilling civic duties guided by their Christian consciences, they "exercise their proper task of infusing the temporal order with Christian values, all the while respecting the nature and rightful autonomy of that order and cooperating with other citizens according to their proper competence and autonomy."[36] Although the document reaffirms the established differentiation of political and ecclesial spheres and the imperative that Catholics actively participate in public life, it goes on to warn against cultural relativism, moral pluralism, and promoting or voting for laws that attack human life.[37]

In the U.S. context in particular, the bishops' 1986 pastoral, "Economic Justice for All," emphasizes the moral function of government in protecting human rights and in securing basic justice for all its citizens.[38] This moral function of government operative in both *Gaudium et spes* and the social encyclicals more generally reflects a Thomistic understanding of Christians and the political order, based on (considerable) trust in human reason and on optimism concerning the potential of natural humanity to establish a just and peaceful political order governed by law.[39] Although American Catholics inevitably debate the size and role of the state in society and the economy, Catholic teaching insists that government should play an active role, particularly in defense of the poor.[40] Furthermore, in addition to the fact that Catholic social teaching always encourages the works of mercy and working for justice on the community level, it also clearly affirms the need to advocate for justice at the structural level. Explicit in Pope Pius XI's articulation of the principle of subsidiarity is his affirmation that "owing to the change in social conditions, much that was formerly done by small bodies can nowadays be accomplished only by large organizations."[41]

For the past thirty years, the U.S. bishops have issued quadrennial statements on political responsibility. These documents repeatedly make clear that, in the Catholic tradition, "responsible citizenship is a virtue; participation in the political process is a moral obligation."[42] The bishops connect the gospel's social mission with political responsibility, again emphasizing that whereas the words and example of Jesus Christ on earth require individual works of mercy and acts of charity, they also require wider-scale action in pursuit of peace and justice. They point out that the latter necessarily entails the "institutions and structures of society, the economy, and politics."[43] They urge Catholics to measure political policies and platforms by whether they enhance or diminish human life, human dignity, and human rights, and how they advance the common good.[44] They make explicit the implications for Catholicism and American political participation: "[The Catholic] view of the church's ministry and mission requires the church to relate positively to the political order, since social injustice and the denial of human rights can often be remedied only through governmental action. In today's world, concern for human life, social justice and peace necessarily requires persons and organizations to participate in the political process in accordance with their own responsibilities and roles."[45]

The bishops stress that they do not seek to form a religious interest group or endorse any partisan positions or candidates. Rather, they write, Catholics are called to be a "community of conscience within the larger society" and as such to disclose the moral and religious dimensions of social issues and examine them in light of gospel values.[46] As they put it, "We hope American Catholics, as both believers and citizens, will use the resources of our faith and the opportunities of this democracy to help shape a society more respectful of the life, dignity, and rights of the human person, especially the poor and vulnerable."[47] The bishops' statements typically point to basic principles at the heart of the tradition of Catholic social teaching that should guide policymaking, such as the life and dignity of the human person; human rights and responsibilities; family and community life; dignity of work and rights of workers;

the option for the poor; and (global) human solidarity.[48] The bishops remain aware of the necessary balance between political participation and the dangers of politicization highlighted above in the conciliar documents. As they articulate the task, "The challenge for our church is to be principled without being ideological, to be political without being partisan, to be civil without being soft, to be involved without being used."[49] The bishops' statements together with the body of Catholic social teaching link Catholic convictions to an active role in public life and civic responsibility, and they defend the role of the government in enacting structural change.[50] The legacy of Vatican II and the Catholic social tradition taken together is one of depoliticized public engagement. Within this social mandate, one can begin to identify several dimensions of the aforementioned tensions: tensions between church and world, social and political action, and between religious vision and ethical principles.

## Catholic Social Principles as a Framework for Catholic Political Engagement

It is up to Christian communities to analyze with objectivity the situation which is proper to their own country, to shed on it the light of the Gospel's unalterable words and to draw principles of reflection, norms of judgment and directives for action from the social teaching of the Church.[51]

The documents of Vatican II and the broader social tradition reveal a Catholic call to social engagement with political dimensions. What does the social tradition have to say about which particular principles should guide such engagement? Catholic social documents throughout the past century have brought the tradition's resources to bear on the signs of the times. In the U.S. context, perhaps most relevant are the Catholic social principles spelled out and applied in the most recent "Faithful Citizenship" documents. These principles, culled from the body of social encyclicals, offer directives for political advocacy and policy analysis. The bishops often pair themes from Catholic social teaching with contemporary social and political issues to which they apply, in order to help believers connect the faith tradition to everyday concerns as they vote or advocate. For example, the bishops typically point to a similar litany of principles or priorities: human dignity, the call to family, community and participation, human rights and responsibilities, the dignity of work and rights of workers, the options for the poor and issues of social justice, global human solidarity, and concern for God's creation. The political responsibility documents then apply such principles to issues relevant to that particular election year, be they conflicts in the Middle East, welfare reform, or school vouchers.

In addition to these principles, two other background assumptions from the Catholic social tradition have traditionally entered into Catholic political advocacy and policy analysis, in particular: common good and subsidiarity. The Catholic notion of the common good is intrinsically connected to some of the aforementioned principles such as human dignity and participation, and reflects the social and communal nature of human existence. The idea of the common good in Catholic social thought is generally formulated in structural terms as "the sum total of conditions of social living whereby persons are enabled more fully and readily to achieve their own perfection."[52] Promoting the common good in society entails protecting the human rights of all, both civil and political immunities as well as social and economic empowerments, for full participation in the life of the community. So, for example, in their pastoral on the economy, "Economic Justice for All," the U.S. bishops write that "the dignity of the human person, realized in community with others, is the criterion against which all aspects of economic life must be measured," linking dignity, participation, and the common good as standards against which to assess economic policies.[53]

As we have seen above, the government has an indispensable role to play in defining and helping bring about the common good in Catholic thought.[54] Yet Catholic thought affirms the role of smaller groups and voluntary associations in meeting needs and pursuing the common good. Pope Pius XI articulated this principle of subsidiarity in *Quadragesimo anno* as the idea that the government should not replace or absorb smaller forms of community, but should provide them with help (*subsidium*) when they are unable or unwilling to contribute to the common good on their own. The government directs and coordinates the activities of these smaller units or voluntary associations as needed.[55] Nevertheless, "subsidiarity does not mean that the government that governs least governs best. It calls for as much government intervention as necessary to enable the other parts of civil society to contribute to the common good."[56] Subsidiarity should be understood in relationship to solidarity, socialization, and justice in considerations of Catholic policy analysis, not as an independent value on its own. The principles outlined above form the Catholic social framework that generally informs Catholic public theology, political participation, and policy analysis.

These Catholic social principles reflect and flow from biblical and theological foundations. For example, the tradition grounds its fundamental commitment to human life and dignity in the sacredness of all human persons as revealed in their creation in *imago Dei* and the consecration of humanity in the Incarnation. A commitment to human rights flows from this fundamental human dignity. The Catholic principles of justice (commutative, distributive, economic, and social) are grounded in the fundamental Christian norm of love of God and neighbor, for charity must manifest itself in just structures that respect human rights and facilitate human development.[57] The option for the poor is rooted in the special concern God shows for the poor and vulnerable as revealed in the Hebrew scriptures (e.g., prophetic texts and the context of God's liberation of and covenant with Israel), and in Jesus' own practice of seeking out the powerless during his time on earth as well as his teachings regarding attention to suffering and material wealth.

Catholic social principles are also rooted in philosophical natural law arguments, because such arguments are presumed to be universally accessible and therefore apt norms for cooperating with others of goodwill toward solving common problems.[58] For example, human dignity is also rooted in assumptions about humans' rationality and moral agency. Most social encyclicals rely to varying degrees on natural law reasoning, particularly those written prior to Vatican II. These principles have both theological and secular warrants, and the two types of warrants relate positively, following from the Catholic understanding of faith and reason. The Catholic tradition generally understands human reason as reflecting the *imago Dei*, such that faith and reason (and in this case, theological and philosophical warrants) are not understood to be opposed or radically incompatible. This view reflects a Thomistic commitment to reasonable moral order knowable in principle by all humans—an affirmation that grounds hope for forging a common human morality.

Yet different understandings of the relationship between faith and reason recall the incarnational and eschatological humanist distinctions outlined above, and such differences affect interpretations of the legitimacy of secular or philosophical methodology in the service of theological pursuits. In contrast to the more Thomistic appreciation of human reason, a more Augustinian approach focuses on the divine basis of order and its disruption by sin; this perspective therefore remains suspicious of human reason or of any secular efforts. Different understandings of the relationship of faith and reason reflect the underlying tensions within the tradition highlighted throughout this chapter and lead to different understandings of the relationship of philosophical or natural law principles within the Catholic social tradition to theological foundations such as those articulated above.[59]

The manner in which Catholic social principles relate to biblical and theological foundations or the extent to which they constitute unacceptable philosophical translations is disputed by some theologians and ethicists. Methodist theologian Stanley Hauerwas objects, for example, that closely identifying the gospel call with abstracted values such as natural law principles risks cooptation by the violence of the nation state.[60] The just-war framework that Hauerwas denounces, in particular, could also be counted among a basic list of Catholic social principles (with both theological and philosophical warrants).[61] Hence, overall, the social principles that typically guide Catholic political engagement have both theological and secular warrants. These two warrants relate positively on the whole, but disagreements persist over the extent to which the philosophical warrants are consistent with the theological foundations. This survey of Catholic social principles highlights several aspects of the tensions inherent in the mediation of theology to reasoned ethical principles. We shall return to the consequent methodological differences below, but we first turn to Pope John Paul II's stance on political activity, which exhibits both the conciliar legacy of engagement as well as these tensions that have begun to come into view.

## POPE JOHN PAUL II'S LEGACY FOR PUBLIC ENGAGEMENT

The person and writing of Pope John Paul II also point to a church that joins personal and sacramental ministry to a social and public presence, as he himself exemplified a public Catholic posture.[62] Coming to his papacy with the consequences of Vatican II for an activist church already under way, John Paul II distinguished the church's role from political institutions per se, but he promoted a social agenda—increasing the church's social mandate and activity in areas of human dignity and human rights—that had a political impact and indirect political consequences.[63] His activism is noteworthy for both its range and specificity on positions, reflecting more generally the mediation of the general ethical approach we have encountered into the policy domain. Hehir identifies three key themes throughout John Paul's writings and speeches:

> 1. The relationship of technology, politics and ethics; this theme is the way in which he approaches the issues of nuclear weaponry, medical technology and automation in the workplace; 2. The relationship of East/West and North/South issues: under this rubric he criticizes the leading ideologies of the day, the dominance of the major powers and the diversion of resources to weapons rather than human needs; 3. Human Rights: under this theme he addresses international politics as a whole (e.g., the 1979 U.N. address) and human rights within countries.[64]

Whereas Hehir admits that popes since Pius XII have spoken on similar issues, he asserts that John Paul II's specificity on positions and charismatic style placed him center stage in world affairs and enabled him to engage more effectively public attention and policymakers.[65]

In her recent book on Pope John Paul II as prophetic politician, Jo Renee Formicola echoes this idea that, although he grounded church-state relations in the independence of the church, John Paul moved the church into a broader arena of concern, attempting to implement transcendent values by way of political activity (broadly understood) in the global arena.[66] She argues that he used "prophetic politics" to accomplish moral change in the world. She points to such examples as his expansion of the Holy See's diplomatic involvement in Russia, the United States, the Middle East, in African and Asian countries, and in most developing countries; efforts at achieving religious reconciliation with Israel, Palestine, and Cuba; and his sustained witness to developing and developed nations' political, social and economic problems.[67] His actions strengthened the papacy, she contends, because he requested "moral but *realistic* solutions" to various economic problems throughout the globe.[68] Formicola concludes that "John Paul has set himself apart from other popes by merging his positions as religious and geopolitical leader to reach out and make meaningful moral change. He has accomplished so much because of his special abilities and characteristics: charisma, intellect, resourcefulness, creativity, courage, empathy, and understanding of the use of power. Rarely has the world seen a leader with this combination of qualities."[69]

Samuel Huntington has argued that Pope John Paul's visits to countries transitioning to democracy significantly affected the third of three waves of democratization, from 1974 to 1989.[70] This third wave witnessed more than thirty countries move from authoritarian to democratic forms of government, and Huntington notes that most of these countries had Catholic majorities and cultures shaped by Catholicism.[71] Although higher economic growth rates in Catholic countries played a role in the overwhelmingly Catholic third wave, he attributes the shifts more fundamentally to changes in the church deepened at Vatican II and to "Pope John Paul II's move of the church to the central stage in the struggle against authoritarianism."[72] Huntington observes that John Paul II "seemed to have a way of showing up in full pontifical majesty at critical moments in democratization processes. . . . The purpose of these visits . . . was always said to be pastoral. Their effects were almost invariably political."[73] John Paul II joined this diplomacy with extensive papal teaching addressing a wide array of issues during the past two decades. In his social teaching, John Paul II combined a theological vision with moral and political specificity, addressing not only the church, but the world at large as well.[74] His travel to local churches often embroiled in political conflict and his expansive understanding of Catholic social teaching constitute, to Hehir's mind, "the most activist papacy since the High Middle Ages."[75]

Whereas, on the one hand John Paul II joined his religious mission to a public presence with public consequences, on the other hand some of his actions seem to condemn close connections between religious and political realms. For example, he warned clergy to refrain from political involvement and took actions against priests and members of religious orders who occupied political office.[76] Some suggest this reflects a desire to maintain church unity by ensuring that clergy, in particular, avoid politically divisive disputes.[77] Similarly, John Paul issued an apostolic letter in 1998 that set forth new rules requiring all 108 bishops' conferences to be unanimous on any matters of policy or dogma on which they speak.[78] In doing so, he limited the authority of bishops in relating religious doctrine to public policy and ensured little deviation from papal policies, on contentious moral issues in particular.[79] Nevertheless, such actions may point to John Paul II's broader efforts to centralize authority or his preference for the church and church officials to play indirect roles in political advocacy rather than opposition to public theology or public religious engagement per se.

Whereas he has been hailed as a catalyst for democratic change by some and perceived as retrogressive in his antidemocratic actions by others, John Paul II perceived his own role as social, not political.[80] He insisted on the importance of the institutional separation of the church from political systems (perhaps as especially visible in the roles that the pope and clergy play in particular), and he maintained that his own role was a social one, if globally so. Thus, although his many international visits and diplomatic efforts may have had significant political impact, he insisted that he was not political but simply serving his role as "pastor of huge flocks."[81]

Within his encyclicals (*Redemptor hominis, Sollicitudo rei socialis, Centesimus annus*) John Paul II exhibits a certain ambivalent posture revealed in the tensions between his use of explicitly theological doctrines as well as more universally accessible philosophical arguments. On the one hand, he asserts that we are unable to grasp the depth of the social question or generate the will to address it without an "explicit appeal to concepts of sin, grace, and God's call to conversion and reconciliation." John Paul II was also very involved in preparation of *Gaudium et spes*, which is more theological than other social documents. Hehir writes that there exists a tension between John Paul's call to enter scriptural discourse to find moral direction in *Evangelium vitae* and "the secular pluralistic culture which the encyclical never acknowledges."[82]

On the other hand, some of his teachings stress the need for individuals and societies to realize that an objective moral order knowable by human reason is universally binding (grounding his teachings on human rights, bioethics, social teachings, and opposition to totalitarian regimes—as revealed in *Vertiatis splendor* and *Fides et ratio*). Hehir acknowledges that John Paul reaffirmed both sides of social teaching methodological debate but overall was "closer to public theology than public philosophy."[83] These methodological tensions are not limited to his writings, but are illustrative of the complexity of his stance on engagement with the world.

In line with this somewhat ambivalent legacy of John Paul II regarding political engagement and ethical methodology, Catholics from all sides have drawn on Pope John Paul II in different ways—often selectively—to defend divergent models of public engagement.[84] As we have seen, in one sense the person and writings of John Paul represent a collaborative posture in line with a church type. In various addresses to U.S. Catholics and Catholics around the world, he explicitly urged believers to carry out the temporal duties to which all are called, even in the political sphere.[85] He was a player on the world stage dealing with the powers that be, and in his addresses to the United Nations, and in his teachings on market economy, international relations, and social policy, he stood "securely in the *media via* between total confrontation with the state and simply collapsing before the state."[86]

Whereas he functioned as such across every level of society, John Paul II also embodied a more prophetic style or sect type at times. On occasion, he communicated the sense that there may be little common ground between the church and modern culture, or that there is much more of the cross than the shared resurrection vision in church-society interaction. For example, his emphasis on the need to oppose a culture of death and modern consumer culture reveals more of a countercultural stance.[87] Likewise, Pope John Paul II's criticism of the moral relativism promoted in liberal democratic cultures and the tyrant state that can arise absent virtuous citizens in a democracy reflect a prophetic stance that parallels his more collaborative one.[88]

Perhaps prophetic politician is an apt descriptor for the John Paul II, in the sense that his writings, speeches, and actions made a significant impact on public life, yet he maintained his distance from particular political systems and visions, persisting with the critiques of an outsider. At once John Paul II embodied distinct postures toward the state and methods of engagement with the world. Underlying these different postures, however, he sustained a public presence for theology and the Catholic faith: Whether in a collaborative or prophetic posture, in diplomacy or challenging encyclicals, he brought the resources and priorities of the Catholic faith to bear on social issues of the day.[89] These gestures had political impact, however indirect, and his statements regarding the responsibilities of the laity are fully in line with the Vatican II legacy of a public church. The legacy of John Paul II sustains public engagement, yet his writings and activity also reflect the tensions within the tradition to which we have alluded as well: methodological tensions between philosophy and theology, and tensions inherent in the mediation of theology and ethical principles to policy applications or political platforms.

## Ambivalence within Public Catholicism

The ambivalence that John Paul II displayed toward political engagement and that we have glimpsed in different theological emphases above is also evident in the (documentary) Catholic social tradition. Although one outcome of Vatican II was certainly to plunge the church more deeply into concern for and collaboration with the outside world, other changes at the Council reflect a more evangelical strain, such as its call for moral theology to become more thoroughly nourished by scripture. As a result, Catholic social teaching has shifted toward more of a theological mode, but tensions between philosophical and theological approaches persist within the documents, reflecting, in part, the tensions between the possibilities and dangers or shortcomings of mediated collaboration. Similarly, the U.S. bishops' embrace of both just-war theory and pacifism within their peace pastoral exhibits a tension between philosophical and theological (or, more broadly, church and sect) approaches that remains sustained rather than unambiguously solved.

Prior to Vatican II, a philosophical style of discourse was dominant in Catholic social teaching, grounded in the aforementioned distinction between natural and supernatural orders. In this view, natural law governs life in this world, and faith and grace govern the supernatural order, with little to say about life in this world.[90] In this way, much of Catholic social teaching has been cast primarily in philosophical rather than in theological categories, proposing principles that apply to all people: human dignity, justice, and the common good. This has been the case, in part, because most social teaching addresses dual audiences of the church and all people of goodwill and seeks to form alliances to address social problems. Some contend, as well, that natural law argumentation is preferable because on its own the evangelical teaching of the scriptures does not offer sufficient guidance for complex social problems.[91] Where scriptural references or evangelical approaches do appear in Catholic social teaching prior to Vatican II, they are not well integrated; references to the role of Jesus Christ, grace, and the gospel often appear only intermittently or at the very end of the documents. Although a natural law approach has clear advantages for extraecclesiastical dialogue, some contend that it fails to highlight the central role of Jesus Christ in Christian morality and that natural law optimism fails to disclose or attend to the power of sin and evil in the world.[92] Some Catholic theologians object that such gospel ideals should determine how laity and clergy alike live now, and translations into philosophical, accessible categories, or dialogue with others on intermediate human goals dilute the distinctive gospel call to which we are all subject.[93]

One consequence of the emphasis on moral theology becoming more nourished by scripture at Vatican II was to legitimize "a style of Catholic social teaching that approximates the language of public theology more closely than the previous century of Catholic teaching had done."[94] In his recent book analyzing the historical, ethical, and theological dimensions of Catholic social teaching during the past century, Charles E. Curran asserts that "the significant shift in theological ethical methodology at Vatican II involved the realization that grace, faith, redemption, the Gospel, Jesus, and the Spirit affect and influence life in the world. The world and social issues do not involve the realm of the natural only."[95] *Gaudium et spes* represents this shift well, with its ecclesiological focus, biblical tone, and its moral analysis with little attention to a natural law ethic. Although the document retains a classical church model approach in its address to wider society about the moral dimensions of public life, *Gaudium et spes* casts its moral critique in the biblical-theological categories of the Christian tradition, with appeals to scripture and Christology, for example.[96] Conciliar teaching on conscience and this call for the renewal of moral theology "emphasize the essentially religious and apostolic qualities of moral life."[97]

Some maintain, however, that even after Vatican II the use of scripture and theology in social teaching has been instrumental or poorly integrated. For some social ethicists, the Sermon on the Mount remains an ideal or goal but not normative in a full-throated way for political morality or social justice.[98] Even in "The Challenge of Peace," the bishops refer to eschatological peace, but only as something toward which we must urgently go.[99] In part, this lack of integration persists because Catholic social teaching generally focuses on changing structures and institutions, so its principles are not very evangelical.[100] In pre–Vatican II documents, the need for a change of heart is emphasized in the documents' conclusions alone (along the lines of the sentiment that an outpouring of Christian love will aid social change or the impact of grace on natural law more generally). Postconciliar documents give more importance to this interior change, because biblical language suffuses the documents more, yet they still do not make this central to the church's social teaching.[101] Curran explains this uneven attention by pointing out that the field of social ethics primarily deals with structures and institutions, addresses all people of goodwill, and demands cooperation with those outside the church, given the gravity of contemporary social ills.[102] Social change requires both changes of heart and institutions, however, and Curran concludes that the papal documents of Catholic social teaching exhibit a methodological split personality. That is, in his view they lack a well-integrated theological methodology in addressing ethical issues. Even post–Vatican II, the sections of documents that on occasion treat the roles of faith, grace, Christ and the gospel are never well integrated into the ethical sections dealing with specific issues.[103]

Curran's diagnosis reflects the tensions that persist in the Catholic social tradition between scripture and natural law, and, more broadly, between the collaborative church and more evangelical sect type approaches that have now come into view. A look at the U.S. bishops' peace pastoral provides a final example of this tension. Although "The Challenge of Peace" displays a dominant church-type ecclesiological posture, some of its themes betray these very moral tensions in the church-society relationship.[104] In the pastoral, the bishops affirm pacifism within an overall promotion of a just-war framework, deliberately remaining open to such pluralism. They go beyond earlier universal documents by asserting that some Christians have committed themselves to a nonviolent lifestyle based on the life of Jesus from the earliest days of the church, and that a tradition of nonviolence has persisted within Catholicism.[105] The bishops assert that pacifism and just-war theory are complementary strands within the tradition, although some have questioned whether these two positions can, in fact, be considered complementary or whether they are ethically opposed.[106] Whether or not the bishops are ultimately convincing in showing a workable complementarity of the positions on ecclesiological or moral levels, this inclusion of both positions demonstrates a deliberate openness to a pluralism of individual stances and highlights the ambiguities and tensions inherent even within Catholic social documents that call for specific courses of action.

Moral thought on war presents a pronounced example of the difference between church and sect approaches (and between philosophical and theological approaches): On the one hand, a just-war framework is a refined philosophical expression (while theological in grounding) and "The Challenge of Peace" reflects a church type (in its audience, mode, ecclesiology). On the other hand, pacifism is rooted in an absolute prioritization of the gospel call to peacemaking, and "the emergence of the nonviolent position within Catholicism was tied to some degree to a more explicitly evangelical interpretation of the problem of warfare."[107] The peace pastoral acknowledges this long history and the legitimacy of individual pacifist positions. Hehir asserts that the crucial analytical move, however, is the pastoral's reassertion of the just-war ethic as the church's public position on the morality of warfare, signaling "a continuation of the ecclesiological-moral posture that has characterized the church-type."[108] Although The Challenge of Peace grants normative status to a public church approach and affirms the just-war majority position, in that document's section on discipleship the bishops emphasize the minority status of Christian disciples in the world and the significant differences between prevailing cultural standards and a Christian conception of life.[109] This move, along with the pastoral's opening extensive biblical reflection on war and peace and its allowance for individual pacifist stances, illustrates the overall thrust of post–Vatican II Catholic social ethics: a basic endorsement of public engagement along with the persistence of a more evangelical strain and ambivalence regarding how to best relate the fullness of the tradition to social life.

## PUBLIC THEOLOGY IN THE U.S. CONTEXT: DIVERSE FORMS AND MODES

A variety of approaches to the engagement of Catholic Christianity with public culture persists. In the U.S. context, debate over the proper approach to such engagement has increased since Vatican II placed social engagement in a more central role vis-à-vis the church's overall mission. In his historical study of the public role of the U.S. Catholic Church, *Public Catholicism*, David O'Brien outlines several broad historical styles to describe different modes of Catholic public engagement. These styles include a republican style, which celebrates religious liberty and the separation of church and state, and accepts relegation of distinctly Christian concerns to private sphere; an immigrant style, marked by group consciousness or defensiveness, working through parish-based ethnic organizations to facilitate advancement in the New World; and an evangelical style, emphasizing the integration of all aspects of life through complete commitment to gospel values, marked by interiorization of spiritual life and commitment to serving the poor.[110]

In a piece written around the same time as the above-cited document, but looking toward the future prospects for American Catholicism, O'Brien articulates four different options that the church might pursue, based on where the U.S. church was in the 1980s and where he saw it headed. O'Brien's options include (1) a subcultural restoration option (hopes for a return to pre–Vatican II Catholicism with its traditional missionary agenda); (2) evangelical radicalism (sectarian opposition to or withdrawal from the world); (3) comfortable denominationalism (support of privatization of religion and political marginalization of the church); and (4) public church (engagement on institutional and policy-making levels, vocation entails active citizenship).[111] In *Public Catholicism*, O'Brien concludes that a potentially creative dialogue might emerge from the tension between integrity, responsibility, and effectiveness, but that there is no escape from public Catholicism, because even an approach that claims to confine its attention to spiritual matters influences wider society by its very stance.[112] In his later discussion of various options, O'Brien spells out ways in which that tension and dialogue may play out.

In the 1990s, theologians across the spectrum also articulated different classifications to describe how they perceived various U.S. Catholic approaches to the question of public religious engagement. For example, in a 1990 article in *America* magazine, Avery Dulles outlines four different strategies that correspond to how different groups related the Catholic tradition to American culture. He outlines a traditionalist strategy, which seeks to restore a more centralized and authoritarian Catholicism and is critical of dominant American culture; a neoconservative strategy, which believes that the Catholic tradition provides unique resources for renewing the American experiment in ordered liberty; a liberal strategy, which suggests that Americanism can help to modernize the Catholic Church along lines of participatory democracy and selective adherence to doctrine; and a radical strategy, which advocates countercultural, prophetic witness against American capitalism, consumerism, and militarism.[113] Dulles maps these four strategies onto a square of opposition with positive and negative perceptions of both Catholicism and American secular culture functioning as the axes, such that for neoconservatives Catholicism and American culture are basically sound, and such that for radicals both are fundamentally corrupt.[114] Although he advises that each has its strengths and weaknesses and all should be pursued concurrently, Dulles hints that the neoconservative program has the greatest potential for the needed evangelization of American culture.

Finally, Hehir outlines models that correspond more specifically to the role or mode of Catholic involvement in society. He identifies an educational-cultural model, where religion's task is to shape the religion-culture conception of society and to focus on broad themes of public philosophy, personal character, and family values; a legislative-policy model, which goes beyond the first model to advocate concrete policies, as the U.S. bishops' pastorals do; and a prophetic witness model, which creates a counterpoint to existing society within the church, and where transformation is only possible or desirable as a product of prior conversion.[115] Hehir notes these different approaches were catalyzed by the debates surrounding the NCCB pastorals on the war and the economy in the 1980s. His insights that the first two models share a view of a transformationist view of the role of church in society, whereas the prophetic witness model draws a distinct line between ecclesial and civil communities, anticipate his more recent articulation of a growing rift in U.S. Catholicism between Troeltschian church and sect types, and the challenge the latter poses to the former.[116] We shall return to this idea in chapter 3 as we examine Hehir's stance in detail. We shall also encounter echoes of all of these various classifications in the following chapters as we examine the methodologies of several contemporary Catholic theologians, as well as the motives and practices of those who engage in Catholic political advocacy work on the ground.[117]

The legacies of Vatican II, Catholic social teaching, and John Paul II yield a Catholic stance that is institutionally depoliticized yet socially and politically active in service of protecting human life and dignity and pursuing the common good. On this civil societal level, Catholic public theology and political participation should be guided by the priorities set forth in Catholic social documents during the past century. Nonetheless, practical divergences persist in how the church's social mission plays out amid the pilgrimage that is life between the times and among the challenges that we face living in the American Empire and the globalized world. The following chapters will investigate just how the social mandate outlined here plays out in contemporary theologies and practices of engagement, and how these theories and praxes might inform an authentic and responsible American Catholic public theology.

## NOTES

1. See 1971 Synod of Bishops, *Justitia in mundo*, in David O'Brien and Thomas A. Shannon, eds., *Catholic Social Thought: The Documentary Heritage* (Maryknoll, NY: Orbis Books, 1992), 288–300 at 289.

2. John A. Coleman, S.J., "Two Pedagogies: Discipleship and Citizenship," in Mary C. Boys, ed., *Education for Citizenship and Discipleship* (New York: Pilgrim Press, 1989), 35–78 at 57.

3. Ibid., 58.

4. The terms *social ministry, public engagement, political engagement,* and *religiopolitical engagement* will be used throughout this and subsequent chapters. These terms are distinct, yet related. The church's social ministry refers more broadly to the institutional church's vocation and duty regarding the wider world. (The social mission or social teachings of the church generally encompass church-state, church-society, and church-world relationships.) Public engagement refers to the interaction of the church (the institutional church and its individual members) with society, and is generally on the civil-societal level. Political engagement of Christians or religiopolitical engagement similarly refers to the interaction of the church, institutionally, or of its members with society (i.e., lobbying, public demonstrations, and efforts to influence public opinions or culture) at the civil-societal level. Political engagement will not refer to partisan involvement unless otherwise noted.

5. Ernst Troeltsch, *The Social Teaching of the Christian Churches*, 2 vols. (New York: Harper Torchbooks, 1960. Orig. 1912, first trans. 1931.).

6. Troeltsch's mystical type, characterized by fellowship of life in the Spirit on a more individual level is less relevant to our investigation here of models of ecclesial relationships to wider society. A more comprehensive overview of the broader American Christian context would also include the category of denomination. See, e.g., Sidney E. Mead, "Denominationalism: The Shape of Protestantism in America," in Russell E. Richey, ed., *Denominationalism* (Nashville: Abingdon, 1977), 70–105.

7. See J. Bryan Hehir, "The Right and Competence of the Church," in John A. Coleman, S.J., ed., *One Hundred Years of Catholic Social Thought: Celebration and Challenge* (Maryknoll, NY: Orbis, 1991), 55–71 at 69–70; Hehir, "The Prophetic Voice of the Church," lecture given at Boston College sponsored by the Boisi Center for Religion and American Public Life, April 1, 2002. Transcript available at www.bc.edu/bc_org/research/rapl/word/hehir_lecture.doc (accessed May 27, 2005).

8. Such Catholics are frequently engaged in lay groups such as Catholic Worker communities, Pax Christi, and the Pro-life movement. We will take up Pax Christi USA in detail in chapters 4 and 5. Hehir, "A Catholic Troeltsch? Curran on the Social Ministry of the Church," in James J. Walter, Timothy E. O'Connell, and Thomas A. Shannon, eds., *A Call to Fidelity: On the Moral Theology of Charles E. Curran* (Washington, D.C.: Georgetown University Press, 2002), 191–207 at 202.

9. See David O'Brien's treatment of immigrant Catholicism in his *Public Catholicism* (New York: Macmillan, 1989), 34–61 and 247–52. For a recent study of

how U.S. Latino and Latina Catholicism might navigate a public theology amid struggles to preserve historical and cultural identity while claiming membership as active and legitimate citizens, see Benjamin Valentin, *Mapping Public Theology: Beyond Culture, Identity and Difference* (Harrisburg, PA: Trinity Press International, 2002).

10. This distinction grew out of Murray's debates with Paul Hanley Furfey over intercredal cooperation in the 1940s. See Murray, "Christian Humanism in America: Lines of Inquiry," *Social Order* 3 (May–June 1953): 233–44; reprinted with only slight changes as chapter 8, "Is it Basket Weaving?: The Question of Christianity and Human Values," in Murray, *We Hold These Truths: Catholic Reflections on the American Proposition* (New York: Sheed & Ward, 1960, 1988), 175–196.

11. For example, St. Paul counsels that righteousness is based on faith, not works (Rom. 9:30–32) whereas James warns that faith without works is dead (James 2:17). Mark recounts Jesus' "Render unto Caesar what belongs to Caesar . . . and to God what belongs to God," 12:13), whereas Peter declares "We must obey God rather than any human authority" (Acts 5:29). Paul recommends we obey local authorities (Rom. 13:1–7), whereas elsewhere in the New Testament (Rev. 13:1–10) government is portrayed as demonic in nature.

12. H. Richard Niebuhr has described the sources that inform different stances toward culture in this way: Those who rely on Scripture alone tend toward more a sect type, whereas those whose chief source is reason or reason's interaction with Scripture tend toward a church type or transformationist model. See Niebuhr, *Christ and Culture* (New York: Harper & Row, 1951), where he, too, articulates classic typologies describing different conceptions of the relationship between Christianity and culture.

13. See Charles E. Curran, *Catholic Social Teaching 1891–Present: A Historical, Theological and Ethical Analysis* (Washington, D.C.: Georgetown University Press, 2002), 23.

14. See United States Catholic Conference [USCC] Administrative Board, "Faithful Citizenship: Civic Responsibility for a New Millennium," *Origins* 29, no. 20 (October 28, 1999): 309–18.

15. National Conference of Catholic Bishops [NCCB], "The Challenge of Peace: God's Promise and Our Response" in O'Brien and Shannon, eds., *Catholic Social Thought*, 492–571. For the bishops' discussion of their distinct styles of teaching and dual audiences, see no. 16–20; for an illustration of eschatological humanism; see esp. no. 276–77.

16. For an analysis of the shift in the understanding of the relationship between faith and reason or sacred and secular realms at Vatican II, see William Dych, S.J., "The Dualism in the Faith of the Church," in John C. Haughey, S.J., *The Faith that Does Justice: Examining the Christian Sources for Social Change* (New York: Paulist Press, 1977), 47–67. Dych writes, "the negative and extrinsic relationship between faith and the secular of Vatican I is replaced by a positive and intrinsic relationship [at Vatican II]," 55.

17. Hehir, "The Implications of Structured Pluralism: A Public Church," *Origins* 14, no. 3 (May 31, 1984): 40–43 at 41.

18. Vatican II, *Gaudium et spes: Pastoral Constitution on the Church in the Modern World* in O'Brien and Shannon, eds., *Catholic Social Thought*, 164–237 at 167 (no. 3).

19. Richard McBrien, "Catholic Social Action," *National Catholic Reporter* 14 (March 3, 1978): 7–8, as cited in Timothy G. McCarthy, *The Catholic Tradition: The Church in the Twentieth Century*, 2nd ed. (Chicago: Loyola Press, 1998), 260.

20. Hehir, "Right and Competence of the Church," 59–60.

21. Vatican II, *Gaudium et spes*, no. 39.

22. Ibid., no. 43.

23. Ibid., no. 41–42.

24. Ibid., no. 76.

25. Ibid., no. 40–42.

26. Hehir, "Church-State and Church-World: The Ecclesiological Implications," *Catholic Theological Society of America Proceedings* 41 (1986): 54–74 at 58–59.

27. Vatican II, *Gaudium et spes*, no. 74.

28. Vatican II, *Dignitatis humanae*, in Walter M. Abbott, S.J., and Very Rev. Msgr. Joseph Gallagher, *The Documents of Vatican II* (New York: Guild Press, 1966), no. 4, 683.

29. John Courtney Murray, S.J., in notes to *Dignitatis humanae* in Abbot and Gallagher, *The Documents of Vatican II*, 683, no. 11.

30. Hehir, "Church-State and Church-World," 58; In Hehir's words, "One way to interpret the conciliar theology is to say the church has become less political but correspondingly more active in its social witness. . . Freedom [from interference by the state], however, is not an end in itself, but a pre-condition for the church to fulfill its social witness." See Hehir, "Continuity and Change in the Social Teaching of the Church," in John W. Houck and Oliver F. Williams, C.S.C., eds., *Co-creation and Capitalism: John Paul II's* Laborem Exercens (Washington, D.C.: University Press of America, 1983), 124–40 at 135–36.

31. As Edward Schillebeeckx has suggested, this commitment to engagement to the world was the most lasting and significant change of the council. In his words, the implication was that there was to be "No salvation outside the world." See Schillebeeckx, *Church: The Human Story of God* (New York: Crossroad, 1990), 5.

32. Hehir, "Continuity and Change in Social Teaching," 131.

33. 1971 Synod of Bishops, *Justitia in mundo* in O'Brien and Shannon, eds., *Catholic Social Thought*, 288–300 at 289.

34. For a detailed analysis of the legacy of *Justitia in mundo* and *Evangelii nuntiandi* and the relationship of the church's religious mission of redemption and programs of human liberation or work for justice, see Charles M. Murphy, "Action for Justice as Constitutive of the Preaching of the Gospel: What Did the 1971 Synod Mean?" *Theological Studies* 44, no. 2 (2001): 298–311.

35. *Evangelii nuntiandi* also warns against the danger of reducing the church's mission to simply a temporal project or man-centered goal, emphasizing that salvation is the gift of God's grace and mercy, and is not an imminent salvation restricted to temporal existence and struggles. These links are anthropologically, theologically, and evangelically grounded: "anthropological, because the man who is to be evangelized is not an abstract being but is subject to social and economic questions; theological, since one cannot disassociate the plan of creation from the plan of redemption which applies to very concrete situations of injustice; evangelical, which refers to charity and justice included in it." Murphy, "Action for Justice," 206, paraphrasing *Evangelii nuntiandi*, no. 31. For text of *Evangelii nuntiandi* see O'Brien and Shannon, eds., *Catholic Social Thought*, 301–46.

36. Congregation for the Doctrine of Faith, "Doctrinal Note on Some Questions Regarding the Participation of Catholics in Public Life," *Origins* 32, no. 33 (January 30, 2003): 537–43 at 539.

37. These latter sections of the document sparked great controversy regarding the permissibility of Catholic politicians receiving communion whose voting records depart from church teaching on particular matters, particularly during the months leading up to the 2004 U.S. presidential election. I treat this matter further in chapter 4 by examining the responses of the U.S. Conference of Catholic Bishops.

38. The bishops write, "It is the responsibility of all citizens, acting through their government, to assist and empower the poor, the disadvantaged, the handicapped and the unemployed." See NCCB, "Economic Justice for All: A Pastoral Letter on Catholic Social Teaching and the U.S. Economy," (Washington, D.C.: USCC, 1986), no. 122–23, 55–56.

39. In Aquinas's view, Christians may be at home in the political order, and the sanctification by the Spirit in Christ takes place within that order, not over and against it. In contrast to Augustine and the reformers' stance, Aquinas holds that political authority and law do not exist due to original sin alone, but rather correspond to needs and purposes inherent in human nature itself (e.g., our social nature). Finally, government's task is to establish and maintain conditions—principally matters of justice—that allow citizens to lead the good life, rather than serving simply as dikes against sin. See Lisa Sowle Cahill on the Thomistic synthesis of Aristotle and Augustine in her *Love Your Enemies: Discipleship, Pacifism and Just War Theory* (Minneapolis, MN: Fortress Press, 1994), 82–85. For Aquinas's treatment of law as it relates to our argument above, see Aquinas, *Summa Theologica*, trans. Fathers of the English Dominican Province (New York: Benziger Bros., 1948), I–II, Q 90–94.

40. Hehir, "Implications of a Structured Pluralism, 42.

41. Pope Pius XI, *Quadragesimo anno,* in O'Brien and Shannon, eds., *Catholic Social Thought*, no. 79: 60.

42. USCC, "Faithful Citizenship," 312.

43. USCC Administrative Board, "USCC Statement on Political Responsibility" (full title: "Political Responsibility: Proclaiming the Gospel of Life, Protecting the Least Among Us, and Pursuing the Common Good," dated November 5, 1995), *Origins* 25, no. 22 (November 16, 1995): 369–83 at 375.

44. Ibid., 373.

45. Ibid., 375.

46. USCC, "Faithful Citizenship," 312.

47. USCC, "Statement on Political Responsibility," 374.

48. Ibid., 376. The "Faithful Citizenship" version in 1999 adds environmental stewardship to these principles.

49. USCC, "Statement on Political Responsibility," 373–74. That said, the bishops' record on de facto partisan endorsements by way of a single-issue focus in twentieth-century electoral politics has been widely debated. We shall return to this topic in our case study of the United States Conference of Catholic Bishops (USCCB) in chapter 4.

50. In addition, the bishops note that the Catholic community of faith brings particular assets to American political life and public discourse: a consistent set of moral principles (tradition of Catholic social teaching, consistent ethic of life); long-

term, broad experience in serving those in need (Catholic schools, hospitals, social service agencies, and shelters) that occasions practical expertise and everyday experience that enriches public debate; and the diverse community of citizens that Catholics comprise, ranging as they do across the political and socioeconomic spectra, and yet sharing a common commitment to stand with the poor and vulnerable.

51.  Pope Paul VI, *Octogesima adveniens*, in O'Brien and Shannon, eds., *Catholic Social Thought*, 265–86 at 266, no. 4.

52.  John XXIII, *Mater et magistra*, in O'Brien and Shannon, eds., *Catholic Social Thought*, 84–128 at 146, no. 60. For an in-depth analysis of the common good tradition and its relevance for addressing contemporary problems like globalization and urban poverty and isolation, see David Hollenbach, S.J., *The Common Good and Christian Ethics* (Cambridge: Cambridge University Press, 2002).

53.  NCCB, "Economic Justice for All," no. 28, 31.

54.  As the full theological vision of the common good consists in the communion of all persons with God, Catholic social thought denies any theory that gives absolute sovereignty to the state. Nevertheless the Catholic vision of the common good is not antistatist. For a Catholic account of this denial of the absolute sovereignty of the state, see Jacques Maritain, *Man and the State* (Chicago: University of Chicago, 1951), esp. 194–95.

55.  Pope Pius XI, *Quadragesimo anno*, in O'Brien and Shannon, eds., *Catholic Social Thought*, 42–80 at 60 (no. 79).

56.  David Hollenbach, "The Common Good," in Judith Dwyer, ed., *A New Dictionary of Catholic Social Thought* (Liturgical Press: Collegeville, MN, 1994), 195.

57.  For an analysis of the foundations of justice in Catholic social teaching, see David Hollenbach, "Modern Catholic Teachings Concerning Justice," in John C. Haughey, S.J., *The Faith that Does Justice: Examining the Christian Sources for Social Change* (New York: Paulist Press, 1977), 207–31.

58.  For a recent overview of the theological and philosophical methodology of Catholic social teaching, and the relation of one to the other, see Curran, *Catholic Social Teaching*. We shall return to a discussion of these methodological tensions below.

59.  In his discussion of the debates at Vatican II (particularly in connection with the drafting of *Gaudium et spes*), Joseph Komonchak explicates these underlying differences in a helpful manner: "The typically Augustinian approach works with a sharp and unmediated distinction between sin and grace, natural reason and faith. The natural world appears to have no solidity or substance except as a sign pointing beyond itself to the spiritual and supernatural. The dramatic contest between sin and grace monopolizes attention, distracting it away from the natural, or rather subsuming the natural under the religious categories so that on the one hand we are *natura filii irae* and, on the other, our 'true' nature is only recognized in the supernatural. The typically Thomist approach, in contrast, effects a theoretical distinction of the natural, not only in order to deny that the drama of sin and grace is the only real drama in human history but in order to promote a more accurate understanding of it. 'Nature,' if you will, theoretically mediates the practical drama. It has its own solidity or substance, its own laws, its created autonomy. Sin is what falls short of or contradicts nature, and grace is what heals and transcendently fulfills nature. This permits one at once to differentiate the

genuine limitations of nature without having to label them as sinful and to affirm the power of grace as the fulfillment and not the destruction of nature." See Komonchak, "Vatican II and the Encounter between Catholicism and Liberalism," in R. Bruce Douglass and David Hollenbach, *Catholicism and Liberalism*: *Contributions to American Public Philosophy* (Cambridge: Cambridge University Press, 1994), 76–99 at 87.

60.  See Stanley Hauerwas, *The Peaceable Kingdom* (Notre Dame, IN: University of Notre Dame Press, 1983), esp. chap. 6, part 5, "The Social Ethics of the Church," 111–15.

61.  Hauerwas served as the director of Baxter's doctoral dissertation at Duke University. We shall revisit differences between just-war and pacifist approaches in detail below and in chapter 3. We shall also encounter in chapter 3 the related objections to philosophical mediations grounded in similar theological foundations (such as the Augustinian or eschatological humanist orientations outlined above) in our exploration of Baxter's stance.

62.  Hehir, "Implications of a Structured Pluralism," 41.

63.  "In the perspective of generations of Christian scholarship it will come to be noted that the evolving papal stress on the dignity of man received its most notable and swift expansion in the prepapal and papal pronouncements of Pope John Paul II." George H. Williams, *The Mind of John Paul II*: *Origins of His Thought and Action* (New York: Seabury Press, 1981), 264; Hehir, "The Social Role of the Church: Leo XIII, Vatican II and John Paul II," in Oliver F. Williams, C.S.C., and John W. Houck, eds., *Catholic Social Thought and the New World Order*: *Building on One Hundred Years* (Notre Dame, IN: University of Notre Dame Press, 1993), 29–50 at 39. Hehir notes that John Paul links the social tradition's emphasis on the person and a definition of the church's pastoral ministry that places the person at its center. "The defense of human dignity and the protection of human rights are not simply humanistic and moral truths, they are today for the Catholic Church an ecclesiological imperative. From this imperative flows the need for a social ethic . . . [and] the function of a social ethic is to specify the challenges confronting the church in defense of human dignity." Hehir, "Continuity and Change in Social Teaching," 132.

64.  Hehir, "Church-State and Church-World," 66.

65.  Ibid., 66. Hehir notes, "Commentators as different in their perspective as George Will and Tad Szulc both agree that John Paul II is the most significant single figure on the world stage." Hehir, "Continuity and Change in Social Teaching," 133. Hehir cites Tad Szulc, "Politics and the Polish Pope," *New Republic* (October 28, 1978): 19–21.

66.  Jo Renee Formicola, *Pope John Paul II, Prophetic Politician* (Washington, D.C.: Georgetown University Press, 2002), 217.

67.  Ibid., 217–18. For an assessment of John Paul II's diplomatic role, see Hehir, "Papal Foreign Policy," *Foreign Policy* 78 (Spring 1990): 26–48.

68.  Formicola, *Pope John Paul II*, 220 (Formicola's emphasis).

69.  Ibid., 218.

70.  Samuel P. Huntington, "Religion and the Third Wave," *National Interest* 24 (Summer, 1991): 29–42 at 34.

71.  Huntington (ibid., 30) notes that "roughly three-quarters of the countries that transitioned to democracy between 1974 and 1989 were Catholic," including

Portugal, Spain, Chile, the Philippines, Poland, and Hungry. Some might argue that Huntington's more recent work on the salience of cultural and national identity amid a multicivilizational global reality and what he perceives as threats to Anglo-Protestant culture in the U.S. context point to the weight of our broader discussion of discipleship-citizenship identities and church-sect tendencies. See Huntington, *The Clash of Civilizations and the Remaking of World Order* (Simon & Schuster, 1996); *Who Are We? The Challenges to America's National Identity* (New York: Simon & Schuster, 2004), esp. chapter 5.

72. Ibid., 34.

73. Ibid. David Hollenbach points out that this judgment is reinforced by Mikhail Gorbachev's statement in 1992 that "everything that took place in Eastern Europe in recent years would have been impossible without Pope John Paul II's efforts and the enormous role, including the political role, he played in the world arena." See Mikhail S. Gorbachev, "My Partner, the Pope," *New York Times* (March 9, 1992), A17, as cited by Hollenbach, "Freedom and Truth: Religious Liberty as Immunity and Empowerment," in J. Leon Hooper, S.J., and Todd David Whitmore, eds., *John Courtney Murray & the Growth of Tradition* (Kansas City: Sheed & Ward, 1996), 129–74 at 131.

74. Hehir, "The Right and Competence of the Church," 61–62.

75. Hehir, "The Social Role of the Church," 39.

76. John Paul II activated the canon in 1917 Canon Law that is opposed to priests in public office (except by permission of superior), ordering, for example, the removal from office of Congressman Robert F. Drinan, S.J., of Massachusetts, and prohibiting the direct involvement of priests and nuns in liberation movements and radical theology in Latin America and elsewhere. See G.H. Williams, *The Contours of Church and State in the Thought of John Paul II* (Waco, TX: Baylor University Press, 1983), 66. The 1983 Code of Canon Law Can. 287 §2 states: "Clergy and religious are not to have an active role in political parties and in the direction of trade unions unless the need to protect the rights of the Church or promote the common good requires it in the judgment of the competent ecclesiastical authority." See James A. Corriden, Thomas J. Green, and Donald E. Heintschel, eds., *The Code of Canon Law: A Text and Commentary* (New York/Mahwah, NJ: Paulist Press, 1985), 227. Richard McBrien points out, however, that political involvement by clergy may take many forms, and the (prohibited) holding of appointed and elected public office or playing an active role in political parties makes up only one level of political involvement. He points to seven other levels on which it remains permissible for clergy to be involved in politics (or that are governed by prudence, rather than law), including participation in public debate, personal association with officeholders, public demonstrations, direct and indirect support of candidates for public office. See McBrien, *Caesar's Coin: Religion and Politics in America* (New York: Macmillan, 1987), 47–49.

77. In her overview of church-state theory in the Christian tradition, Leslie Griffin concludes that while the "primacy of the priest's spiritual mission prevents his undertaking a political role in the world," the laity are called to political involvement at every level. As figures of unity, clergy should not be involved in political controversy, but the laity's sphere of competence extends to the political arena of the secular world. See Griffin, "The Integration of Spiritual and Temporal:

Contemporary Roman Catholic Church-State Theory," *Theological Studies* 48 (1987), 225–57 at 248.

78. Pope John Paul II, *Apostolos suos*, May 21, 1998, *Origins* 28, no. 9 [July 30, 1998]: 152–58, esp. no. 20.

79. Formicola, *Pope John Paul II*, 216.

80. Some, like Griffin, have concluded that his encyclical *Evangelium vitae* not only challenges ethical relativism, but also confirms his opposition to democracy and religious liberty. See Griffin, "Evangelium Vitae: The Law of Abortion," in Charles E. Curran and Richard A. McCormick, S.J., eds., *Readings in Moral Theology #10: John Paul II and Moral Theology* (New York: Paulist Press, 1998), 92–108 at 101; in my view, John Paul II's position is one that is supportive of human rights and democracy, but is also concerned about the culture that liberal democracy and capitalism engender, and is committed to maintaining the church's independence from any one system of government.

81. Williams, *Contours of Church and State*, 67.

82. Hehir, "Get a [Culture of] Life: The Pope's Moral Vision," *Commonweal* 122, no. 10 (May 19, 1995): 8–9 at 9. Furthermore, Hehir notes that John Paul II's proposals for civil law and policy to reflect moral law "do not struggle with the conditions which Catholic politicians, administrators, and professionals face even if they are wholly convinced of the moral vision of The Gospel of Life. . . There is much to criticize in the cultural presuppositions of post-industrial society, but the dynamic of politics and culture requires more attention than even this long, welcome encyclical provides."

83. Hehir, "Public Theology in Contemporary America: Editors Forum," *Religion and American Culture* 10, no. 1 (Winter 2000): 1–27 at 26. John Paul's teaching uses explicitly biblical and theological categories more extensively than does Hehir's own approach, as we shall see in chapter 3.

84. Hehir, "The Prophetic Voice of the Church."

85. In his departing statement in Baltimore during his October 1995 visit, John Paul II noted that "democracy serves what is true and right when it safeguards the dignity of every human person, when it respects inviolable and inalienable human rights, when it makes the common good the end and criterion regulating all public and social life." See Pope John Paul II, "Departing Statement," Baltimore, MD, October 8, 1995, *Origins* 25, no. 18 (October 19, 1995): 317–18 at 318. Even in *Evangelium vitae*, where he decries a culture of death and the moral relativism sometimes promoted in liberal, democratic cultures, John Paul II writes, "As a firm and persevering determination to commit oneself to the common good, solidarity also needs to be practiced through participation in social and political life." See Pope John Paul II, *Evangelium vitae*, *Origins* 24, no. 42 (April 6, 1995): 689–727. In his 1980 address in Nairobi, Kenya, he emphasized the importance of political participation as well: "An important challenge for the Christian is that of political life. In the state, citizens have a right and duty to share in the political life. For a nation can ensure the common good of all the dreams and aspirations of its different members only to the extent that all citizens in full liberty and with complete responsibility make their contributions willingly and selflessly for the good of all." See Pope John Paul II, May 7, 1980, address in Nairobi, Kenya, *Origins* 10, no. 2 (May 29, 1980): 26–28 at 27.

86. Hehir, "A Catholic Troeltsch?" 201; Hehir, "The Prophetic Voice of the Church."

87. Ibid., 202.

88. Pope John Paul II, 1993, *Veritatis splendor* (Washington, D.C.: USCC); *Evangelium Vitae*, no. 20. *Evangelium Vitae* perhaps most clearly illustrates John Paul II's opposition to the culture of death prevalent in some contemporary societies and his call for all societies to return to the truth taught by the church.

89. As Hehir sees it, although Pope John Paul II did oppose specific forms of church engagement in politics such as the participation of institutionally representative figures in elected office, "there is no basis for using these specific limits to say that John Paul II is eroding or constraining the church's social witness." See Hehir, "Continuity and Change in Social Teaching," 135–36.

90. Curran, *Catholic Social Teaching*, 25.

91. Hehir, "Church-Type Reinvigorated: The Bishops' Letter," in Paul Peachey, ed., *Peace, Politics, and the People of God* (Philadelphia: Fortress Press, 1986), 47–70 at 59.

92. Curran, *Catholic Social Teaching*, 29. We shall explore these different interpretations of the value of natural law methodology further when we examine Hehir and Baxter's approaches in chapter 3.

93. Under pre–Vatican II theology, clergy and religious were understood to have left the world and chosen to follow evangelical counsels, whereas the laity, who remain in the world, were understood to have a subordinate calling and were understood to be subject simply to the natural law. See Curran, *Catholic Social Teaching*, 31. Vatican II's *Lumen gentium* signals a shift to a new focus on an active role for laity and the universal call to holiness. The conception of the church as the people of God moves beyond separate directives or counsels for the laity and the clergy, such that the laity living in the world are also called to holiness or perfection and called to follow gospel demands, not just the natural law. This move reflects the conciliar shift in understanding of the relation of the sacred and secular and further informs (perhaps complicates in the sense that our focus on ambivalence signals such complication) our understanding of the responsibilities that all Catholics bear.

94. Hehir, "Public Theology in Contemporary America," 25.

95. Curran, *Catholic Social Teaching*, 33–34.

96. Hehir, "Public Theology in Contemporary America," 21–25. See also Curran, *Catholic Social Teaching*, 21–52, on the history of this evolution.

97. Walter J. Woods, "Liturgy and Social Issues," in Peter Fink, ed., *New Dictionary of Sacramental Worship* (Collegeville, MN: Liturgical Press, 1990), 1198–1201 at 1200. See Vatican II, *Gaudium et spes*, no. 16–17, for conciliar teaching on conscience.

98. Curran charges John Courtney Murray with this, for example.

99. Curran, *Catholic Social Teaching*, 45.

100. Ibid., 45.

101. Curran notes that *Evangelii nuntiandi* gives greater centrality to interior change, but that its subject matter is evangelization and its audience the church itself (e.g., *Evangelii nuntiandi*, no. 18, 36). He adds that *Sollicitudo rei socialis* gives one chapter to a theological reading of social problems (chapter 5 of 7, regarding

structural sin's obstruction of development), and that *Centesimus annus* addresses the theological dimension for identifying and solving social problems only in its last chapter (human being as the way of the church). See Curran, *Catholic Social Teaching*, 46–47.

102. Ibid., 46–47.

103. Ibid., 48–49. Curran calls *Evangelii nuntiandi* an exception but it is addressed to a church audience and does not consider many specific issues. Again he attributes this to the documents' dual audiences (members of church and all people of good will) and thinks the tension pervades most Catholic social ethicists' work as well noting Michael Himes and Kenneth Himes, *Fullness of Faith: The Public Significance of Theology* (New York/Mahwah, NJ: Paulist Press, 1993) as an exception.

104. Hehir, "Church-Type Reinvigorated," 58.

105. Here the bishops affirm the pacifist allowance made in *Gaudium et spes* on an individual conscience level without including the Vatican II document's provision that nonviolence will not incur injury to others' rights and duties or the community. See Vatican II, *Gaudium et spes*, no. 78.

106. The bishops assert that just-war thinking and pacifism can coexist as complementary approaches on several grounds: The positions share a presumption against the use of force (no. 120), they are both rooted in the Christian theological tradition (no. 121), and the two strands often converge in their opposition to methods of warfare (no. 121). NCCB, "The Challenge of Peace," in O'Brien and Shannon, eds., *Catholic Social Thought*, at 518; see Kenneth R. Himes, O.F.M., "Pacifism and the Just War Tradition in Roman Catholic Social Teaching," in Coleman, *One Hundred Years of Catholic Social Thought: Celebration and Challenge* (Maryknoll, NY: Orbis, 1991), 329–44.

107. Hehir, "Church-Type Reinvigorated," 60.

108. Ibid. As Joseph Cardinal Bernardin puts it, "Despite the radical moral skepticism of the pastoral letter about ever containing the use of nuclear weapons within justifiable limits, the bishops were not persuaded that this moral judgment should lead to an ecclesial posture of withdrawal from dialogue or participation in the public life of the nation. Rather, in accord with the traditional Catholic conception, they affirmed a posture of dialogue with the secular world. I am the first to say . . . that it is a precarious posture, but one I found more adequate than either total silence within society or absolute separation from society." See Bernardin, "Church Impact on Public Policy," *Origins* 13 (February 2, 1984), 566–69 at 567.

109. Eager to affirm that the peace pastoral reinvigorates the church type, Hehir notes that this reflects differences between the existential conditions in which Christians live and the (proper) institutional presence of the church in the world. Yet changes in the contemporary character of war and violence in some ways call such a "realism/idealism" distinction into question.

110. O'Brien, *Public Catholicism*.

111. David O'Brien, "Choosing Our Future: American Catholicism's Precarious Prospects," in *Annual Proceedings of the College Theology Society* (Chico, CA: Scholars Press, 1986); McBrien, *Caesar's Coin*, 46–47.

112. O'Brien, *Public Catholicism*, 252.

113. Avery Dulles, "Catholicism and American Culture: The Uneasy Dialogue," *America* (January 27, 1990): 53–59.

114. Ibid., 57.

115. Hehir, "The Right and Competence of the Church," 66–70.

116. Hehir, "A Catholic Troeltsch?" 191–207.

117. An earlier version of portions of this chapter appeared as "Insights from Catholic Social Ethics and Political Participation," in Ronald J. Sider and Diane Knippers, *Toward an Evangelical Public Policy: Political Strategies for the Health of the Nation* (Grand Rapids, MI: BakerBooks, 2005), 101–15.

# CHAPTER THREE

# Divergences within American Catholic Social Ethics

## *J. Bryan Hehir and Michael J. Baxter, C.S.C.*

The conciliar and episcopal statements surveyed demonstrate that the official stance of the Catholic magisterium, as it has developed post–Vatican II, is one of church engaged with state and society. We have also encountered a certain ambivalence in such documents and the broader tradition, exhibiting a tension between the call to such collaboration and a more evangelical ethic. J. Bryan Hehir notes that, overall, the Catholic Church understands itself as a public church, in the sense that its basic understanding of pastoral responsibility includes participation in the wider civil society.[1] He locates his own view in this vein, yet, given the tensions entailed in worldly activity, he thinks Catholics must continually reexamine such collaboration lest it turn into co-optation.[2] Contemporary Catholic social ethicists and theologians, such as Charles E. Curran; Michael Himes; Kenneth Himes, O.F.M.; and David Hollenbach, S.J., support a similarly collaborative model of a public church, although with differing methodologies, to some degree.[3] According to these scholars, this model withstands a degree of internal pluralism, both in specific moral judgments and in the different roles that the church plays.[4]

As we have begun to see, however, some Catholics question the legitimacy of this public church model, representing a prophetic sect type and a rigorist, evangelical social ethic. For example, Michael J. Baxter, C.S.C., objects that if the church participates in the agenda of the state or attempts to provide an ethic for wider society, it will end up aligning itself with the interests of the nation at the expense of fidelity to the gospel. He believes that in collaborative efforts the church adopts wider secular policy debates' standards of success, which exclude gospel standards, making it more difficult for the Christ-centered radicalism of prophetic movements within the church to be heard.[5] Those who share this perspective assert that the church's social ethic should consist only of the witness of the church community itself, which should serve as a contrasting model to the state.[6] Hehir objects that this position creates too great a chasm between the call to discipleship and the call to citizenship.[7]

The present chapter explores the social ethics of Hehir and Baxter to provide an overview of these two major strands in contemporary Catholic social ethics. A critical comparison of their methods, theological foundations, and attitudes toward church and state helps probe the distinct forms of Christian witness that each draws from the Catholic tradition. Due to their differences in theological emphases and the ambivalent nature of different social contexts, proper discernment emerges as a particularly important practice in considering public theological stances. Many argue on theological and sociological grounds that the church should encompass pluralistic methods for vocation and witness.[8] Some Catholics have called the presence of those who feel a special call to witness to peace or to voluntary poverty or to life itself as keeping the larger church faithful and honest, but assert that, by definition, such groups will remain minorities.[9] Ultimately, the strengths and shortcomings of each methodology suggest promising ways in which the two might inform one another, rather than living with substantive pluralism or relegating one to minority status.

It is important to note at the outset that the work of Hehir and Baxter are not coequal in terms of influence in the contemporary Catholic landscape. Nevertheless, Baxter well represents the evangelical critique encountered in American Catholicism, exhibited, for example, by Dorothy Day and the Catholic Worker Movement, and, as we saw in chapter 2, certain aspects of the work and posture of Pope John Paul II.[10] Surveying the stances and foundations of Hehir and Baxter side by side will help illuminate the tensions within the church's social mission and clarify the possibilities and limits of public theology and political engagement.

## REV. J. BRYAN HEHIR AND THE PUBLIC CHURCH

As a policy advisor to the United States bishops at the United States Catholic Conference (USCC) for many years, dean and professor at Harvard Divinity School, and recent president of Catholic Charities USA, Hehir has exercised one of the most influential public roles in recent American Catholic history.[11] Hehir is perhaps best known for his work as policy analyst and advisor at the USCC (1973–92) where his work was extremely influential on the bishops' policy agenda.[12] He played a major role in formulating the bishops' policy proposals on the economy, Central America, and abortion as well as influencing the overall direction of the bishops' social policy agenda in the 1970s and 1980s.[13] Hehir was also the principal author of the bishops' pastoral on nuclear weapons in 1983, "The Challenge of Peace: God's Promise and Our Response." He notes that he has lived his priesthood "overwhelmingly at the intersection of the Church and the political arena and the Church and the academic arena," and that being engaged with the world has been a major emphasis all his life, because he wanted to study politics and diplomacy even before he was sure about theology or the priesthood.[14] Reflecting on theology in the Catholic tradition, Hehir named four themes running through the fabric of his own sense of vocation: "Ideas count. Institutions are decisive. Politics are about life and death. Prayer is critical."[15] We encounter the effects of these points of departure in Hehir's social ethic and its theological foundations, because he understands that his faith commits him to pursue justice and peace at structural levels.

## Social Ethic

Hehir's own approach to social ethics exemplifies a public church, accepting social responsibility for the common good and envisioning its teaching role as encompassing participation in the wider societal debate.[16] In his view, the Catholic Church should remain engaged with the wider society, and, whereas its role is distinct from that of the state, part of the church's vocation entails collaboration with the state and other secular actors.[17] Hehir maintains that the church enters the policy debate in the United States as a social institution and a community of believers, with the challenge to "live with a vision which makes a difference for the world."[18] Entering into dialogue with the wider society by way of issuing pastorals on social issues or lobbying Congress on behalf of the vulnerable, the Catholic Church not only addresses specific political questions, but also creates space for moral analysis and clarifies the human consequences of the technical and policy choices we make as a society.[19] The church also calls the state to a different standard. For example, "The Challenge of Peace" called for quite a different posture and policy than the United States was following at the time. Hehir allows that within the Catholic Church there should remain room for different models of engagement that may diverge from this dominant model, for such inclusivity is appropriate to the character of Catholicism. He admits there should be room for the type of prophetic or evangelical posture we encounter in Baxter's stance. Nevertheless, Hehir asserts that, for the sake of institutional coherence, there should be a dominant model, and that he is "absolutely on the side of a Troeltschian church type model."[20]

Hehir has been profoundly influenced by *Gaudium et spes*, calling it the church document that most animates and symbolically represents his work.[21] He highlights many of the themes from *Gaudium et spes* that we reviewed in chapter 2, including the balance between the church's depoliticization and engagement, its proper competence to address the religious and moral significance of political questions, and its task of protecting human rights and dignity.[22] In line with *Gaudium et spes,* Hehir understands his role as engaging the world in a spirit of dialogue and service in a reciprocal manner undertaken in what he calls "confident modesty," or remaining mindful that the church both teaches and learns from the world.[23] The document's emphasis on this respectful engagement with the world and then its transformation by the penetration of gospel values drives Hehir's work in social ethics.

Hehir describes his own approach to Catholic social ethics in this way: "First of all to understand the world in all its complexity; second, to respect it in its secularity; third to be restless about its infirmities and limitations; and fourth, to feel driven to lay hands on it, which is what Catholic social ethics calls the world to do—to lay hands on a world you respect but are not ready to accept in its present form."[24] This sequence highlights a major difference between Hehir's and Baxter's approach: Starting with the world on its own terms positions Hehir on a different trajectory than do Baxter's suspicions about the world outside of the church community and his Lindbeckian sympathies that would begin (and end) with scripture and the Christian community that it engenders alone.[25]

Hehir's articulation of his own vocation brings us to his position on how the church is to engage wider society. Whereas his stance has evolved somewhat over the years, he continues to favor a natural law–based or philosophical mode of dialogue when the church is addressing those outside its own community. Hehir insists that the church's public voice should be expressed in terms the larger public can understand, so it should rely on a philosophical style of discourse in the tradition of John Courtney Murray, S.J., and Pope John XXIII's *Pacem in terris.* He notes that when the church engages the world, it should marry its theology to a philosophy with empirical grounding.[26] Hehir believes that the church's effectiveness and credibility at the level of complex policy recommendations depend on its ability to understand relevant empirical data from disciplines outside of theology (e.g., data on the economy, foreign policy, weapons systems, and so on). He notes that, in part, this is "how a teaching Church becomes a learning Church."[27] Hehir continues to distinguish between using religious language to address the church community but not for issues directly affecting law and policy. Hehir insists that "one ought not seek to use coercive civil law for a society as a whole and draw upon resources that are unintelligible to large parts of that society. When the issue is church and society, the broader framework of civil society, it is perfectly acceptable in the American context to draw upon any and all resources, philosophical, religious or otherwise. But when you turn to law and policy, there needs to be a way to find the common ground of discourse that a law can have access to."[28] Hehir concedes that in pastoral letters or when otherwise addressing the internal

church it is appropriate to use the full range of religious and philosophical resources and language.[29] He admits that his colleagues such as Hollenbach have
convinced him on the value of using theological language (at least on the civil-
societal level), and he suggests that with church-society discourse there is
plenty of room for religious language and symbols. He maintains, however,
that when you get into any church-state or policy issues when you are going to
use the coercive power of the state to enforce a policy or to prohibit action, "the
religious tradition ought to explain, justify, and present their positions in terms
that others who do not share our faith may be persuaded by our moral wisdom."[30] Natural law argumentation, in discussions with those outside the
Christian community, Hehir contends, provides a philosophical matrix that
bridges the vision and values of a faith community with the complex sociopolitical reality. "This mediating function of the natural law is matched by its
second role: to provide a faith community with categories, principles and rules
that are intelligible beyond the boundaries of the church."[31] He notes that after Vatican II the documents of the Catholic social tradition shifted from using
the philosophical language that had dominated pre–Vatican II encyclicals toward a greater emphasis on public theology.[32] Especially after the conciliar
charge to dialogue with all people of goodwill, many church encyclicals address both internal and external audiences, and thus, on Hehir's model, they
combine theological and philosophical argumentation.

We recall how "The Challenge of Peace" combines philosophical and theological argumentation in addressing different audiences. Evidencing the
post–Vatican II shift, however, it is, overall, much more theological than is
*Pacem in terris*. Whereas the peace pastoral sought to appeal to society as a
whole and to shape public policy on highly technical issues (and so used mediating language and detailed policy analysis), it also appeals to scripture and
the way of life of Jesus. In light of charges that the lack of integration between
natural law and references to scripture and the life of Jesus in pastorals such
as "The Challenge of Peace" evidences a methodological split personality,
Hehir denies any sharp distinction between an ethic of reason and an evangelical ethic in the pastoral. He insists that "the trade-offs made in shaping
this letter are similar to those which have been debated for centuries in the
Christian Church. To choose to speak to *both* the Church and the world is to
lose some of the 'prophetic edge' of the scriptures."[33] Hehir admits that there
is a tension in the way the bishops shape their dialogue in "The Challenge
of Peace," but insists that speaking simultaneously to the ecclesial and civil
communities comes closest to their sense of pastoral responsibility.[34] Thus,
Hehir's social ethic embodies a public-church model that highly values the
mutual informing of church and society by taking empirical data seriously
on its own terms and communicating in modes accessible to those beyond
the faith community in the course of its public witness.

## Theological Foundations

In many ways, Hehir represents the incarnational humanist approach depicted and embodied by John Courtney Murray, S.J. The theology that grounds Hehir's commitment to a public church is deeply influenced by incarnational and social principles, as well as by a transformative view of ecclesiology and eschatology. The starting point for Hehir's social ethic is his conviction that "the theological perspective of Catholicism calls us in every age to give public witness to our faith."[35] The incarnational principle begins with the event of the incarnation and includes an all-encompassing conviction that God works through humanity. God enters humanity not just to accompany us, Hehir notes, but rather Christ transforms human nature, so that transforming the human and whatever is of human significance is part of the Christian vocation and continues the ministry of the kingdom.[36] The sacramental principle complements this idea, confirming this conviction that the incarnation is extended in time and the transformation of the human in the liturgical life of the community. The sacramental principle also extends beyond the liturgical community, however, because according to Hehir, "to be touched sacramentally is to see the incarnational principle at work in the world," and "the work of the kingdom being carried on in the midst of history."[37] According to Hehir, even the secular character of social service and advocacy should be understood as the extension of the scriptural and liturgical work of the church, in light of this sacramental vision. Finally, the social principle points to the deeper meaning of public and political existence, setting the context for the "transformative ministry of the kingdom" that Hehir favors.[38] This principle grounds ecclesial public ministry in Christian convictions of common creation, human consecration through the incarnation, and the expectation of a common destiny, such that the public church's defense of human rights and dignity and pursuit of just institutions makes historically manifest God's creative and redemptive historical interventions.[39]

Hehir's position on the theological bases for a public church also echoes the foundation laid out at Vatican II in *Gaudium et spes*: a religious conviction of the transcendent dignity of the human person, the protection of which propels the church to address issues of social and political significance.[40] *Gaudium et spes* integrates incarnational themes in Catholic thought on Christology, ecclesiology, and sacramental theology into a strong endorsement of the role of the church in the world.[41] As Hehir summarizes it, "The structure of the conciliar argument is anthropological in its foundation, eschatological in its culmination, ecclesiological in its focus and christological in its content."[42] By grounding Catholic social teaching and social ministry in the service of the human person and relating social ministry to the eschaton, Hehir notes, Vatican II provides a theological foundation for church-world engagement for the first time.[43]

Hehir also adopts Yves Congar's eschatology, a transformative view that closely connects ecclesiology and eschatology and in which human efforts consecrated and transformed by the Holy Spirit help bring about the kingdom.[44] Hehir asserts that this perspective structures the church-world problem and points to the foundations of *Gaudium et spes*: "The kingdom is both present in history and transcends history: it is within us and ahead of us. The created world, while ambivalent and ambiguous in terms of its orientation toward the kingdom because of sin, provides the raw material for the heavenly Jerusalem. The work of human intelligence and creativity that perfects the created order points toward the culmination of history in the eschaton— hence the lasting value of human work. Both the church and world are destined for the kingdom, both serve the purposes of the kingdom but using different means with different purposes in the overall design of God."[45]

Most of Hehir's work does not rely explicitly on biblical foundations, because he favors philosophical and empirical approaches in the analysis and advocacy that comprise the majority of his own work. Hehir is far more likely to draw on the tradition of Catholic social teaching and conciliar documents than he is to draw directly on scripture, even in his more theological moments. He does allow that there exist inherent tensions in biblical texts addressing God and Caesar, or Christianity and the world.[46] He concludes that the Christian tradition over time is charged with addressing these tensions and the church-world question. He moves to a discussion of how this has ensued in Christian history, naming Augustine's two cities, in particular, and Aquinas's more positive conception of state and society (from his integration of Aristotelian political philosophy with Christian teaching). Hehir notes that "the power of Augustine's sense of sin, grace and history and Aquinas' sense of the dual resources of reason and faith will be part of any Catholic understanding of the church-world problem."[47] This relative inattention to the use of scripture to inform the complex particulars of social problems stands in contrast to Baxter's more evangelical approach. Baxter charges that, for Hehir and others like him, scripture does not have a normative function, because it provides attitudes and directives without adequately informing concrete actions and decisions or "giving us a world to inhabit."[48] Baxter recently repeated his criticism of this dominant phenomenon, that is, that scripture informs ethics only paranetically in Catholic social ethics.[49]

Without a doubt, the single most important analytical influence on Hehir, theologically or philosophically, remains Murray.[50] Theologically speaking, Murray's own outlook is well characterized by his own depiction of incarnational humanism that we encountered in chapter 2, and as we have begun to see, this reflects Hehir's own theological approach and foundations, as well. Beyond that, Murray's method of respecting secular disciplines on their own terms and of engaging the world in terms it can understand are apparent in

Hehir's own work and style.[51] Hehir describes the influence of Murray's approach on his own methodology: "Murray's method has always made the most sense to me: to take the world on its own ground, with all its complexity, and respect people who help you understand the world in its empirical density. The content of his theology and the meaning of his life remain an abiding reality for me. He once said that to be a theologian in the Catholic church is to stand on the growing edge of tradition, the place where the tradition encounters the rest of reality; the more you understand the center of the tradition, the better you stand creatively at the growing edge."[52]

Hehir refers to Murray as representing one end of the spectrum in how Christians should address a pluralistic world about what we know and believe, because Murray's approach was "ascetical about the use of theological terms in projecting the Catholic social vision," in Hehir's view. Murray thought that the church should speak a language that the state can understand when it speaks on public issues, and his own approach relied on natural law rather than theological arguments. Hehir points to the emergence of public theology as a reaction to Murray's asceticism, an insistence that such an approach gives away too much and the fact that it makes the state normal and bids the church figure out a way to speak its vision to the state "even though it regards the state as a relative passing entity in history."[53] Although since Murray's death much debate has ensued on the most faithful continuation of Murray's work, Hehir maintains that the philosophical method at the heart of Murray's approach remains the most appropriate one for Catholic social ethics today, given the facts of pluralism and increasing interdependence.[54]

Hehir's own methodology and distinctions about which modes Catholics should use in public reflect this philosophical legacy. Some have found his theologically ascetic, natural-law ethic (particularly in its defense of just-war theory) to be morally minimalistic. Thomas Merton's critiques of Christian realist theologians in this vein reflect a discomfort with Murray's approach (that could apply to Hehir, by extension). Writing in response to a 1961 *America* magazine article justifying the use of force in particular circumstances, Merton demands, "Are we going to minimize, and fix our eyes on the lowest level of natural ethics, or are we going to be Christians and take the Gospel seriously?"[55]

Thus, Hehir's approach remains theologically ascetic yet deeply grounded in incarnational and social principles and a transformative view of ecclesiology and eschatology. His method is relatively inattentive to scripture in the service of the universality and accessibility of the church's public voice. His embrace of Murray's metaphor of the growing edge of tradition also reflects Hehir's commitment to truly letting his theological outlook and its social implications be informed by the signs of the times and the integrity of relevant disciplines.

## The Role of the Church

Within Hehir's model, the U.S. church engages society through ideas, institutions, and a constituency. This means that the church acts through its systematic social tradition of relating religious values and moral principles to public policy, its social and educational institutions, and the power of its membership taken as a whole ("with the capacity to share a vision, a set of values and a perspective on personal and public life with their members").[56] In particular, Hehir contends that the church's role in the public arena is as a teacher first and an advocate second. Therefore, he maintains, one cannot measure the success of the church's public mission by totaling its wins on legislative issues at the end of a legislative term. Although Hehir supports the church's role in addressing specific policy issues, he asserts that the long-term significance of the church consists in its efforts to shape the mode of discourse. He adds that, in that respect, those who emphasize the culture-shaping role of the church (as opposed to the legislative role) are important, because the legislative agenda can be exhausted. An activist church must retain more long-term goals than that.[57]

Nevertheless, contentious debate has ensued within the church over the degree of specificity that should characterize ecclesial policy statements, such as particular recommendations made in the economic and peace pastorals of the 1980s.[58] These pastorals provoked a debate about the scope and authority of episcopal documents and freedom of conscience.[59] Avery Dulles, S.J., among others, cautions against specificity in policy recommendations lest the bishops cease to be seen as spiritual leaders (rather than citizens with particular views on politics), deprive the laity of their distinctive responsibility, and restrict the legitimate range of options open to Catholics on concrete social and political issues.[60] Against Dulles's objections, Hehir defends the legitimacy of church leaders' detailed policy recommendations in the Catholic tradition, provided that "adequate room for disagreement is guaranteed within the church."[61] He writes, "In terms of moral argument the Catholic church is committed by both its ecclesial and moral premises to be an 'activist' agency of public discourse. The goal of engagement is not only to maintain a unified vision on key moral themes within the church, but also to engage civil society in moral dialogue. The instrumentality of engagement remains a natural law ethic and the debate will be carried on at the level of both principle and policy conclusions."[62] Furthermore, Hehir believes that the significance and illuminative power of moral principles appear fully only as they are incarnated in the fabric of concrete social problems, and that stating such principles too abstractly risks engendering wildly divergent conclusions among people all claiming to support the same principle.[63]

## Hehir's View of the Government and Its Role

Although Hehir often emphasizes that his public church posture does not imply complete identity of church with society or culture, his is an embrace of the world on its own terms and openness not only to collaboration with governmental structures, but also to learning from secular society. Hehir frequently repeats that, despite inevitable debates about the precise nature and scope of the state's role, the fact that the government has an active, positive role to play is beyond question in Catholic social teaching. His stance reflects a Thomistic perspective on the necessary connection between law and morality and the role of the government in helping secure minimum demands of justice, fundamental human rights, and the common good. In the consistent ethic of life framework that he worked out with the late Cardinal Joseph Bernardin, Hehir articulates a particular conception of the state, one that is activist but not totalitarian, and whose activism is limited by the concepts of public order and subsidiarity.[64]

Hehir maintains that pluralism of power in American society presents an opportunity for the social role of the church, in line with the Catholic principle of subsidiarity, for the "variegated institutional structure of Catholicism in the U.S. (including schools, universities, health care systems and social welfare organizations) fits well with the ideal of a pluralism of power. A pluralistic social structure invites collaboration from nongovernmental agencies." Furthermore, the wide range of social issues requires both private and public funding and engagement to effectively address them.[65] Whereas in the latter part of the twentieth century Hehir believes American social policy has moved from a view of government as the answer (to social crises) to government as the main social problem, Catholic teaching "*combines* a positive conception of the state's social role with an equally positive view of the need for other agencies in the social arena."[66]

Thus, Hehir calls for the church's engagement with the state and wider society both in the capacity of institutional presence in civil society and as an advocate in policy making. In Hehir's view, addressing domestic issues today requires both advocacy on the public policy level and seeking just investment of public funds (e.g., for housing or health care needs) and matching efforts by "a clear strategy of how Catholic institutions are prepared to play a larger role in concert with public institutions."[67] Thus, Hehir's views on the potentially positive role of government and opportunities for church engagement made possible by the pluralism of power in the United States directly inform his social ethic, encompassing church-society and church-state collaboration on the levels of public debate, policy analysis and advocacy, and institutional contributions.

Although he thoroughly endorses a public church model, Hehir himself concedes that critics on the left and the right find a public church model such as his insufficiently prophetic and countercultural. The left objects that such a via media between witnessing chiefly in contrast to society and co-optation with the power of the state is insufficiently prophetic in its critique of society; the right objects that the approach risks secularizing the church.[68] Objections from the left often arise around the issues of war, capitalism, and consumerism, and highlight the "inherent tension between modern war and Christian convictions, between accepting the going premises of global capitalism, and between living the sort of standard American consumerist life, and discipleship."[69] Such critics object that a public church or collaborative model risks compromising too much on such issues. On the right, critics generally focus on issues such as abortion, sexual standards in society, and secularism. Such critics warn that "there is a great gulf between what Catholics would expect or should expect and what goes on in the wider culture and society and therefore, the chance of common ground is very slim."[70] In Hehir's view, prophetic minorities from both the right and left stand against society as witness rather than witnessing via participation, due to the nature of either military and corporate (on the left) or media and educational (on the right) institutions. Hehir describes this inclination as entailing the following elements: "(1) a drive for clear and radical gospel teaching (e.g., no to [nuclear] deterrence and to abortion without any saving exceptions); (2) following upon clear teaching, the call for a sharp break by the Church with society; (3) as a consequence of this ecclesial break, a call for discipleship to be lived over against society."[71] We now turn to the work of Baxter, who embodies these very prophetic critiques of a natural law–based, reformist ethic such as Hehir's, in ways that largely defy categorization as right or left.

## MICHAEL J. BAXTER AND CATHOLIC RADICALISM

Baxter serves as assistant professor of theology at the University of Notre Dame and is a member of Peter Claver House, a new Catholic Worker community in South Bend, Indiana. His formation took place at Notre Dame's seminary in the 1980s, under Professor Stanley Hauerwas of Duke University, and at a hospitality house that he cofounded in Phoenix, Arizona. Baxter's social ethic, in large part, serves to challenge the "Catholics to the rescue" mentality (as he puts it) that the dominant strand of contemporary Catholic social ethics embodies. Baxter objects to Hehir's approach on the grounds that a public church inevitably aligns itself with the interests of the state and drowns out the Christ-centered radicalism of prophetic movements within the church. In addition to founding and expanding Andre House of Hospitality and its satellite job service, St. Joseph the Worker, in Phoenix, Baxter has worked extensively with draft counseling, from educating young people in the military, to teaching ROTC employees the Army regulations when Notre Dame students he counseled had an awakening of conscience and became pacifists.[72] Baxter has recently resurrected the Catholic Peace Fellowship, originally founded in 1964 to support Catholics committed to peacemaking (including draft resisters, antiwar activists and conscientious objectors). Baxter's courses such as "A Faith to Die For" (organized around the parts of the Roman Catholic liturgy), "The Dynamite of the Church," and "The Rise and Fall of Catholic Social Ethics" focus on the development of Catholic radicalism in the United States as an alternative and point of resistance to the violent and acquisitive character of the modern state and market.[73] Baxter's past and present experiences opposing violence, enacting the works of mercy, and embracing and teaching the Catholic faith in its rigorist form have contributed to a prophetic posture that calls the public church model into question and departs significantly from what we have encountered in Hehir's approach.

### Social Ethic

One of Baxter's chief objections to the shape and focus of contemporary Catholic social ethics lies in its emphasis on the very approach we have encountered in Hehir, a commitment to a public church that enters legislative debates and makes concrete policy recommendations.[74] Baxter finds this emphasis disproportionate, arguing that "in the field of Catholic social ethics, 95 percent of the thought goes into what the policies should be, and 5 percent into doing the works of mercy in a personal way. It should be just the reverse. Our emphasis should be on what actual people can do."[75] Baxter's position, influenced by Dorothy Day and the Catholic Worker movement, corresponds to the evangelical radicalism stance we encountered above in David O'Brien's typologies: Whereas Baxter does not see his position as sectarian or withdrawing from the world, he describes it as rigorist discipleship that embodies Christian practices rather than translating the scriptures' mandates into accessible principles (or, worse yet, political policies). Baxter's critique of a public church model focuses on several related objections: In his view, Hehir's model rests on the false assumption of a fundamental harmony between Catholic and American interests that risks co-optation, and it stems from an outdated nature-grace dualism and therefore attempts to mediate Christian theology. Baxter's opposition to such mediation leads him to propose alternative ways of cultivating in Christian communities a contrast society as a means of resisting such accommodation.

Baxter objects to what he terms the central assumption of the Americanist tradition in mainstream Catholic social ethics (neoliberal and neoconservative versions alike). The idea that "there exists a fundamental harmony between Catholicism and the political arrangement of the United States of America." He argues that this assertion "has been espoused by such a broad spectrum of theorists that it has become difficult to imagine an alternative to this Americanist tradition."[76] As such, the dominant reformist model limits its concern only to those aspects of Christianity that easily translate into principles that can be applied to an American policymaking agenda. Mainstream Catholic social ethics therefore generates a domesticated version of Christianity that too willingly conforms to conventional American political protocols. Paraphrasing political theologian Johann Baptist Metz, Baxter worries that in this way the public church actually does not transform American society but that, rather, "U.S. society does not rest until the public church fits in with itself and with what it considers reasonable."[77] Baxter suggests that the only way to prevent the type of accommodation and co-optation he perceives in a public church approach is "to conceive of the church itself as a culture, with its own languages, practices, conventions, and forms of life."[78] In his view, the dominant public church models do not sufficiently attend to ways in which Christians are called to be far removed from some societies ("even liberal democratic ones") and the ethics of discipleship should become public only through the witness of the church community itself, which serves as a contrasting model to the state or secular citizenship.[79] Hence, Baxter's concerns about the grave differences between the American polity and Christianity lead him to countercultural witness and practices of resistance.

In articulating his own social ethic largely in opposition to this dominant model of social ethics, Baxter repeatedly defines himself against those following in the tradition of Murray. Baxter narrates a historical account of American Catholics' desire to move (and their success in moving) from ghetto to mainstream, and ways in which this desire and successful transition have tempted Catholic social ethics into co-optation with national interests.[80] Since the 1960s, Baxter notes, American Catholics have finally perceived themselves as capable of contributing to national public life, and, as a result, they have tailored social ethics to this undertaking.[81] He asserts that various camps within contemporary social ethics aim to provide a social ethic for the nation, and in so doing, they subordinate the church to the state's agenda. In Baxter's view, the public church stance that dominates Catholic social ethics, while purporting to reform injustices, simply serves to legitimate the dominant role of the state and capitalism by participating in the present social structures. Baxter notes that a public church model is rarely sufficiently inclusive when public is understood in terms of the mechanism of the state—because it excludes those who live in economic depression, those uncounted in censuses, and the homeless.[82] To those who would suggest public theologians and social ethicists seek to reform precisely such inequities and injustices, Baxter replies that "this kind of reformist agenda only serves to reinforce the assumption that the only effective mechanism for implementing justice in the modern world is the modern state."[83]

Baxter frequently decries the efforts by Murray (and those writing in his tradition today) to demonstrate the consonance between U.S. political structures and Catholicism.[84] He specifically points to Murray's attempt to demonstrate the American constitutional separation of church and state as something to which Catholics can and should give moral and intellectual assent, as an article of peace, not an article of faith.[85] He also names Murray's restriction of discussions about politics and public discourse to the confines of natural law at the expense of theological realities or categories.[86] Baxter critiques Murray's distinction between the spiritual and temporal orders as the foundation for affirming religious liberty and American political structures as an untenable dualism or two-tiered understanding of nature and grace.[87] Baxter criticizes Murray and his followers not only for seeking (impossible) consonance between American and Catholic values and structures, the exclusion of theology (by some), and of ultimate ends (by most) in their vision of public discourse, but also for identifying this nature-grace dualism as the root of their problems.[88]

Baxter charges that the nature-grace dualism at the root of Americanists' misguided attempts to seek consonance between American and Catholic values causes them to exclude theology or ultimate ends in public discourse. In his view, approaches such as Hehir's rest upon standard neo-Scholastic assumptions that segregate the natural from the supernatural, faith from reason, theology from politics, and that therefore privatize faith. Consequently, he claims, these ethicists assume that only reason independently grounded from revelation (autonomous reason) can gain currency amid religious pluralism. For Murray and his successors, this means that religious beliefs and practices must be privatized, and that those associated with ecclesial practices such as liturgy are too tradition-specific to ground a public ethic for American society.[89] He laments that, as a result, "theology is limited to functioning as a kind of conceptual reservoir providing ideals, principles, and themes to be applied to the policy issues facing the larger public called 'society'."[90] Baxter objects to any such mediation of theology by social ethics, whether by the natural law approach one encounters in Hehir, in more public theological approaches, or in the very principles that pervade Catholic social encyclicals.[91] Baxter believes that such translation only contributes to the false separation of theology and politics and fails to overcome this neo-Scholastic dichotomy between sacred and secular.[92] He rejects such separation of theological elements that disclose public truths and those that do not, and the consequent task of the social ethicist to make truth claims that can be tested in public discourse without the public signing on to the entire belief system grounding those claims.

Baxter is likewise suspicious of any rules or standards for public conversation as put forth by social ethicists who call on fellow Christians to respect rules for public discourse.[93] In stark contrast to Hehir's own methodology and belief that the absence of criteria for public discourse (such as technical competency, civil intelligibility, and public courtesy) constitutes an assault on pluralism, Baxter rejects such rules and their standard justification. He disputes the rationale that allowing unmediated theological influence of politics amid pluralism is fundamentalistic or invites dangers of sacralized politics or theocratic claims. He argues that adherence to rules for civil discourse simply supports the liberal democratic state, which is itself responsible for equally deplorable moves to manifest destiny or religious wars, such as sustaining slavery, killing the indigenous peoples of the Americas, and unleashing weapons of mass destruction.[94] Baxter criticizes such theologians for their insistence on translating eccleisally specific practices and beliefs into terms that a pluralism of groups can accept.[95] Baxter charges that the adoption of the liberal conceptual framework that would confer rules for civil dialogue as well as the mode of social ethics implicitly buying into the same framework's segregation of politics from religion evidences how a public church stance necessarily falls too easily into uncritical embrace of the surrounding society.

Hence, in contrast to Hehir's aim to provide a public ethic for the nation, Baxter asserts that social ethics should begin in contemplation, and that the most important thing we can do is to invite the faithful to observe the Sabbath. Contemplation, he suggests, is a form of seeing, and only then can we begin to imagine and to walk away from a lot of the things from which we should walk away.[96] As concrete alternatives to the dominant approach he opposes, Baxter advocates enacting the works of mercy on local levels and embodying alternatives to the surrounding culture of violence (such as the aforementioned conscientious objector counseling or liturgical sites of resistance) and mounting social criticisms from these alternate contexts alone. Thus, Baxter's overall social ethic lies in a substantial critique of mainstream social ethics that mediates visions that are fully theological visions of reality via theological and philosophical principles and dialogue with the wider society toward common goals.[97]

## Theological Foundations

In contrast to these theological emphases on the goodness of creation, Baxter's own appropriation of the Christian story and liturgical tradition focuses on the radical demands of Christian discipleship. Baxter's work is more scripturally

grounded and is imbued with the supernaturalism and personalism of Dorothy
Day and the Catholic Worker Movement, the movement's theologian, Paul
Hanly Furfey, and the work of Virgil Michel, O.S.B. These figures' emphases
on the Sermon on the Mount and a perfectionist ethic in imitation of the life
of Jesus have significantly affected Baxter's method. As the incarnational-
eschatological humanism debate outlined in chapter 2 illustrates, the differences between Murray and Furfey are reflected in the distinct theologies of
Hehir and Baxter several decades later.[98]

A major influence on Baxter's outlook is the Catholic Worker Movement,
which was started by Dorothy Day and Peter Maurin in 1933. Baxter summarizes the Catholic worker as a "non-state-centered, theologically-informed, radicalist perspective."[99] Its program is threefold: clarification of thought through
*The Catholic Worker* newspaper, houses of hospitality (Catholic worker houses
established throughout North America that meet the needs of the poor), and
self-sufficient farming communes. Baxter has been influenced by Worker radicalism in the sense of grounding the roots of social construction in the work of
Christ, and in refusing to conform to the order (or disorder) imposed by the
modern nation-state.[100] Day rejects a merely reformist agenda in collaboration
with the state in favor of a localist understanding of government and politics
grounded in the power of the cross.[101] Baxter is also influenced by Day's pacifism, and has continued to remain active in concrete work for peace.[102]

Baxter's ethic has also been influenced by Day's supernaturalism. In contrast to those writing in the Murray tradition who, Baxter argues, prescind
from consideration of final ends in discussing of social ethics or politics, "the
Catholic Worker embodies an instinct within Catholicism against confining
final ends to a sphere called 'the supernatural' and then divorcing them from
'the natural,' 'the social,' the 'political,' or 'the economic'."[103] Such supernaturalism permeates Day's writings (she bookends her autobiography, *The Long
Loneliness*, with accounts of the sacraments of confession and communion),
and she articulates particular practices that constitute a supernaturalized life
in her "thick descriptions of feeding the hungry, clothing the naked, giving
hospitality to the stranger, instructing the ignorant (that is, picketing), growing food on the land." Baxter notes that this reveals how Maurin's "new society within the shell of the old" where "it is easier for people to be good" is
entirely attainable in the present via the power of the Holy Spirit and saints'
intercession.[104] Day connects the works of mercy and the concrete service of
Christ in the poor to Matthew 25 and the Second Coming, leading some to
describe her spirituality as eschatological in theory and praxis.[105] Nevertheless, Baxter notes, such a new society departs from the current understandings
of mainstream Catholic social ethics, and thus this approach has remained
marginalized. He posits that such a society was considered to be "'spiritual'
rather than 'temporal,' 'supernatural' rather than 'natural,' 'ecclesial' rather

than 'social.' It embodied 'charity' rather than 'justice.' These terms are false oppositions, of course, produced by the separation of theology and social theory that dominated Catholic scholarly discourse in the preconciliar era, but the effect, as Peter Maurin saw so clearly, was to confine the power or the *dynamis* of Christ to an asocial sphere where it lay dormant."[106] The supernaturalist approach of the Catholic Worker movement and its founders have had a deep impact on Baxter's own ethic in his attempts to integrate theology and politics and subsequent contrast-society stance.

Similar to Day, Paul Hanley Furfey—another major theological influence on Baxter—presents a more integrated understanding of the relationship between the natural and supernatural. Furfey's radicalism is rooted in scripture's hard sayings; he warns that we must have the courage to follow Jesus and suffer as he did and not to water down the Lord's sayings.[107] Furfey insists that all Catholics are called to holiness and he distinguishes between two moral codes: the authentic Christian moral code based on the New Testament ideal and the popular code based on what is socially respectable or acceptable, using the latter in an ironic, pejorative sense.[108] In Furfey's view, Jesus summed up his message when he dared his disciples to be perfect even as the heavenly Father is perfect.[109]

Furfey's ecclesiology reflects the triumphalistic understanding of his day, that the Catholic Church is the one true church of Jesus Christ, so grace and the kingdom of God are identified with (but not coterminous with) the Catholic Church, for practical purposes.[110] He charged that intercredal cooperation based on natural law was an unacceptable form of Catholic conformism.[111] In his debates with Murray on the subject, Furfey criticized Murray's approach for emphasizing only those aspects of Catholic teaching that are in concert with liberalism and downplaying distinctively Catholic, supernatural (unpopular) teachings such as the significance of the Eucharist, the union of church and state, or hell as a penalty for social evil.[112] Furfey stresses the radical incompatibility between grace and sin, the kingdom of God and that of Satan, and between the pistic society and the positivistic society. As Curran has summarized it, "Furfey, the radical, opposed intercredal cooperation because Catholics must use their own unique supernatural means and not the natural means that are common to all."[113] Unlike Murray who excludes ultimate ends from the realm of political activity, arguing that natural law could serve to carve out and achieve limited human goals amid the real situation of religious pluralism, Furfey calls fundamentally deficient the depiction of any human activity that did not order it to our supernatural end.[114]

Furfey advocated a Christian personalism that is motivated by charity and takes the form of the spiritual and corporal works of mercy, including worker's cooperatives, projects promoting racial integration, and agrarian reform. Baxter supports Furfey's duty of bearing witness and technique of nonparticipation, efforts that call into question existing social orders and engender Christian alternatives to those orders.[115] Furfey contextualizes such strategies eschatologically, "thereby relativizing the demand for effective action, for immediate and wide ranging results," maintaining that the mystical body is largely hidden and its effects only "faintly traceable through the clamor of history."[116] Furfey's supernatural sociology[117] orders morality to the supernatural, because natural law morality (otherwise) "quickly degenerates to a minimalism that promotes conformity to the status quo. A supernatural morality, on the other hand, nourished by the life of the church, calls on Catholics to live heroic lives patterned after the example of Christ and the saints."[118] This operative eschatology stands in contrast to Congar's transformative eschatology that influences Hehir.

Another influence on Baxter's theological foundations is one of the founders of the liturgical movement in the United States in the 1920s, the Benedictine monk Virgil Michel, whose work Baxter has attempted to reintroduce into contemporary discourse.[119] Michel's social theory similarly imagines a non-state-centered society, "one regenerated by the Christ-life, not through the bureaucratic organization of secular power, but through small-scale, practice-based communities."[120] Baxter emphasizes that Michel does not use theological ideas as symbols performing functions, but rather as virtues and practices to be embodied in particular ways.[121] Baxter contrasts Michel's vision (and his own) to those who follow a public church model whose adherents would find this untranslated understanding of justice too particularistic to contribute to the public discourse of a pluralistic society.[122] Baxter has been influenced by this call for "the creation of an alternative space from which the body of Christ can mount a critique of the debilitating life-forms produced by capitalism and the nation-state and at the same time generates forms of life exemplifying the true nature and purpose of God's creation."[123] Such a liturgy-cast social theory, Baxter argues, would allow Christians to discern all that exists beyond the liturgy and distinguish all that advances human flourishing from all that diminishes it. He says that this does not preclude reading the signs of the times, but he does insist that the liturgy itself is indispensable for reading them correctly.[124]

The supernaturalism and personalism of Day, Furfey, and Michel have a significant impact on Baxter's social ethic.[125] Their scripturally informed ethic, based on radical gospel teachings that highlight differences between church and world and discontinuities between grace and human efforts, is evident in Baxter's approach. Baxter's perfectionist ethic prioritizes cultivating Christian community to convincing others of a Christian approach to social life. As Baxter himself puts it, "theologically, scripturally, sacramentally, from the Acts of the Apostles and patristic writings, we are clearly called to a distinctive Christian ethic."[126]

## The Role of the Church

According to Baxter, the church's task lies in formation and education. In other words, in appropriately Hauerwasian fashion, he holds that the most important task for the church is to be the church, to be rather than to adopt a social ethic.[127] Baxter himself notes that Catholic disciples, as followers of Jesus, should embody the teachings and the life of Christ in the world and as members of a body united in communion with one another in such a way that the world is able to see in its midst the actual life of Christ. He believes that such embodiment is how Catholics should also understand politics, first and foremost. He argues that when national allegiance trumps Christian identity and discipleship, the body of Christ "gets dismembered," and so "the first task of the followers of Christ is simply to bring that life to the world."[128] He refers to the judgment scene in Matthew 25 and the idea that our salvation seems to rest on works of mercy, to suggest constructing a new society based on Christ and performing works of mercy within the old. As we have seen, he notes that the most important thing we can do is to invite the faithful to keep the Sabbath. Baxter emphasizes the importance of Catholics spending time with their families, reading the Bible, and gathering for liturgy so that the Body of Christ is not dispersed and absorbed into American culture.[129]

The impression that Baxter's ecclesiology is implicitly triumphalistic is well founded. Less characteristic of Catholic ecclesiology today perhaps than it was in Furfey's time, this understanding of the Catholic Church as the one, true church has implications for the importance of rightly embodying the faith and safeguarding the ecclesial community from wider society. Furthermore, Baxter seems to emphasize more discontinuity with this world and the world that is to come than the continuity emphasized in Hehir's view. The role of the church with respect to the world in Baxter's view, then, may be described as being a light to the nations.

A related key role for the church, from Baxter's perspective, lies in resistance to the agenda and mechanism of the nation-state, a resistance to the accommodation he deems inevitable when engaging the state as a public church. In his view, the church's only public role should lie in the example it sets by being church. Some have depicted this stance as necessarily setting the church over and against the world or succumbing to a sectarian temptation.[130] Yet Baxter believes the term *sectarian* is invoked as a way to dismiss the very claims he and other Catholic radicalists make: "that Christian discipleship entails a form of life that is embedded in the beliefs and practices of the Church and therefore cannot serve as the basis for universal, supra-ecclesial ethical principles that are then applied in making public policy."[131] A public church model "runs counter to the consistent claims of [Peter] Maurin and

[Dorothy] Day that true society is rooted in the supernatural life of Christ and cannot be abstracted from the beliefs and practices of the Church."[132]

Thus, in Baxter's view, the ghetto-to-mainstream arrival of American Catholicism signals failure rather than success, because he perceives mainstream Catholic ethics to be unchristian accommodation.[133] Rather than getting Congress to enact legislation based on Catholic social principles, the genuine success of U.S. Catholicism should narrate the personalist movements advocated by Furfey and Michel and resistance, such as pacifism, conscientious objection, and nonparticipation.[134] Baxter's understanding of the church's role is inextricably linked to his perception of government and the dangers it poses to the church when the church undertakes involvement beyond what he has proposed here—being church, cultivating an alternate space that embodies the Christ life.

## Baxter's View of the Government and Its Role

In rather stark contrast to Hehir's Thomistic view of the state as a vital instrument in helping to achieve the common good, Baxter views the state as a tool of violent coercion, an impersonal bureaucracy likely to denigrate human dignity, and a danger to Christians who choose to engage it as a competing object of loyalty. In Baxter's words, "We have to remember that Christ died at the hands of the state—and that drama is being reenacted, one way or another, again and again."[135] He is suspicious not only of fitting Catholicism and American democracy too neatly together, but also of Catholic social ethicists' eagerness to affirm democratic pluralism.[136] Baxter criticizes the tendency in political discourse to affirm pluralism as an inherent good and pluralism's subsequent immunity from any fundamental critique, and holds that theologies captured by Catholic liberal values—such as Hehir's public church approach—are "simply incapable of challenging the political order in the way that Catholic radicalism does."[137]

Baxter believes that a public church model, whether it uses natural law or public theology, cannot avoid endorsing the nation-state in an unchristian way, and so it must be avoided. He especially warns that the kind of civic participation affirmed by the bishops in their "Faithful Citizenship" documents is a risky business for Christians. According to Baxter, "We should be very careful to identify ourselves as Catholics first and as American way down the line. And we should remember that our very catholicity, the universal character of our church, calls into question the local allegiance of any nation-state."[138] Activities of a public church fail to attend sufficiently to Christians' status as aliens in this life and their citizenship in another patria.[139] Rather, in his view, "A truly Christian politics, one that resists accommodation to the nation-state, can be fostered only by an account of the incarnation that draws on the specific practices taught and exemplified by Christ."[140] In a recent address, Baxter nuances a view of total dissonance between church and state to argue that church teaches the legitimate nature of the state in principle but not in fact, warning that the actual state can veer from natural law, misuse reason, fail to protect the universal common good and thereby lose legitimate authority.[141]

In his profile of Furfey and the Worker movement, Curran notes that in practice Furfey tries to distinguish between different aspects of government in discerning what to oppose and what support is permissible. He explains that their opposition to the depersonalizing aspects of government is generally rooted in the biblical injunction to obey God rather than human beings, so they oppose federal but not local taxes (the latter provide services that benefit the entire community). They also oppose defense spending and civil defense procedures in light of their pacifist stance and the Catholic Worker generally holds that voting only contributes to the perpetuation of the state.[142] Baxter notes similarly that he does not reject everything American, but that *American* and *public* often serve to exclude, and he does support the forgotten Americans. He points to Howard Zinn's historical accounts of the wobblies, radical leftists, socialists, and Communists in Zinn's *People's History of the United States*, noting that some of these forgotten groups exhibit parts of the Christian vision. Baxter consequently qualifies the need to reject all things American.[143] Nevertheless, Baxter maintains that the bishops' "Faithful Citizenship" documents "drive him nuts" and that his overall stance toward the nation-state is one of suspicion, viewing it as a tool of violence and temptation to cooptation for Christians who directly engage it.

Baxter points out that the major difference between a radicalist approach such as his and an Americanist one such as Hehir's lies in different understandings of the nature of the polis in social ethics: "[In] the Americanist tradition, the *polis* is identified with the modern state, in particular with the United States of America, and as a result, the state is seen as the primary mechanism for the implementation of justice. In the radicalist tradition, by contrast, the *polis* is identified with Christ and the church, and with smaller, practice-based communities whose forms of life are closely patterned after the body of Christ and the church."[144] The theological foundations and perspectives on the state undergirding Hehir's and Baxter's approaches further elucidate their dissimilar methodologies. A comparative analysis of the two approaches will help to clarify each in light of the other.

## CRITICAL ANALYSIS OF HEHIR AND BAXTER

Hehir and Baxter present two fairly divergent approaches to living out the social aspect of our Christian duty. What are the limitations and insights of each? We have encountered different conceptions of the state and politics, as well as divergences in theological emphases and the role of secular or empirical sources. Does Hehir's natural law approach give away too much of Christian distinctiveness or does Baxter's stance risk irresponsibility to the range of social problems in a pluralistic environment? Does Baxter too starkly separate discipleship and citizenship, or does Hehir risk not allowing our discipleship to be sufficiently normative? Do their approaches simply reflect an ethic of ultimate ends and an ethic of responsibility, which Max Weber characterizes as fundamentally and irreconcilably opposed, or do their common foundations promise hope for mutual illumination?[145] Having explored the social ethics of Hehir and Baxter, let us now turn to a comparative analysis of the two approaches, considering the benefits and liabilities of each approach. Taken together, what do they reveal about the proper limits and possibilities for public engagement?

As the preceding overview suggests, Hehir and Baxter conceive of politics differently, something that significantly affects their distinct stances. Baxter charges that a public church model presupposes that theology is not inherently political, and consequently perceives a need to rely on political structures that are nonecclesial and that use modes of mediation (natural law, social principles, public theology). His approach reflects a Christian understanding of politics that must be "presented through historical texts and images which have no permanent, transcendental place apart from the practices and forms of life that produce them."[146] In contrast to the institutional and theoretical separation of theology from politics out of which Hehir operates, the Catholic radicalist tradition "promotes interaction between theology and politics and economics based on its claim that philosophical reason becomes too easily distorted when it is not elevated and corrected by the truths of revelation."[147]

Thus, unlike Hehir who perceives points of contact between the American national project and Catholicism that enable fruitful engagement (e.g., commitments to justice, equality, and participation), Baxter finds no such harmony between the Catholic and U.S. agendas. In addition to the reasons we have explored above, Baxter fears that American politics relegates religious truth claims to a separate sphere such that, in Augustinian terms, American politics is not genuine politics at all. He writes, "A genuine politics, by contrast, is grounded in the service of 'true religion' from which flow 'true justice' and 'true peace' as embodied by the citizenry, not of any earthly city but of the pilgrim City of God."[148] This difference in conception of politics, related to different ecclesiologies, underlies the disparities between a public church and radicalist evangelical model.[149]

A more localist approach such as Baxter's is frequently charged with being ineffective or irresponsible to wider society, in contrast to models that engage in ecumenical and interreligious cooperation or wider-scale advocacy.[150]

Amid the complexities of the contemporary global situation, the impact and scope of smaller-scale efforts will pale in comparison to the effects that federal budget priorities, laws, and programs will have on the lives of the majority of those in need. This is not to say that both charity and advocacy do not constitute our call as Christians. Rather, given the problems posed in a globalized economy, local efforts alone (or nonparticipation alone) may not advance justice (or, arguably, peace) as effectively as structural forces can advance justice and peace.

Baxter would respond, however, that this critique misunderstands radicalism. He notes that George Weigel's and Curran's depictions of Day and the Catholic Worker movement similarly deem radicalist methods irresponsible and ineffective in terms of institutional change. Although both praise the Worker movement as an inspiring example, they restrict its significance to the realm of individual witness.[151] He stresses that both are indebted to the dominant paradigm of politics, which associates religion with an ethic of ultimate ends and politics with an ethic of means amid a world of conflict and violence, and they therefore view the Catholic Worker approach through a distorted lens.[152] Baxter objects that such critiques emanate from this dominant paradigm rather than looking to gospel imperatives as standards of judgment. He writes that "the [Catholic] Worker *is* effective, once it is clarified that effectiveness must be measured not in terms of public policy making but in terms of achieving the good as displayed in the incarnate life of Christ. . . . The Worker *is* responsible, precisely because 'responsibility' should be construed not in terms of participating in the political machinery of the United States, but in personalist terms of serving the Mystical Body of Christ. True Christian responsibility means performing the works of mercy on behalf of the poor, the homeless, and others of the least among us who are Christ in our midst."[153]

Baxter thus insists that meanings and standards of success must be determined not by national politics but by the politics of our supernatural end. Yet how do the two interact? It seems that at their best both models entail bringing the consequences of our supernatural end to bear on our shared life together in different ways (rather than an inevitable selling out of gospel distinctiveness by anyone who engages structures) amid de facto pluralism. Furthermore, these same government structures that Baxter dismisses out of hand as tools of violence or impersonal bureaucracy can serve as tools of distributive justice; it seems we should at least (or at worst) refer to them as ambivalent. Baxter contests the Catholic tradition's efforts to characterize certain governmental institutions as natural or divinely ordained, yet it is difficult to deny amid the complexities of modern life that, in some cases, the government serves as a means to accomplish together just and charitable measures that we cannot accomplish alone.

Hehir concedes that Christians could easily arrive at Baxter's position, that there should remain room in the church for that model. He grants that prophetic critiques offered by someone such as Baxter positively serve to test the motives and tactics of a public church.[154] Hehir notes that he does not think it necessary for Christians to arrive at Baxter's position, however, because it is not necessary theologically, ecclesiologically, or morally to conclude that there is little common ground between church and society, or between nature and grace.[155] Conversely, Baxter argues that "theologically, scripturally, sacramentally, from the Acts of the Apostles and patristic writings, we are clearly called to a distinctive Christian ethic."[156] Hehir is quick to emphasize, however, that there is no simple identity between the two methods and that "someone in a collaboration stance does have the responsibility of constantly testing that collaboration: on what issues, with what stance, by what justification." He ultimately maintains that Baxter's stance draws too great a chasm between the traditions of reason and revelation, and between the church's witness to the kingdom and its participation in helping shape history in the direction of the kingdom.[157]

In fact, Hehir and Baxter each charge the other's stance with segregating faith and reason or theology and politics too greatly, with Baxter maintaining that his own supernaturalist view does not separate either and Hehir arguing that our faith compels us to participate in the public sphere. So, for Hehir, supernatural concerns impel us to have a concern for natural or temporal matters, and action in the latter realm remains implicitly supernatural (e.g., advocacy for just wages reflects the concern for human dignity rooted in *imago Dei* and God's creation and Incarnation, and the prophets' call for enacting justice for the vulnerable and the poor). For Baxter, the supernatural cannot at all be distinguished from the natural in this way, and such mediation dilutes the richness and fullness—and radicalism—of the Gospel's call. In his view, such advocacy would likely detract from the urgency of meeting workers' needs on a direct, personal level and would imply complicity with the capitalist system and nation-state, structures that are antithetical to Christian values.

Although Baxter's concerns about accommodation and the complete lack of harmony between church and culture are overdrawn, as Hehir rightly suggests, Baxter's instruction about the dangers of some parts of culture to Christian identity and the need for constant discernment are well taken. Hehir sometimes errs on the side of insufficient hesitation and a related insufficient attention to sin. For example, Hehir rarely speaks of dangers associated with public engagement. It is telling that at a panel discussion on the First Amendment and Religious Liberty Clauses and American Public Life at the University of Virginia, held April 11–13, 1988, when the participants were asked what dangers they perceived in others' religious engagement, Hehir responded, "For myself, I would rather not focus on the dangers of contending, but on the criteria we should set for participation in the public argument."[158] On the one hand, Hehir's warnings against overdrawing the divisions between church and world, between the sinfulness of the state and secular society and the saintliness of the church community are important.[159] Drawing a sharp line between church and society in such a manner is increasingly untenable. On the other hand, Baxter's insights instruct that at the least a public-church model must install mechanisms to prevent overly optimistic participation or accommodation.[160] Hehir's hesitations to focus on the dangers to Christianity of an activist church highlight this risk. Hehir is more attentive to the possibilities of public engagement, often at the expense of due attention to its limits.

The rules of discourse that Baxter perceives as undue accommodation to the dominant liberal paradigm are criteria that Hehir promotes, not only to facilitate respectful engagement, but further because he believes that the absence of them (and the efforts to translate that Baxter so strongly opposes) constitutes an assault on the real pluralism that exists. Amid the complexity of social issues and the challenges of pluralism, Hehir advocates the following criteria for such discourse: technical competency, civil intelligibility, and public courtesy.[161] Hehir's rules recall the standards of engagement outlined in chapter 1. Baxter would undoubtedly object to any such rules, not to mention any efforts to translate Christian insights or understand political courtesy as secular charity. Nevertheless, Hehir emphasizes that although "there is legitimacy to proposing a sectarian argument within the confines of a religious community . . . it does violence to the fabric of pluralism to expect acceptance of such an argument in the wider public arena."[162] These criteria for modes of engagement highlight significant divergences between the two approaches.

## Purity and Compromise

In examining the stances of Hehir and Baxter in terms of degrees of purity and compromise one might immediately polarize their two positions: Hehir risking undue compromise for the sake of dialogue and relevance and Baxter remaining too preoccupied with the purity and uniqueness of Christian doctrine to fully attend to the ways that Christianity is shaped by culture and the universality of Catholics' call. Those who oppose an activist public church generally presume that compromise and risks of cooptation are entailed whenever the church attempts to address a pluralistic audience, much less engage the state.[163] In particular, Hehir's methodological commitment to taking empirical data on its own terms and allowing it to inform theology (and not simply vice versa unidirectionally) would raise concerns about undue compromise.

In contrast to the mode of scriptural interpretation and triumphalistic ecclesiology that we encountered in surveying Baxter's influences, Hehir advocates a characteristically Catholic complementarity over dialectical tension: grace *and* nature, faith *and* reason, church *and* world.[164] Baxter might view this, too, as undue compromise or undue concern with the relation of Christianity to non-Christian entities and ideas. Hehir writes, "As we face the mystery of God or infinite intelligibility, there is a sense that, while we can't pull it all together, it does all belong together, and so we don't end up being sectarians."[165] Similarly, he focuses on the transformative role of the church in the world: "Things do belong together even if they don't easily fit together, and so we work at the intersection of what should be together but is not yet. . . I am doing what I am doing because the world is what it is, and it should be something different . . . that gives reason and purpose to the whole theological endeavor."[166] The mediation or translation that ensues in such efforts, however—as borne out in natural law language in encyclicals, attention to the search for coherence with outside knowledge, or overt engagement in the political discourse or agenda of the United States—risks compromise, in Baxter's view. He holds that the scandal of particularity or the specificity of Christian realities untranslated cannot be removed in such ways without compromising authentically Christian convictions.[167] Hehir insists, however, a public church model must predominate, because "to forsake this style of public presence is to purchase clarity and certainty [or, we might add, purity] at too high a price pastorally and publicly."[168]

Baxter's position is a rigorist one that could be classified as embodying or prizing purity exclusively and avoiding any compromise. He promotes a perfectionist ethic and judges the use of natural law or mediating principles prevalent in Catholic social documents, social ethics, and advocacy as reflective of more compromise than he deems authentic.[169] In contrast, Catholic radicalism appeals directly to theological realities, scripture, and spirituality.[170] The radicalist integration of faith and social action, then, is certainly more explicit than implicit, and some would argue as such that it is a more purist endeavor.

Baxter is particularly suspicious of the efforts of the United States Conference of Catholic Bishops (USCCB) to affect public policy as risking accommodation and undue compromise, and points to the origin of the conference in war efforts as "illustrative of the way the bishops' agenda has been shaped by a paradigm of serving the nation-state."[171] Baxter laments that although Catholic teaching on life issues such as abortion, euthanasia, capital punishment, and war contradict North American theory and practice, many Catholics continue to accommodate themselves to that political order.[172] Baxter identifies abortion, in particular, as a telling example of Catholic accommodation to the American political order. He notes that, even among those who claim that they oppose abortion, if they genuinely believed abortion was the de-

struction of human life they would not be as ready to accept it as one position among others.[173]

Abortion is certainly one issue that poses a particular challenge to
Catholics' engagement in political life. The direct move from opposition to
abortion on the basis of faith to nonparticipation in American political life as
a consequence of its current laws, however, is not self-evident. Could not opposition to abortion on a public church model—lobbying against abortion
laws, working to shape and change the public cultural consensus about abortion through dialogue and debate, for example—constitute a form of prophetic,
countercultural resistance to abortion? Conversely, it is unclear to me how nonparticipation constitutes a stronger opposition to abortion than do such legislative and educational efforts. Hehir has called abortion the most dramatic
test for the dual challenge the public church faces, "(1) how to address the
wider civil society by using a religiously grounded tradition to produce moral
wisdom persuasive to those outside the community of faith, and (2) how to
maintain a coherent community of faith when its members are influenced significantly by the wider cultural pattern of pluralism." Now, thirty years into
the debate, Hehir notes, Catholicism has maintained a coherent position without persuading the wider culture.[174] This case of antiabortion advocacy challenges Baxter's claim that the public church will necessarily fit itself into the
liberal paradigm risking cooptation. The issue of abortion presents one example of the public church advocating for a marginal position in terms of contemporary American political life and having to negotiate conscience clauses
for Catholic institutions (mirroring more of a nonparticipation tactic), both posing challenges to the way Baxter has contrasted the public church stance to a
prophetic one.[175] The example of abortion raises the subject of the range of
social issues Baxter and Hehir address.

### Range of Issues Addressed

One issue that both Baxter and Hehir consistently address is that of the use of
force. As Baxter puts it, this is where the rubber meets the road in terms of
differences of approach, and the matter is particularly revealing of theological differences between the two models. Baxter's pacifist stance serves to remind the wider church that we should subordinate human values to a transcendent center of value, and that, on the face of it, violence and coercion are
antithetical to the way of Jesus.[176] Hehir's just-war position seeks to utilize the
Christian framework dating back to Augustine and Aquinas to restrain force
and to determine when its use should serve as a regrettable last resort to protect human rights and defend the common good.[177]

The just-war/pacifism debate rests on fundamental theological quandaries
that also lie at the heart of the broader questions investigated here and that

reflect the aforementioned ambivalence in the Christian tradition. As Hollenbach puts it, "at the heart of the divergence between pacifist and just war traditions within the Church lies the basic theological question of how the poles
of belief in the gospel and the conclusions of social understanding are to be
synthesized with each other."[178] We might understand pacifism and just-war
approaches as conflicts between the pursuits of absolute peace and justice. The
theology grounding just-war theory understands Jesus' nonviolence in light of
the reality of sin and the demands of justice in this life, and holds that pacifism
absolutizes the value of human life at the expense of other human values, such
as justice, freedom, and human rights.[179] Hollenbach describes well the theological questions at the heart of the just-war pacifist debate: "Does the com-
mandment to love one's neighbor imply that the incarnation of love in a just
social order should take priority over the love of enemies which is expressed
in nonviolence? Does the death of Jesus on the cross imply that nonviolent,
suffering love is the only authentically Christian response to the reality of injustice? Does the victory of Christ over sin and death in the resurrection imply that Christians are now empowered by God to participate in the shaping
of a new and more just earthly society, or is its primary meaning the bestowal
of grace to follow Jesus Christ in the way of the suffering servant? Does Christian hope in the ultimate fulfillment of God's reign of justice and love mean
that Christians should look toward that triumph in a spirit of total nonviolence
or that they should seek to work toward that fulfillment even through the use
of force? The way one answers these religious questions will have a significant
impact on how one is disposed to interpret the interconnection between the
values of peace and justice in political life."[180]

Similarly, whereas Jesus' crucifixion, as Baxter's Protestant influences
(John Howard Yoder and Hauerwas) have emphasized, points to self-sacrifice,
conflict, and nonviolence in the face of worldly rejection, the resurrection that
follows points to the inauguration of God's love and justice and God's desire
for the communion of all humanity. These underlying theological differences
of emphasis are implicitly and explicitly evident in the stances of Hehir and
Baxter. Baxter's pacifism and suspicion of worldly values reflect more attention to the cross whereas Hehir's pursuit of justice in collaboration with others
and his just-war stance are rooted in creation and an incarnational theology
along with hope of helping to bring about God's reign.

In terms of the range of issues each addresses, however, many credit
Hehir's efforts at the USCC with broadening the bishops' pro-life agenda,
from what was perceived as a narrow antiabortion focus to a wider-ranging
consistent ethic-of-life agenda that situated abortion concerns within a broader
framework.[181] Hehir was able to exercise so much influence at the USCC on a
wide range of policy issues, in part because he "provided the intellectual
framework within which [the bishops] came to understand and evaluate ma-

jor policy questions," and these efforts helped enhance the church's credibility in public policy debates.[182] Hehir describes the consistent ethic as "an attempt to provide a coherent framework and rationale for the public policy positions of the Catholic Church" rather than as a detailed blueprint on the issues themselves.[183] Although Hehir has acknowledged the assets and the liabilities of using the consistent ethic framework at the levels of principle and strategic or tactical levels, he clearly opposes single-issue approaches. Although single-issue approaches have strategic advantages in some cases, such as gun control or civil rights legislation, Hehir maintains that "on ecclesiological and moral grounds . . . the logic of the Consistent Ethic compels the church to resist a single issue strategy. Ecclesiologically there is the responsibility of the church to set a tone and an atmosphere in the civil life of society that it cannot do by focusing exclusively on a single-issue. Such a posture risks depicting the church as simply an interest group in a political struggle. The effect of single-issue voting strategies is to reduce the chance that parties and candidates will be judged by standards that test their vision of society and their capacity to address the basic needs of the common good. Morally, a single-issue strategy forfeits many of the resources of the moral teaching of the church. To highlight one question as the primary and exclusive objective in the policy process is to leave too many issues unattended and risks distortion on the single issue itself."[184] Hehir's work at the USCC served to bring the richness of the Catholic social vision to bear on issues across the spectrum cutting through typical political alliances. Thus, on theological and moral grounds, Hehir favors a more comprehensive approach to the range of social and political issues that the church addresses.

Baxter's stance, in its opposition to dangers of the nation-state, focuses mainly on opposition to war, abortion, and market-driven capitalism. In practice, this plays out in opposition to a culture of violence through a strategy of nonparticipation and education (draft counseling) and embodying works of mercy to address socioeconomic needs via local efforts, rather than the large-scale policy advocacy that Hehir would engage. Even in the aftermath of September 11, the response Baxter advocated (from an admittedly pacifist stance) was to counter terrorism and war with the works of mercy and a willingness to die rather than kill others.[185] In the case of the conflict begun in the aftermath of September 11, other Catholic theologians and activists across the spectrum considered addressing related economic and foreign policy issues as essential to attaining a just peace. Immense global economic disparities, conflict and injustice abroad, especially in the Middle East and developing world, and American involvement in the oil and arms trades were among the related factors and underlying conditions contributing to the violence. Catholic advocacy on behalf of the vulnerable and toward articulating and achieving the global common good related to such policy issues would better address the

range of issues related to instances of violence, without necessarily competing with pacifist efforts to resist violent retaliation.[186]

Despite this response typical of Baxter's stance, he has critiqued David
Schindler's communio ecclesiology and civilization of love for being too
vague. In his review of Schindler's book, *Heart of the World, Center of the
Church*, Baxter challenges Schindler to demonstrate how his proposal "translates into a public ethic that draws directly on substantive theological convictions without at the same time underwriting the kind of religious intoleration
disavowed in *Dignitatis humanae*."[187] He goes on to note that "a flurry of questions are unanswered. What does a state under the sway of a 'civilization of
love' look like? Does it prohibit capital punishment? Does it follow church
teaching in the waging of wars? Do its people enjoy basic economic rights,
such as the right to a living wage? Abortion? Crisis pregnancies?"[188] Considering Baxter's own work, the same questions might indeed be posed to him. In
his review he does hint that only local forms of political association can address these issues, citing Alasdair MacIntyre's suggestion that the modern
state is incapable of embodying substantive agreement on the good and genuine community and that virtues can only be cultivated on this smaller
scale.[189] Yet addressing issues such as capital punishment and a living wage
suggest a national or at least larger-scale, structural approach to translate a civilization of love into a concrete public ethic. His critique also seems to imply
novel attention to the dangers posed by a supernaturalized ethic and an imperative to make concrete theological convictions. This suggests potential for
at least limited common ground with an approach such as Hehir's.

Moreover, Hehir has shown signs of understanding the gravity of what
Baxter proposes (more accurately or even sympathetically than some of the
Americanists Baxter repeatedly claims misunderstand or dismiss his approach) and has even raised questions about the ability of his own model to
address certain social questions. Many reformists refer to theological and ethical sectarianism as a seductive temptation, because it provides Christians
with clear distinctiveness in behavior and an unambiguous identity, yet falls
short on social responsibility or commitments to universality and mediation.
James Gustafson worries that it isolates Christians and limits their participation in not only the ambiguities of moral and social life, but also in global patterns of interdependence.[190] He doubts the possibilities of internal or external
critique on such a model, worrying that doctrine becomes idolatry, because
"it isolates theology from any correction by other modes of construing reality."[191] Although Hehir seems to sympathize with Gustafson's concern that
such sectarianism "isolates Christians from taking seriously the wider world
of science and culture and limits the participation of Christians in the ambiguities of moral and social life in the patterns of interdependence in the
world," he asserts that Gustafson fails to fully appreciate the sectarian per-

spective.[192] Hehir writes that Catholic and Protestant advocates of a sectarian position would likely respond that Gustafson does not address their fundamental insight: "Dispelling the ambiguity surrounding military service on a nuclear submarine or medical practice in a university hospital where abortions are performed is necessary because ambiguity masks unacceptable compromise. Legislators whose voting records on war or abortion legislation depict a pattern of *sic et non* are not regarded as holding the moderate middle but having a misguided sense of tolerance and a flaccid conscience."[193] As we shall see below, Hehir similarly challenges those such as Curran who characterize Baxter's stance as a necessarily minority position in the church that the larger church should tolerate but not incorporate.

Furthermore, Hehir has recently acknowledged the inadequacies of restricting theological arguments and claims in the public square. Although he strongly favors public philosophy in matters of law and policy, he has recently alluded to the failure of philosophical and empirical approaches to illuminate the human consequences in policy debates such as those about health care, welfare reform, and foreign aid. He notes that the issues in such debates entail premoral questions that his preferred methodology cannot address, but that religious traditions can and do: convictions about the ties that bind us, our responsibilities to one another, and our rights and duties that are grounded in the prior reality of our shared humanity.[194] Hehir adds that religious communities hold a distinct advantage in being able to address such embedded convictions more readily than empirical or philosophical modes, and that such "theological convictions . . . can illuminate contemporary questions that are being poorly stated."[195] He reasserts that such "theological license is severely restricted" once we address the state on the levels of law and policy, but confesses that "prior to stating the policy issue we can and should expansively engage the wider civil community in the deeper questions that undergird policy choices, and that may take theological argument to the surface, because they are about our basic relationships as a society and a human community."[196]

Hehir also suggests that some social issues are in fact divided precisely along the lines of theological conviction. He points to abortion and assisted suicide, and wonders how to build moral consensus if believers' positions on such issues are directly affected by such Christian tenets as belief in afterlife, an acceptance of suffering as having religious significance, or a profound sense that our lives are in hands of larger mystery or the full human status of the embryo.[197] These steps by Hehir beyond a strict exclusion of theological categories from policy discussions indicate a hint of common ground with some of Baxter's concerns. Thus, although we encounter a degree of difference in the range of issues each addresses, we also encounter recent moves by Baxter and Hehir alike that might suggest prospects for mutual clarification, if not rapprochement.

## Catholic Universalism: Challenges to Baxter's Stance

Roman Catholic understandings of mediation, creation, the universality of Catholic concern and the limits of human understandings (or Catholic conceptions) of God pose several fundamental challenges to Baxter's overall approach. As Hehir's own position and critique suggest, the Catholic theological approach is characterized by mediation, as evidenced in Catholic ecclesiology (our relationship to Jesus takes place through the visible mediation of the church) and the ways in which God's word and love are mediated in the Incarnation and sacraments. Curran rightly points out how Catholic radicalism's division between sin and grace, or church and world, "fails to give enough importance to the reality of the goodness of creation which is present in the world, overestimates the presence of sin in the world, fails to recognize that grace is already present and to a limited extent redeeming the present, and sees only discontinuity between the present and the eschatological fullness."[198] The Catholic emphasis on mediation highlights more of a continuity between nature and grace, reason and faith, the world and the kingdom of God (without denying some discontinuity) than we encounter in Baxter. Grace and nature are not opposed; rather, grace is mediated through the natural and the human. "So too with faith and reason," Curran notes, "No one relying on the Catholic tradition can theologically propose a radical incompatibility between this world and the kingdom of God."[199]

The U.S. bishops suggest that, because human understanding and religious faith are not opposed (though they are not identical, either), constructive dialogue and interaction can ensue between the Catholic community and wider culture. In their pastoral on the economy, they summarize the reasons for this optimism: "Biblical and theological themes shape the overall Christian perspective on economic ethics. This perspective is also subscribed to by those who do not share Christian religious convictions. *Human understanding and religious belief are complementary, not contradictory.* For human beings are created in God's image, and their dignity is manifest in the ability to reason and understand, in their freedom to shape their own lives and the life of their communities, and in the capacity for love and friendship."[200]

In the Catholic tradition, grace builds upon rather than destroys nature. In a critique of Furfey that also applies to Baxter, Curran charges that, although Furfey attempts to ground his radicalism in traditional Catholic theology, "traditional Catholic theology and ecclesiology cannot be consistently radical." Viewing the world at least partly in relation to creation, as the Catholic tradition does, disallows any total opposition between the kingdom of God and this world.[201] Unlike emphases on mediation and their social and ecclesiological consequences, a narrativist approach to Christian identity and engagement considers mediation between the Gospel and other systems of meaning as "fraught with the dangers of blunting its critical edge by lessening its distinctiveness, and of depriving it of its liberating power by treating it as a key to a theoretical interpretation of reality rather than as an inspiration to ethical praxis."[202] The universality of the Catholic Church and its understanding of mediation conflicts with the absolute radicalism of an approach such as Baxter's that is ecclesiologically sectarian (even if the term has come to have connotations that he would resist).

In addition to this tradition of mediation, God's creation and redemption of all of humanity and God's transcendence of human communities' comprehension (even Christians') challenges an excessive ecclesiocentrism. As Hollenbach puts it, the same God in whom Christians believe is the God of all creation, and "for this reason it is possible to hope that the Christian story as told in the scriptures is not entirely foreign or strange to those outside the church. It can raise echoes and perhaps recognition among all who share in the quest for the human good."[203] A self-contained model (that Baxter's approach at least risks) contradicts the catholicity, because the God we believe in is God of all that is. Hollenbach's own proposal is one of public theology in collaboration and conversation with others (intellectual solidarity) toward articulating and achieving the common good. In a proposition that might, in fact, challenge both Hehir and Baxter in different ways, he argues that "theology can contribute to the common good of a pluralist society by being simultaneously fully theological and fully public. Only in this way will it illuminate the meaning of the good with the depth and breadth demanded by those limit questions that drive us into the religious domain." Whereas our status as pilgrims leads Baxter to call for distancing ourselves from the fleeting earthly community beyond the church and its temptations, it leads Hollenbach to conclude that we are always on the way toward an adequate understanding of the full human good and therefore we should seek to "articulate the meaning of biblical faith in dialogue with other traditions' answers to the ultimate questions about the human good," which cannot adequately ensue in closed communities.[204]

This provisional quality of our grasp on the fullness of God's revelation and its directives for how we should live in between times serves to remind us that it is not only collaboration with the state or secular forces that risks idolatrous tendencies. Baxter assumes that such collaboration rests in Catholics' desires to become relevant on secular terms (vis-à-vis the state and in the academy), to continue to move from ghetto to mainstream in a way that he implies compromises Christian distinctiveness and purity. It is important to attune ourselves to the risks equally inherent in a model such as Baxter's, however, such as spiritual pride. Insofar as Baxter's stance reflects Furfey's triumphalist ecclesiology, Catholic understandings of salvation and John Paul II's own affirmation that each human is included in the mystery of redemption challenge its implications for the status of other religions.[205] Christians do not have a monopoly on grace (or on salvation).[206] In short, it risks an exclusivity challenged by Catholic universalism.

In his discussion of religious radicalism in public life in the wake of September 11, J. Leon Hooper, S.J. suggests that true radicalism involves inclusivity, not bright line-drawing to distinguish groups and stake exclusive claims.[207] He calls Dorothy Day most radical not when she was actively demonstrating against nuclear bomb shelter drills or committing to live with the poor and encounter Christ there, but "when she would not allow her religious values to exclude anyone from God's redeeming presence."[208] He argues that "we are learning that any faith that traps the God of love, God compassionate and merciful, within our moral and doctrinal commitments, is a form of idolatry." Although his discussion occurs in the context of Day and Murray in the wake of terrorist attacks in the name of Islam, his sentiments regarding sectarian temptations speak to our topic as well: "To claim only the full realization of justice, or only the full realization of mercy, is always an attempt to play God, and thus to deny the God who continues to create and reveal. . . . The corrective to this idolatry is not abandonment of our hard fought moral discriminations, but lies in a willingness to live with them while simultaneously we acknowledge that God's embracing love reaches beyond them."[209] The type of public engagement that Baxter decries might serve to help resist such ideological distortion from within rather than focusing on deterring the threat only from without.[210] Radicalist claims that realizations of mercy and justice will occur only within Christian communities (particularly when they come together as the Body of Christ rather than when they engage outsiders) at least risk the idolatry Hooper signals.[211]

In a recent address, Baxter signaled renewed attention to several of these risks, arguing that his approach need not imply ecclesial narrowness and underscoring the fact that grace perfects nature rather than destroys it.[212] Baxter noted that belief in the divinity of Christ need not lead to the denial of creation or ecclesial narrowness; rather, the fact that all things are made through God should open us up to other cultures. He referred to a dialectical task in which recovering our true nature entails letting go of our false natures, citing Aquinas, yet reminded his audience that grace sometimes disturbs (false) nature. This approach seems to depart from his characteristically operative grace-sin dichotomy (rather than a nature-grace interaction), which works only to the extent that the world is sinful. Yet Baxter notes that a mode such as that of Anthony of the Desert does not necessarily suggest mere withdrawal, but rather "the desert becomes the city."[213] This conception is suggestive of how Baxter understands the responsibility of a radicalist approach in contrast to accusations of sectarian withdrawal.

## THE MODELS OF HEHIR AND BAXTER: BEYOND COEXISTENCE

In the end, then, does there simply exist an irreducible tension between the two models that Hehir and Baxter exemplify? Is such tension and coexistence theologically necessary, given the character of life between the times? Must a prophetic critique such as Baxter's remain a minority position by nature? Some perceive the Catholic Church as a big church that must include room for such divergent approaches to social ministry and public life. As we saw in Murray's description of incarnational and eschatological humanism, from his perspective the approaches are complementary and not mutually exclusive. Others, such as Hehir, counter that understanding the Catholic Church in the United States as a collaborative, public church that simply tolerates a more radically prophetic minority is becoming increasingly insufficient. Rather, the truth claims and theological foundations grounding each call for the mutual clarification or creative combination of each, rather than polarizing the two approaches, relegating one to minority status, and living with substantive pluralism.

In Hehir's view, it is appropriate for pluralism to exist within the Catholic moral framework: "In the Catholic tradition, pluralism is not anarchy; it has content, limits and rules of discourse which produce a structured pluralism. The meaning of structured pluralism is being worked out in theory and practice in the postconciliar church."[214] He points to episcopal, theological, and political pluralism, evidenced in the differences in specific judgments among international bishops' conferences, room for the tradition of nonviolence amid an affirmation of just-war tradition, and differences in specific conclusions of the peace pastoral, among others. Hehir insists that amid such pluralism principles should be evident and the categories should remain clear.

Although Hehir allows room for multiple models of Catholic witness, he has questioned the adequacy of invoking inclusivity on sociological grounds alone. For example, Curran refers to Catholic prophetic minorities on the left and right who embody the approach Baxter advocates as prophetic shock minorities, and argues that, whereas such Christians who believe that a "special call to witness to peace or to voluntary poverty or to life itself" might "help keep the larger church honest and faithful," they will remain minorities by definition.[215] Hehir acknowledges that this model of a church type encompassing a sect minority group is creative and functional, in that "a big church [Curran's term] needs pluralistic choices for vocation and witness." Yet Hehir notes that Curran fails to acknowledge that such prophetic Catholic groups "often define their position as the minimum the church should adopt. They seek not simply a seat at the table but a chance to define the agenda of the meeting."[216] Furthermore, Hehir thinks we cannot simply invoke a big church model on sociological grounds, i.e., that the majority of members will not adopt a sectarian stance; rather we must have normative reasons why the ecclesial and ethical modes of a big church model are grounded in the Christian tradition.[217] Hehir, too, thinks that the church-sect debate will remain a part of the Catholic landscape and that the medieval model of keeping both within the church must be renewed if not replicated, while reaffirming that the church model should remain the public position of Catholicism.[218]

Hollenbach argues that such coexistence is not only sociologically inevitable, but also theologically necessary. Considering the coexistence of the two approaches in terms of absolute pacifist and just-war approaches (characteristic, as we have seen, of the larger divide), he notes that the tension between justice and nonviolence will never be fully overcome in history, but that its total reconciliation remains an eschatological reality. According to Hollenbach, this implies the necessity of both pacifist nonviolence and self-sacrifice as the route to justice and (just-war) commitment to justice as the way to peace and mutual love. In another sense, it implies the concurrent pursuit of Hehir's and Baxter's approaches. Only the simultaneous presence of both ensures the "full content of Christian hope is to be made visible in history," because each "bears witness to an essential part of the Christian mystery." Hollenbach concludes that both are legitimate and necessary Christian expressions and that their coexistence is a theological necessity, given the reality of Christian life between the times.[219] The coexistence of dual approaches that reflect our public church and radicalist ones remains theologically necessary during Christians' pilgrimage in this life.

Whereas these sociological and theological assessments might, in fact, remain inevitable between the times, my own claim for the mutual clarification of each by the complementary insights of each stance is perhaps best represented by Catholic historian David O'Brien's call for a combination of the two approaches. In *Public Catholicism* O'Brien advances his hope that the responsibility of the Republican type, the effectiveness of the Immigrant type, and the integrity of the Evangelical type "will foster creative interaction whereby a better, richer theoretical framework and a more effective pastoral style might emerge."[220] The U.S. bishops' 1993 "The Harvest of Justice Is Sown in Peace," for example, reflects an attempt to move beyond the mere coexistence of just-war and pacifist approaches. They write, "One must ask, in light of recent history, whether nonviolence should be restricted to personal commitments or whether it should also have a place in the public order with the tradition of justified and limited war."[221] O'Brien thinks that Catholicism is at its best when republicanism and evangelicalism are held in creative tension—and finds this most successfully the case in the bishops' pastorals of the 1980s.[222] We turn now to possibilities for such creative tension or common ground between the two, in light of my analyses of Hehir and Baxter.

Despite their significant differences, hints at some overlap in recent moves by Baxter and Hehir, along with complementary theological emphases in each, suggest that at their best the two approaches need not be competing ones. In at least three areas, the two might clarify and inform one another, cultivating more of a creative than a destructive tension and dismissal that sometimes prevails. This could be achieved by underscoring (1) the Christian call to both charitable and structural justice efforts; (2) the significance of discernment in any social engagement; and (3) prospects for joining liturgical or sacramental renewal to social justice efforts.

Any adequate social ethic calls for a change of heart and a change of institutions.[223] In like manner, with respect to the actions advocated by Hehir and Baxter, each one's emphasis alone remains somewhat one-sided, whether elevating personal conversion or institutional change. Catholic social ethics as a discipline concerns systematic analysis of social issues in light of Christian theology, whereas peacemaking and works of mercy are related but different (and not competing) endeavors. Others would argue that, as a whole, Catholic social teaching focuses too much on structural measures, and that individual practices are underrepresented, such that the latter demand increased focus in social ethics.[224] Whereas this may be the case, many would counter that individual practices fall more into the realm of spirituality or charity than social ethics, or that such underrepresentation points to an imbalance elsewhere such as in catechesis or formation. Baxter would perhaps reply that we cannot separate the Christian call as such, and that such differentiation is part of the problem.

Given the scale and complexity of social problems today, pitting localist, individual practices against structural change falls short, and Baxter's approach alone remains too limited in its ability to adequately address global issues. Similarly, it is not sufficiently evident how local efforts disrupt an entire political system via noncooperation or how they escape reinforcing the status quo by such nonparticipation. Baxter's suggestion that five percent of the efforts of Catholic social ethics should focus on structural change (or that we hire someone such as Hehir to do lobby on discrete issues as they periodically arise) ignores the fact that civic responsibilities are the concerns of every disciple in the Catholic tradition, not simply hired lobbyists, as the bishops are correct to point out.[225] Given the impact of social policies and budget priorities on the lives of the poor (relative to discrete local actions), Catholics are all called to *both* personal and structural activism.[226] Discipleship-informed active citizenship need not be jingoistic or unduly compromise our Catholic identity. Baxter's position as it stands risks political apathy, which de facto serves to reinforce the status quo.[227]

Furthermore, depending on the issue, the church's public witness may be understood as countercultural rather than risking co-optation (e.g., on such issues as abortion, universal health care coverage, or capital punishment). Just as we cannot simply correlate grace and sin to church and world, so we cannot easily conclude that if one advocates on a structural level then she necessarily becomes co-opted by the nation-state. Baxter is correct to warn that political engagement in a culture that contradicts Christian values in many ways (or that prefers the privatization of religion) risks corruption if one does not continually guard against co-optation or form oneself in the Christian tradition. His and others' warnings about conforming Christian ethics in language and approach to a liberal paradigm that seeks to privatize religion (at best) are also important. Yet structural advocacy on behalf of the poor or unborn, it seems, offers a way of responding to the gospel call in an age of complexity, rather than an inherent desire to be respected by or become accommodated to the nation (or liberal paradigm) in the majority of cases. The church not only serves the world by making policy recommendations, but also "by being the sign of God's salvation of the world and by reminding the world of what the world still is not."[228]

Because we are called to engagement on these distinct levels and yet such interaction does entail risks, a crucial aspect of any church-world engagement is proper discernment. This proves to be a particularly promising site for mutual clarification of Hehir's and Baxter's approaches. Any approach taken to its extreme—unrelieved countercultural identity in the face of what is portrayed as total cultural corruption, or merely one path among other equally valid paths—is problematic.[229] As we have seen, each approach draws on different theological strands of the tradition to varying degrees, and understanding which approach is appropriate to given cultural and historical situations will depend on discerning the demands of the given moment. Citing the Barmen Declaration and *Dignitatis humanae* as examples of situations calling for distinct Christian responses, Hollenbach notes that "an assessment of just what the larger culture is up to is essential to authentic Christian identity. There is no *a priori* way to determine whether resistance or learning is called for."[230] Reminiscent of Baxter and Hehir's distinct theological influences, Hollenbach frames this task of discernment as understanding "*when* the affirmation that 'Jesus is Lord' should lead to countercultural resistance and *when* 'God is creator of heaven and earth' should lead to cooperation with non-Christians in pursuit of a universalist agenda." He continues, "Theologically, [both statements are] true. Both are scriptural; both were employed in the formation of Christian identity during the Apostolic age that is still normative . . . it is not possible on theological grounds to grant absolute primacy to one or the other of these two stances on the relation of Christian identity to its intellectual, social and political environment."[231] Thus, we see how prudential discernment can tap into the complementary resources Hehir and Baxter's approaches offer, enabling us to determine when each emphasis is appropriate, and it bridges some of the concerns of Baxter (uncritical embrace of culture) with the engagement that Hehir favors. Because the everyday dilemmas of Christian engagement may be more mundane and less straightforward than the cases of religious liberty or Nazi Germany, attention to formation and discernment becomes more significant.

In fact, Baxter later granted that such questions entail discernment and casuistry, conceding that sometimes one cannot determine in advance which approach will be more Christian—and whether the church is for or against America in certain cases—but that a more useful approach is to focus on practices of discernment in making one's way through moral dilemmas. He nuances Furfey's strategy of withdrawal to argue that one has to determine the relative wisdom of participation and withdrawal on a case-by-case basis.[232] For example, Baxter has delineated certain practices sponsored by the nation-state as unproblematic, such as "obeying traffic laws, putting out the garbage, and using the postal service" and others as "a matter of judgment, voting in elections, for example, or supporting certain political action groups." He insists on actions to be resisted, however, such as "paying federal taxes for war or abortion, and refusing conscription."[233] Even if various reformist lists would look different, therefore, Baxter's affirmation of discernment suggests a promising site of convergence.

One final related point of potential convergence entails the prospects for the role of liturgy in this formation for discernment. As we have seen in Baxter's retrieval of Michel, a liturgy-based ethic is central to his own stance, yet such formation must propel Catholics outward into the world. Baxter contends that Michel's social theory does not call for an in-principled rejection of all social activity external to the church, because it only sets the church against the world in a sectarian way, if by "world" one means the social networks produced by advanced capitalism, the world of autonomous individualism, mass culture, economic oppression, and the rule of secular power.[234] If, as we have argued, discernment is fundamental to determining one's proper response in light of different contexts, perhaps liturgy can serve as a locus and means of formation for such discernment.

Michel holds that liturgy provides a site for helping Christians to embody the Christ-life, and that faith and justice are connected in and through the action of the liturgy, yet that justice is not to be applied to social problems, only embodied. Some have argued that such tendencies to disassociate social engagement from the liturgy are reinforced by the very natural law argumentation in social documents to which Baxter objects.[235] This separation, however, seems to deny the Catholic belief that sacraments point beyond ritual practices out into the world and it falsely opposes embodiment and engagement.[236]

Hehir, too, grounds his work in the sacramental principle that confirms our conviction that the incarnation is extended in time and the transformation of the human in the liturgical life of the community.[237] At the same time, he insists that the sacramental principle must extend beyond the liturgical community, as it commends Christians to help carry on the work of God's reign in history.[238] As Pope John Paul II contends in *Sollicitudo rei socialis*, "All of us who partake in the Eucharist are called to discover, through this sacrament, the profound *meaning* of our actions in the world in favor of development and peace; and to receive from it the strength to commit ourselves ever more generously, following the example of Christ, who in this sacrament lays down his life for his friends."[239] An understanding of liturgy that aids in formation of conscience and educates to action for justice and peace may serve as a point of contact between Baxter's and Hehir's approaches.

Although formation through the liturgy and other sacraments aids in discerning when and how to engage the wider world, however, social, political, and theological analysis remain essential parts of the task of social ethics if the imagination is to be informed by not only the realities of Christian faith, but also of our social environment.[240] Furthermore, holiness may not be hindered but fostered by engagement in the world beyond an ecclesial community. As the late liturgical theologian Mark Searle put it, whereas the liturgy provides a basis for discernment and social criticism, "it neither dispenses with the need for policy planning and programs of social action nor provides us with any specific guidelines for setting about such undertakings."[241] Ideally, proper formation for discernment and mechanisms for guarding against distortion will enable us to better call both church and world to account, and to purify our efforts from distortion from within and without. If the ability to make discriminating judgments is fundamental to determining one's proper response in light of different contexts, then liturgy may serve as a significant locus and means of formation for such discernment. A fully theological and fully public approach guided by liturgically informed discernment will also strengthen connections between spirituality, conversion, and ethics.

The distinct Catholic methodologies profiled here reflect longstanding theological differences and distinct presuppositions. The comprehensiveness of the Catholic call entails a universality and integrity that demand the dynamic, mutual correction of each incomplete approach. A radicalist embodiment of Christian faith severed from any external communication or advocacy limits its witness efforts in the face of internal challenges, just as reformist advocacy severed from embodiment of the norms and practices one promotes significantly undermines credibility. A unidirectional mode of witness (church as teacher but not learner) also discounts the interreligious and ecumenical cooperation to which the post–Vatican II tradition calls Catholics. A commitment to strengthening the connection between embodiment and engagement of Christian norms, principles, and practices will enhance the integrity of Catholic social ethics. Mutual clarification of approaches such as Hehir's and

Baxter's along the lines introduced here should allow for a move away from rigid typologies and toward prophetic, critical engagement that models gospel values and engages the wider world on issues that touch human life and dignity.[242]

## NOTES

An earlier version of this chapter appeared as Kristin Heyer, "Bridging the Divide in Contemporary U.S. Catholic Social Ethics," *Theological Studies* 66 (June 2005): 401–40.

1. J. Bryan Hehir, "Responsibilities and Temptations of Power: A Catholic View," *Journal of Law and Religion* 8, no. 1–2 (1990): 71–83 at 77.

2. Interview with Rev. J. Bryan Hehir, July 13, 2002, Alexandria, Virginia.

3. Charles E. Curran, *American Catholic Social Ethics: Twentieth-Century Approaches* (Notre Dame, IN: University of Notre Dame Press, 1982); Michael J. Himes and Kenneth R. Himes, O.F.M., *Fullness of Faith: The Public Significance of Theology* (New York/Mahwah, NJ: Paulist Press, 1993); David Hollenbach, S.J., *The Common Good and Christian Ethics* (Cambridge: Cambridge University Press, 2002).

4. Curran includes various roles in this model: "teacher and learner, provider for the needy, empowerer and enabler, advocate, and model for society." See Curran, *The Church and Morality: An Ecumenical and Catholic Approach* (Minneapolis, MN: Fortress, 1993), 81–85.

5. Michael J. Baxter, "Blowing the Dynamite of the Church: Catholic Radicalism from a Catholic Radicalist Perspective." Talk delivered at Creighton University, Omaha, Nebraska, on January 26, 1999, cited in John O'Callaghan, "Fr. Michael Baxter on 'Catholic Radicalism,'" in *Center for the Study of Religion and Society* newsletter 11, no. 1 (Fall 1999). Available at http://puffin.creighton.edu/human/CSRS/news/F99-2.html (accessed on November 5, 2002).

6. See John Howard Yoder, *The Politics of Jesus* (Grand Rapids, MI: William B. Eerdmans Publishing Co., 1972).

7. Hehir interview.

8. See Curran, *American Catholic Social Ethics*; David Hollenbach, S.J., *Nuclear Ethics: A Christian Moral Argument* (New York: Paulist, 1983), esp. 31–32; David O'Brien, *Public Catholicism* (New York: Macmillan, 1989).

9. J. Bryan Hehir, "A Catholic Troeltsch? Curran on the Social Ministry of the Church," in James J. Walter, Timothy E. O'Connell, and Thomas A. Shannon, eds., *A Call to Fidelity: On the Moral Theology of Charles E. Curran* (Washington, D.C.: Georgetown University Press, 2002), 191–207 at 202. Hehir rightly objects to this characterization (articulated by Curran, among others), pointing out that such prophetic groups on the right and the left (e.g., Pax Christi USA [PCUSA], Catholic Worker, parts of the pro-life movement) often define their position as the minimum that the church should adopt. In Hehir's words, "they seek not only a seat at the table but a chance to define the agenda of the meeting." See Hehir, "A Catholic Troeltsch?" 202. We shall explore the activities of PCUSA in chapter 4.

10. See also the work of Christian nonviolence scholars James W. Douglass and Gil Bailie.

11. A priest of the Archdiocese of Boston, Hehir was recalled to serve as cabinet secretary for social services, director of social services, and president of Catholic Charities of Boston in January 2004. In July 2004 he was named Parker Gilbert Montgomery Professor of the Practice of Religion and Public Life at the Hauser Center for Nonprofit Organizations, John F. Kennedy School of Government, Harvard University. Hehir has also taught at Georgetown University and at St. John's Seminary, and served as pastor of Saint Paul's Church in Cambridge, MA, and as consultant to Catholic Relief Services.

12. When Hehir worked at the USCC, he served first as director of the Office of International Affairs, then secretary of the Department of Social Development and World Peace, and finally as counselor for Social Policy (in which position he counseled bishops on a broad range of policy areas, but did not manage a staff). For a recent overview of Hehir's work and legacy at the bishops' conference, see William J. Gould, "Father J. Bryan Hehir: Priest, Policy Analyst, and Theologian of Dialogue," in Jo Renee Formicola and Hubert Morken, eds., *Religious Leaders and Faith-Based Politics: Ten Profiles* (Lanham, MD: Rowman & Littlefield Publishers, Inc., 2001), 197–223.

13. Gould, "Father J. Bryan Hehir," 197–98.

14. Ibid., 198.

15. J. Bryan Hehir, "Catholic Theology at Its Best," *Harvard Divinity Bulletin* 27, no. 2–3 (1998): 13–14 at 13.

16. Other contemporary Catholic social ethicists and theologians, such as Charles Curran; Michael Himes; Kenneth Himes, O.F.M.; and David Hollenbach, S.J., support a similarly collaborative model of a public church, although their methodologies are somewhat different. See Curran, *American Catholic Social Ethics*; Himes and Himes, *Fullness of Faith*; Hollenbach, *The Common Good*; J. Bryan Hehir, "Church-State and Church-World: The Ecclesiological Implications," *Catholic Theological Society of America, Proceedings* 41 (1986): 54–74 at 64.

17. Hehir, "A Catholic Troeltsch?" 196; Hehir interview.

18. J. Bryan Hehir, "The Implications of Structured Pluralism: A Public Church," *Origins* 14:3 (May 31, 1984): 40–43 at 40–41.

19. Ibid., 41–42.

20. Hehir interview.

21. Hehir notes that *Gaudium et spes* is "a kind of programmatic document about the Church committing itself to engagement with the world, service to the world, [and] I really see my role as one personal contribution to trying to live out the expectations of that text." See Gould, "Father J. Bryan Hehir," 201.

22. Hehir, "Church-State and Church-World," 58–59. As we noted in chapter 2, Hehir insists that the effort to make the endless distinctions and choices entailed in keeping the church's involvement indirect is essential lest the church retreat (and betray its incarnational dimension) or become politicized (and betray the gospel's transcendence).

23. Gould, "Father J. Bryan Hehir," 201.

24. Hehir, "Catholic Theology at Its Best," 13.

25. In his groundbreaking *The Nature of Doctrine: Religion and Theology in a Postliberal Age*, George Lindbeck articulates a postliberal theology with three major

components: a cultural-linguistic model that seeks to provide a "thick" description of religion as a comprehensive interpretive scheme wherein language functions intrasemiotically; an approach to Scriptural interpretation that stresses the primacy of the biblical narratives and the intratextual hermeneutics of the biblical canon; and the "rule" theory approach to doctrine that views doctrines as non-propositional rules functioning like grammar, governing the confessing community's discourse and practice. Unlike theologies that seek to translate a tradition's symbols into wider categories, Lindbeck's model "redescribes reality" within the scriptural framework so that the text absorbs the world, rather than the world absorbing the text. See George Lindbeck, *The Nature of Doctrine: Religion and Theology in a Postliberal Age* (Philadelphia: Westminster Press, 1984) esp. chapter 6. For an analysis of Lindbeck's methodology with particular attention to the public nature of theology, see Kristin Heyer, "How Does Theology Go Public? Rethinking the Debate between David Tracy and George Lindbeck," *Political Theology* 5:3, July 2004, 307–27.

26. Gould, "Father J. Bryan Hehir," 202.

27. Ibid.

28. J. Bryan Hehir, "Response to Stephen Pope's 'Catholic Social Teaching and the American Experience,'" (Spring 2000 Joint Consultation) Joint Consultation, *American Catholics in the Public Square* initiative, Commonweal Foundation and Faith and Reason Institute (Annapolis, MD: June 2–4, 2000). Available at www.catholics inpublicsquare.org/papers/spring2000joint/pope/popepaper2.htm (accessed May 26, 005). As I made clear in chapters 1 and 2, the focus of my project concerns religious activity on the civil-societal level. Hehir holds that once religious groups directly lobby Congress or otherwise attempt to get the state to shape its policy in a specific direction with laws that coerce, they enter the church-state arena. Some of my findings may pose a challenge to this delineation and some of Hehir's own statements suggest a less stringent distinction than he delineates here between church-state and church-society involvement. For our purposes here, we can understand Hehir's approach as favoring a philosophical or natural law–based approach in matters of policy fairly broadly considered—in my view this "asceticism" extends to the church-society range in Hehir's own work and preferences even though he has changed his view on the permissibility of theological language at the societal level, as we shall see below.

29. It is worth mentioning that the pastoral letters issued by the U.S. bishops (which used both theological and more natural law–based and empirical modes of discourse) were, in part, attempts to change policy.

30. Hehir interview. Hehir resists any direct appeals to biblical discourse and religious discourse when entering the specifics of law and policy choices. He admits, however, that there is a symbiosis between society and state and that discourse on the civil societal level does have the potential to shape perspectives and illuminate issues. He notes that this is why he has come to see the wisdom of using theological language at the civil societal level, and has been convinced by others to distinguish the use of natural law or philosophical discourse for matters of law and policy alone.

31. Hehir, "Responsibilities and Temptations of Power," 77.

32. J. Bryan Hehir, "Public Theology in Contemporary America: Editor's Forum," *Religion and American Culture* 10, no. 1 (Winter 2000): 1–27 at 23–24.

33. J. Bryan Hehir, "From the Pastoral Constitution of Vatican II to *The Challenge of Peace*," in *Catholics and Nuclear War: A Commentary on* The Challenge of Peace, *The U.S. Catholic Bishops' Pastoral Letter on War and Peace*, Philip J. Murnion, ed. (New York: Crossroad, 1983), 71–87, at 80–81.

34. Hehir, "From the Pastoral Constitution," 81.

35. Hehir, "The Implications of Structured Pluralism," 40.

36. J. Bryan Hehir, "Personal Faith, the Public Church, and the Role of Theology," (Convocation Address at the Opening of the 180th Year), *Harvard Divinity Bulletin*, 26, no. 1 (1996): 4–5 at 5.

37. Ibid.

38. Ibid. The work of Henri de Lubac has been foundational for Hehir's conception of this essential sociality of Catholicism. According to de Lubac, Catholicism "is social in the deepest sense of the word: not merely in its application in the field of natural institutions but first and foremost in itself, in the heart of its mystery, in the essence of its dogma." The ways in which de Lubac highlights the social character of Catholicism as expressed in its sacramental life, its conception of community, and its doctrine countered the isolation of theology from social issues, thereby placing Catholicism "at the center of the world." See Henri de Lubac, *Catholicism: A Study of the Corporate Destiny of Mankind* (New York: Sheed and Ward, 1958), x. Hehir notes that, according to de Lubac, "the faith and the church *are* social before they articulate a response to social needs and social questions," and a conception foundational to opening paragraphs of *Gaudium et spes*. See J. Bryan Hehir, "The Church in the World: Responding to the Call of the Council," in James L. Heft, S.M., ed., *Faith and the Intellectual Life: Marianist Award Lectures* (Notre Dame, IN: University of Notre Dame Press, 1996), 101–19 at 103–4.

39. Hehir, "Personal Faith," 5.

40. Hehir, "Responsibilities and Temptations of Power," 73–74.

41. The first four chapters of *Gaudium et spes* discuss the meaning of the incarnation for the human person and human history, transforming our understanding of human dignity (no. 22), deepening our sense of community and solidarity (no. 32), giving new dignity to human work and culture (no. 39), and grounding the church's salvific ministry in history (no. 45). See J. Bryan Hehir, "Church-Type Reinvigorated: The Bishops' Letter," in *Peace, Politics and the People of God*, Paul Peachey, ed., (Philadelphia: Fortress Press, 1986), 47–67 at 50.

42. Hehir, "The Church in the World," 113.

43. Ibid., 114.

44. Yves M-J Congar, *Lay People in the Church: A Study for a Theology of the Laity* (Westminster, MD: Newman Press, 1957), 81, as cited in Hehir, "The Church in the World," 109. Although Congar acknowledges the permanent validity and presence in the church community of the dualist-eschatological view (expressed in the monastic vocation's conformity with the city that is to come), he is more convinced by "a certain continuity between the human work of this world on the one side and the kingdom of God on the other" as a basic position for the church. Congar takes care not to collapse distinctions between church, world, and kingdom, and yet he advocates a "transformative view of ecclesiology and eschatology," wherein "the kingdom ultimately is a work of the Spirit, a gift of God, but the Spirit transforms what has been prepared in history by human work through culture, scholarship, politics, art, economics and law" (Hehir, "The Church in the World," 109).

45. Hehir, "The Church in the World," 109–10.

46. Ibid., 103. To name just one of his examples, "St. Paul's theology of history depicts the whole cosmos awaiting redemption ('. . . the universe itself is to be freed from the shackles of mortality and enter upon the liberty and splendor of the children of God,' Rom 8:21), but he warns the disciples not to be conformed to the pattern of the world (Rom 12:2)."

47. Hehir, "The Church in the World," 103, yet Hehir's own work does not seem to be consistently attentive to sin, in particular.

48. Interview with Michael J. Baxter, CSC, South Bend, Indiana, July 18, 2002.

49. Michael J. Baxter, "A Sign of Peace: The Mission of the Church to the Nations," *Catholic Theological Society of America, Proceedings* 59 (2004): 19–41 at 30.

50. Hehir calls Murray his biggest influence and notes that to this day he rereads Murray repeatedly (Hehir interview).

51. It was Murray himself who advised Hehir to study ethics somewhere where he could get the international relations first, because his theology would be too rigid if he formed it ahead of time; he advised Hehir to "get immersed in the fabric of the problem, then work your way through it" (Gould, "Father J. Bryan Hehir," 199).

52. Ibid.

53. Hehir, "Response to Stephen Pope's 'Catholic Social Teaching and the American Experience.'"

54. J. Bryan Hehir, "The Perennial Need for Philosophical Discourse," in David Hollenbach, ed., "Current Theology: Theology and Philosophy in Public: A Symposium on John Courtney Murray's Unfinished Agenda," *Theological Studies* 40 (1979): 710–13.

55. Letter written by Thomas Merton to James Forest, 21 October 1961, in William H. Shannon, ed., *The Hidden Ground of Love: The Letters of Thomas Merton on Religious Experience and Social Concerns* (New York: Farrar, Straus and Giroux, 1985) 256. The *America* magazine article by L.C. McHugh, S.J. (September 30, 1961) defended the use of force to protect against neighbors from invading one's nuclear air-raid shelter. Merton published a response to McHugh's piece in *The Catholic Worker*, "Shelter Ethics." For an analysis of Merton's critiques of Murray in this vein, see Patricia McNeal, *Harder than War: Catholic Peacemaking in Twentieth-Century America* (New Brunswick, NJ: Rutgers University Press, 1992), chapter 5, "Thomas Merton at the Crossroads of Peace."

56. Hehir notes that "Economic Justice for All" and "The Challenge of Peace" were designed to relate these three aspects and to speak to the ecclesial and civil communities simultaneously. See Hehir, "Responsibilities and Temptations of Power," 75.

57. Hehir interview. Hehir mentions George Weigel among those who advocate the culture-forming rather than legislative roles that the church should play (see Hehir's own description of the educational-cultural typology at the end of chapter 2).

58. Hehir, "Responsibilities and Temptations of Power," 78.

59. Ibid., 75–76.

60. Dulles cites statements from Vatican II's *Apostolicam actuositatem* and *Gaudium et spes* regarding the renewal of the temporal order as the special responsibility of the laity, and noting that clergy should not be expected to provide concrete solutions to complex secular problems. See *Apostolicam actuositatem*, no. 7

and *Gaudium et spes*, no. 43 as cited in Avery Dulles, "Gospel, Church and Politics," in Richard John Neuhaus, ed., *American Apostasy: The Triumph of "Other" Gospels* (Grand Rapids, MI: Eerdmans Publishing Co., 1989), 29–55 at 47–49.

61. Hehir, "Responsibilities and Temptations of Power," 78.

62. Ibid.

63. Hehir, "Church-State and Church-World," 69.

64. J. Bryan Hehir, "The Consistent Ethic: Public Policy Implications," in Thomas G. Fuechtmann, ed., *Consistent Ethic of Life* (Chicago: Loyola University Chicago, 1988), 218–36 at 224–26.

65. Hehir, "The Social Role of the Church: Leo XIII, Vatican II and John Paul II," in Oliver F. Williams, CSC and John W. Houck, eds., *Catholic Social Thought and the New World Order: Building on One Hundred Years* (Notre Dame, IN: University of Notre Dame Press, 1993), 44–45.

66. Ibid., emphasis added.

67. Hehir, "The Social Role of the Church, 45.

68. Hehir, "A Catholic Troeltsch?" 201.

69. J. Bryan Hehir, "The Prophetic Voice of the Church," lecture given at Boston College sponsored by the Boisi Center for Religion and American Public Life (April 1, 2002). Transcript available at www.bc.edu/bc_org/research/rapl/index.htm (accessed June 15, 2003).

70. Hehir, "The Prophetic Voice of the Church."

71. Hehir, "Church-State and Church-World," 71.

72. Andre refers to Andre Bessett, a member of the Holy Cross order who had been recently canonized at the time of its founding. A few years after the house was established, the St. Joseph the Worker job service was founded to help the poor find jobs as an alternative to the day labor agents. I am indebted to Michael Lee at Fordham University for this background information.

73. Baxter's courses have also included texts from the Catholic social tradition. In his "The Rise and Fall of Catholic Social Ethics" he covers *Rerum novarum*, *Quadragesimo anno, Gaudium et spes, Centesimus annus,* and "The Challenge of Peace." That course syllabus also includes *The Fullness of Faith* by Michael Himes and Kenneth Himes, yet its course description notes that "it is the task of Catholic theologians in the twenty-first century to disclose how this violence and acquisitiveness is masked and reinforced by the modern discourse of 'Catholic social ethics.'" Baxter's recent syllabi are available at www.nd.edu/~mbaxter/Classes.htm (accessed February 25, 2005).

74. Baxter is not only at the beginning of his career relative to Hehir, but he mounts a critique of the majority of mainstream Catholic social ethicists' approaches, such that his social ethic will necessarily be presented largely in terms of what he opposes and challenges rather than a chiefly constructive account.

75. Michael J. Baxter, "In the World but Not of It," interview with the editors of *U.S. Catholic* 66, no. 8 (August 2001), 224–28 at 24.

76. Michael J. Baxter, "Catholic Americanism and Catholic Radicalism," in Sandra Yocummize and William L. Portier, *American Catholic Traditions: Resources for Renewal* (Maryknoll, NY: Orbis Books, 1997), 53.

77. Michael J. Baxter, "Review Essay: The Non-Catholic Character of the 'Public Church,'" *Modern Theology* 11, no. 2 (April 1995) 243–58 at 244. "Religion

does not lay claim to the bourgeois; instead, the bourgeois lays claim to religion. Religion does not transform society; rather, bourgeois society does not rest until religion fits in with itself and with what it considers reasonable" (Johann Baptist Metz, *The Emergent Church: The Future of Christianity in a Postbourgeois World*, trans. Peter Mann [New York: Crossroad, 1981], 83).

78. Ibid., 246.

79. See Yoder, *The Politics of Jesus;* or Stanley Hauerwas, *A Community of Character: Toward a Constructive Christian Social Ethic* (Notre Dame, IN: University of Notre Dame Press, 1981), esp. part 2, 89–154.

80. On Baxter's account, those writing in Murray's tradition include most Catholic social ethicists today, whether they employ public philosophy or public theology. He names, e.g., Hehir, David Hollenbach, S.J., John Coleman, S.J., Richard John Neuhaus, Dennis McCann, J. Leon Hooper, S.J., and Todd Whitmore (Baxter interview).

81. Baxter, "In the World but Not of It," 25. He notes that liberal or progressive Catholics have taken up this task by addressing issues of war, economic justice, and race (naming Hehir's involvement with "The Challenge of Peace" and Hollenbach's role in "Economic Justice for All"). Neoconservative social ethicists think we should introduce religious values into public discourse and provide the moral leadership that can return the United States to its founding vision.

82. He criticizes the very notions of freedom, justice, common good, and civil society as also concealing the dehumanizing world the bottom fifth of society inhabit. See Baxter, "'Blowing the Dynamite of the Church': Catholic Radicalism from a Catholic Radicalist Perspective," Michael L. Budde and Robert W. Brimlow, eds., *The Church as Counterculture* (Albany, NY: State University of New York Press, 2000), 195–212 at 207. Hereafter this citation title will refer to the article in the Budde and Brimlow volume rather than the aforementioned talk under the same name.

83. Baxter, "Blowing the Dynamite of the Church," 207.

84. Michael J. Baxter, "Writing History in a World without Ends: An Evangelical Catholic Critique of United States Catholic History," *Pro Ecclesia* 5 (Fall 1996): 440–69 at 442. For a more in-depth look at what Baxter calls this Americanist history (both its historical meaning [or meanings] and his focus on "how Catholic philosophers, political theorists, and historians put forth a vision of harmony between Catholicism and the United States"), see William Halsey, *The Survival of American Innocence* (Notre Dame, IN: University of Notre Dame Press, 1980), especially chapters 3, 4, 8, and 9. Baxter also cites as the "most influential work locating Murray in the Americanist tradition," the work by Donald Pelotte, S.S.S., *John Courtney Murray: Theologian in Conflict* (New York: Paulist Press, 1976).

85. John Courtney Murray, *We Hold These Truths: Catholic Reflections on the American Proposition* (New York: Sheed & Ward, 1960, 1988) 56*ff.*

86. Baxter does note, however, some non-Catholics might charge that despite Murray's claims, the natural law is more Catholic than natural (Baxter interview).

87. Baxter adds that, in Murray's day, there was a major institutional division between philosophy and theology, such that most disciplines were philosophically shaped and not theologically informed (Baxter interview).

88. Baxter himself might be subject to the charge of dualism (grace/sin dualism with a rejection of nature). We shall return to this nature/grace divide later in the chapter's analysis section, as well as in chapter 5.

89. Michael J. Baxter, "Reintroducing Virgil Michel: Towards a Counter-Tradition of Catholic Social Ethics in the United States," *Communio* 24 (Fall 1997): 499–528, at 520–21. He notes that such privatization stems from the historical division of theology and social theory or religion and politics into two separate spheres, that then become mediated by the translations provided by social ethics in the postconciliar era (prior to Vatican II they were mediated by philosophical terms).

90. Ibid., 522.

91. In their *Fullness of Faith*, for example, Michael Himes and Kenneth Himes translate theological concepts and commitments into principles to make explicit their social and policy implications. For example, the Trinity grounds an anthropology of mutuality and relationality, thereby theologically grounding a theory of human rights. See Himes and Himes, chapter 3, 55–73. See "Review Essay" for Baxter's critique of the Himes's approach.

92. Baxter, "Review Essay," 248–51. As an example, Hauerwas charges that "justice as participation" (as endorsed by Dennis McCann and David Hollenbach, in this case) "turns out to be another way to say Catholics should be good Americans." See Stanley Hauerwas, "The Importance of Being Catholic: Unsolicited Advice from a Protestant Bystander," in his *In Good Company: The Church as Polis* (Notre Dame, IN: University of Notre Dame, 1995), 91–108, at 105.

93. Baxter asks "What is truthfulness? Intelligibility? Rightness? And so on." See Baxter, "Review Essay," 251–52. Recall the similar objections raised in chapter 1 that such standards for public discourse will inevitably be political all the way down or at least will unduly burden more evangelical or orthodox approaches that are more suspicious of reason or natural law.

94. Baxter, "Review Essay," 252–53.

95. Michael J. Baxter, "Catholicism and Liberalism: Kudos and Questions for Communion Ecclesiology," *The Review of Politics* 60, no. 4 (Fall 1998): 743–64 at 745–46. He notes that these more liberal Catholic social ethicists are heirs to Murray's tradition no less than ethicists like George Weigel, Michael Novak, and Richard John Neuhaus.

96. Michael J. Baxter, "Rekindling the Spiritual Revolution: Merton and Company on Faith and Reason," address delivered to "New Wine, New Wineskins" conference, Notre Dame, IN (July 22, 2002).

97. Baxter admits that his proposals call for a major shift that requires an intellectual revolution so that Catholics start to think more like Mennonites, who, he insists, also engage the world (Baxter interview).

98. Reaching beyond those predecessors, Baxter notes that scholars in the "Murray Tradition" have Karl Rahner's and Bernard Lonergan's theologies behind their approaches, whereas he stands more in the tradition of Hans Urs von Balthasar, believing that we cannot understand transcendental knowledge without categorical knowledge, or actual material stuff, drama, narrative (Baxter interview).

99. Baxter, "Blowing the Dynamite of the Church," 200.

100. Ibid., 207.

101. Ibid. Dorothy Day, *The Long Loneliness* (San Francisco: Harper and Row, 1981) 268.

102. Day originally founded her opposition to war on historical arguments showing that war profited the rich at the expense of the poor, but by 1940 she had grounded her pacifism in Christian personalist action rooted in the gospel's love command, and she viewed war as the "ultimate objectification of the human person." See Curran, *American Catholic Social Ethics*, 163. See William D. Miller, *A Harsh and Dreadful Love: Dorothy Day and the Catholic Worker Movement*, (Garden City, NY: Doubleday Image Books, 1974), 157–85.

103. Baxter, "Writing History in a World without Ends," 465.

104. Baxter, "Blowing the Dynamite of the Church," 202; Day, *The Long Loneliness*, 170.

105. Patricia M. Vinje, "The Political Holiness of Dorothy Day: Eschatology, Social Reform, and the Works of Mercy," in Ann W. Astell, ed., *Lay Sanctity, Medieval and Modern: A Search for Models* (Notre Dame, IN: University of Notre Dame Press, 2000) 161–72 at 171.

106. Baxter, "Blowing the Dynamite of the Church," 202; Paul Hanley Furfey, *Fire on the Earth* (New York: Macmillan, 1936), 202.

107. Curran, *American Catholic Social Ethics*, 138–39. For an example of this approach, see Paul Hanley Furfey, "Five Hard Sayings Repugnant to Natural Man," *America* 56 (April 3, 1937): 604–5. Curran notes that when Furfey met Day in 1934 he found what he was searching for: the use of supernatural means to achieve the social ideal by taking the New Testament literally. See Curran, *American Catholic Social Ethics*, 134.

108. Ibid., 142.

109. Furfey, *Fire on the Earth*, 135.

110. Curran, *American Catholic Social Ethics*, 137.

111. See Paul Hanley Furfey, "Correspondence," *Theological Studies* 4 (September 1943): 467–72; "Intercredal Cooperation: Its Limitations," *American Ecclesiastical Review*, 111 (September 1944): 161–75; "Why Does Rome Discourage Socio-Religious Intercredalism?" *American Ecclesiastical Review*, 112 (May 1945): 364–74; "Are You Ashamed of the Gospel?" *Integrity* 1 (October 1946): 26–31.

112. These debates led to Murray's aforementioned distinction between incarnational and eschatological humanism. Baxter argues that this distinction between incarnational and eschatological humanism and debate between Murray and Furfey prefigure the subsequent stances of James Gustafson and Dorothy Day. I would add that it anticipates underlying differences in the stances of Hehir and Baxter himself, or as Baxter sees it much of mainstream Catholic social ethics in its philosophical and public theological instantiations on the one hand and a more rigorist, radicalist approach in the tradition of Day, Furfey and many Protestants on the other. See also, Joseph A. Komonchak, "John Courtney Murray and the Redemption of History: Natural Law and Theology," in J. Leon Hooper, S.J., and Todd David Whitmore, eds., *John Courtney Murray and the Growth of Tradition* (Kansas City, MO: Sheed & Ward, 1996), 60–81 at 72. Komonchak notes that Furfey's adjectives for Catholic conformists such as Murray were quite harsh, calling them "dishonest, cowardly, half-hearted, disingenuous, ashamed of the Gospel, deserving of Pius X's mocking question: 'What is one to think of a Catholic who checks his Catholicism

at the door as he enters his study club so as not to shock his comrades?'" (Komonchak, "John Courtney Murray and the Redemption of History," 72).

113. At times he qualifies the incompatibility and it is not total (Curran, *American Catholic Social Ethics*, 144).

114. See Murray, "Correspondence," 472–74; Wilfred Parsons and John Courtney Murray, "Intercredal Cooperation (Washington, D.C.: The Catholic Association for International Peace, 1943); Murray, "On the Problem of Co-operation: Some Clarifications," *American Ecclesiastical Review*, 112 (March 1945): 194–214. Although Murray continuously emphasized that cooperation on the basis of natural law was neither ideal nor adequate (nor did it absolve Catholics from the obligation to pursue a distinctly Catholic program of prayer and organized action), Furfey rejected his attempt to ground political discourse in nature rather than the supernatural, and Furfey challenged "a politics tailored to the exigencies of modern pluralism" (Baxter, "Writing History in a World without Ends," 464; Furfey, *Fire on the Earth*, 79–97).

115. Furfey, *Fire on the Earth*, chapters 6 and 7, as cited in Baxter, "Writing History in a World without Ends," 464.

116. Baxter, "Writing History in a World without Ends," 464; Furfey, *Fire on the Earth*, 92–97, 46–50.

117. Furfey, *Fire on the Earth*, 1–21, 32, 51.

118. Baxter, "Catholic Americanism and Catholic Radicalism," 62.

119. Baxter, "Reintroducing Virgil Michel," 499–528.

120. Ibid., 525.

121. As Baxter articulates it, "for Michel, human dignity, community and participation are not mere 'themes' to be extracted from ecclesial symbols and then applied to 'social' problems; rather, they are to be embodied in specific ways as exemplified in the liturgy itself. And . . . for Michel, it is not necessary to make a connection between faith and justice; that connection is already made in and through the action of the liturgy. . . . In short, for Michel, 'justice' is not *derived* from the Christ-life. It is *embodied* in the Christ-life" (Baxter, "Reintroducing Virgil Michel," 523).

122. Michel's understanding of justice, "justice-as-embodied-in-the-Christ-life," does not fit neatly into the faith-justice dichotomy operating in contemporary social ethics discourse in Baxter's view. Baxter thinks Michel's approach should inform social ethics and not be considered as limited to the liturgical realm alone, but he doubts that will ensue because Michel's "understanding of the social is too deeply embedded in the beliefs and practices of a particular ecclesial body and thus does not speak to the wider 'public'" (Baxter, "Reintroducing Virgil Michel," 523).

123. Baxter, "Reintroducing Virgil Michel," 525. Liturgical theologian Mark Searle points out that, on the other hand, "the liturgical assembly reflects, not the justice of the Kingdom, but the divisions of social groupings," which he says represents a tension rather than an achievement, something given yet always to be realized. See Searle, "Serving the Lord with Justice," in his *Liturgy and Social Justice*, (Collegeville, MN: Liturgical Press, 1980), 13–35 at 25.

124. Ibid., 525. Baxter likens Michel's understanding of the liturgy's function here to George Lindbeck's concept of "absorbing the universe into the biblical

world" in his *Nature of Doctrine*. Similarly, the liturgy functions as "a complex set of gestures, rituals, texts, and images that discloses the destiny of the universe and moves it toward that destiny." See Baxter, "Reintroducing Virgil Michel," 526; and George Lindbeck, *The Nature of Doctrine: Religion and Theology in a Postliberal Age* (Philadelphia: Westminster Press, 1984), 135.

125. For a different understanding of the legacy of Virgil Michel with respect to liturgy and social justice, see Mark Searle, "The Liturgy and Catholic Social Doctrine," in *The Future of the Catholic Church in America: Major Papers of the Virgil Michel Symposium* (Collegeville, MN: Liturgical Press, 1991), 43–73.

126. Baxter interview.

127. Hauerwas, *A Community of Character*, part 2; Hauerwas, *The Peaceable Kingdom: A Primer in Christian Ethics* (Notre Dame, IN: Notre Dame University, 1983), esp. 99–101.

128. Baxter, "In the World but Not of It," 27.

129. Ibid., 28.

130. James Gustafson, "The Sectarian Temptation: Reflections on Theology, the Church and the University," *Proceeding of the Catholic Theological Society of America* 40 (1985): 83–94.

131. Baxter, "Blowing the Dynamite of the Church," 205.

132. Ibid. Furthermore, Baxter notes that such an approach "fails to take seriously a contention that has been central to the life of the Catholic Worker from the beginning, namely that the modern nation-state is a fundamentally unjust and corrupt set of institutions whose primary function is to preserve the interests of the ruling class, by coercive and violent means if necessary—and there will always come a time when it is necessary."

133. Baxter, "Writing History in a World without Ends," 465. I am unsure in the end if Baxter then calls American Catholicism from mainstream to ghetto, so to speak, and, if so, how this avoids risking distortion from within.

134. Ibid.

135. Baxter, "In the World but Not of It," 28.

136. He admits that he read a lot of Karl Marx in college, so he is naturally wary of the state, but also that when he reads Murray and his successors such as Hehir on the state's reach as limited to matters of public order, he wants to ask "where is this limited state?" He adds that this instinct reflects Hauerwas' influence (Baxter interview).

137. Baxter, "Writing History in a World without Ends," 457.

138. Michael J. Baxter, "Is this Just War? Two Catholic perspectives on the war in Afghanistan," interview between editors and Baxter and Lisa Sowle Cahill, *U.S. Catholic* 66, no. 12 (December 2001): 12–16 at 14.

139. Stanley Hauerwas uses the term *resident aliens* to refer to Christians in the world. See Hauerwas and William H. Willimon, *Resident Aliens: Life in the Christian Colony* (Nashville: Abingdon Press, 1989).

140. Baxter, "Review Essay," 255.

141. Baxter, "A Sign of Peace." This distinction was made in the context of a nation such as the United States engaging in a preemptive war with a nation such as Iraq.

142. Curran, *American Catholic Social Ethics*, 164–65.

143. Baxter interview; Howard Zinn, *A People's History of the United States* (New York: Harper & Row, 1980).

144. Baxter, "Catholic Americanism and Catholic Radicalism," 53–54.

145. See Max Weber, "Politics as Vocation," ("Politik als Beruf") *Gesammelte Politische Schriften* (Muenchen, Germany, 1921), 396–450. Originally a speech at Munich University, 1918, it was published in 1919 by Duncker & Humblodt, Munich, Germany.

146. Baxter, "Review Essay," 256. Thus, underlying differences in approach, in part, reside in these theoretical differences about the antifoundationalist challenge. Baxter and those he writes against represent two different routes, in his view, beyond the neo-Thomist dichotomy between the natural and supernatural: "one way seeks *rapprochement* with the Enlightenment and with autonomous secular order through a reconstrual of the 'natural,' while the other finds in Christian tradition resources generating, in counter-Enlightenment fashion, a *theology* of politics grounded in 'the supernatural'" (Baxter, "Review Essay," 256). In George Lindbeck's terms, Baxter is a cultural linguistic type and he thinks most contemporary articulators of Murray are in one way or another experiential expressivists (Baxter interview). Space here does not permit an in-depth analysis of the challenges posed by antifoundationalism or the conflicting claims of experiential-expressivist and cultural-linguistic approaches (and those that would defy either categorization), but these distinctions reveal the depth of the differences between the two approaches.

147. Baxter, "Catholic Americanism and Catholic Radicalism," 60–61.

148. Baxter, "Writing History in a World without Ends," 447.

149. We find an emphasis on the one, true church opposing an emphasis on the church as voluntary society compelled by its mission to interact with other bodies with distinct conceptions of the good that the church can teach and learn from (but not merely one among others or a relativistic tolerance) amid a situation of pluralism.

150. Curran has raised the charge of ineffectiveness against Furfey's approach—and, by extension, that advocated by Baxter (Curran, *American Catholic Social Ethics*, 167).

151. Baxter adds, in "equally condescending and misleading ways" (Baxter, "Blowing the Dynamite of the Church," 204–5). Baxter analyzes Weigel's depiction of Day and the Catholic Worker in his *Tranquilitas Ordinis* (New York: Oxford, 1987) 148–73, and Curran's portrayal of Day and Furfey in his *American Catholic Social Ethics* (Notre Dame, IN: University of Notre Dame Press, 1982), 130–71.

152. Baxter traces this religion-politics dualism through the models that shape social ethics discourse via Ernst Troeltsch, H. Richard Niebuhr and Reinhold Niebuhr, and James Gustafson: "ideal/real, absolute/relative, individual/social, sect/church, love/justice, Christ/culture, kingdom/history" (Baxter, "Blowing the Dynamite of the Church," 203–4).

153. Baxter, "Writing History in a World without Ends," 465.

154. As Hehir puts it, "it's good for Baxter to pull and tug at someone like me" (Hehir interview). Hehir's concession here highlights the tensions within the tradition as a whole that we encountered in chapter 2.

155. Ibid.

156. Baxter interview.

157. Hehir interview.

158. Hehir, "Responsibilities and Temptations of Power," 82.

159. In his *Christian Perspectives on Politics*, J. Philip Wogaman compares different generating centers in the Christian tradition in their approaches to political questions. He argues that those he refers to as mainstream liberals are influenced by the moral realism of Reinhold Niebuhr, and thus believe that with original sin as the great leveler, it is difficult to separate humanity along moral lines. Pacifists, (or radicalist approaches more generally, I might add), "come close to the simple notion that it is possible to avoid sinfulness—and therefore that a kind of moral separation can be made between those Christians who accept the pacifist orientation and those who do not." It should also be mentioned that he finds a similar tendency to divide humanity along moral lines in the other generating centers, if for different reasons and along different particular lines (e.g., liberationists, neo-conservatives, and evangelicals of the left and right). See Wogaman, *Christian Perspectives on Politics* (Louisville, KY: Westminster John Knox Press, revised and expanded edition, 2000), 138.

160. We shall return to this directive in chapter 5.

161. The first combines carefully stated religious and moral principles with the ability to control relevant empirical data in policy arguments in order to ensure sound moral analysis. The second requires that religiously based arguments be translated or rendered persuasive to a wider, pluralistic audience; civil intelligibility "simply establishes a test for religious communities to meet: to probe our commitments deeply and broadly enough that we can translate their best insights to others." The third criterion, political courtesy, is a matter of style and is the "secular equivalent of charity," or a respect for one's adversaries and their arguments (Hehir, "Responsibilities and Temptations of Power," 82). For a study of religious civility in the U.S. context among Protestants, Catholics, and Jews (including a case study of John Courtney Murray, S.J.), see John Murray Cuddihy, *No Offense: Civil Religion and Protestant Taste* (New York: Seabury Press, 1978).

162. Hehir, "Responsibilities and Temptations of Power," 82.

163. A public church stance may be conceived of as grounded in love of a faith community (just as a radicalist stance) rather than necessarily accomodationist or seeking public relevance alone. Baxter's posture might be understood as rooted in love of a faith community that stands apart from the nation-state, whereas Hehir's could be understood as grounded in love of a faith community situated in the United States where Catholics share with others responsibility for a common life.

164. John Carr, Director, Office of Social Development and World Peace, USCCB, remarks that Hehir says that the most important word in Catholic theology is the word "and." Telephone interview with John Carr, April 15, 2003.

165. Hehir, "Catholic Theology at Its Best," 13.

166. Ibid.

167. Scott H. Moore, "The End of Convenient Stereotypes: How the *First Things* and Baxter Controversies Inaugurate Extraordinary Politics," *Pro Ecclesia* VII, no. 1 (Winter 1998): 17–47 at 30.

168. Hehir, "Church-State and Church-World," 72.

169. "Even if our sacrifices aren't as dramatic [as martyrs'] we should have a share in that sacrifice. We're all called to be saints." (Baxter, "In the World but Not of It," 28).

170. Curran, *American Catholic Social Ethics*, 166.

171. He recounts the founding of the National Catholic War Council in 1917 in an effort to mobilize Catholics in support of the war effort. After World War I, the name of the council was changed to the National Catholic Welfare Council, then NCCB/USCC, and now the USCCB. Baxter perceives similar dynamics at work in the colleges and universities and thinks together both reflect a desire by Catholics to bring Catholicism and Catholic social principles to America (Baxter interview). I discuss the origins of the USCCB further in chapter 4.

172. Michael J. Baxter, "Dispelling the 'We' Fallacy from the Body of Christ: The Task of Catholics in a Time of War," *The South Atlantic Quarterly* 101, no. 2 (Spring 2002): 361–73 at 364.

173. Baxter interview. Similarly, Hauerwas has written that "opposition to abortion involves much more than opposition to abortion. In fact, it does nothing less than put Catholics at odds with the primary ethos and institution of the liberal culture that has just accepted [Catholics]." Hauerwas, "The Importance of Being Catholic," 107.

174. Hehir, "The Social Role of the Church, 29–50 at 44. Too often missing from the public debate are several significant links: radical denunciation of abortion linked to an outpouring of compassionate care; on the realist side a convincing argument on the importance of abortion as a public, shared problem; and sustained efforts by policymakers to connect abortion legislation to related issues (e.g., explicitly linking opposition to abortion to concrete poverty-related issues regarding prenatal care, infant feeding programs, health care, and education).

175. Capital punishment or universal health care advocacy are others.

176. Wogaman, *Christian Perspectives on Politics*, 152.

177. Hehir also views this issue as illustrative of the imperative of using non-theological language in public debate. He writes, "Pacifism has a *prima facie* moral attractiveness; for state leaders it is virtually unintelligible as a strategic posture. In debates about assisted suicide, Christian eschatological hope and convictions about the ultimate meaning of human suffering are intrinsic to the Catholic position; can they be shared as reasons in a societal debate? . . . Even if certain theological convictions can be made somewhat intelligible, should they be the basis for law and policy?" Hehir goes on to recount his distinction between the permissible use of theological or religious language in discourse in civil society and its impermissibility in discourse that is designed to shape law and policy (for the latter invokes "the coercive power of the state and touch[es] the lives of all citizens"). See Hehir, "A Catholic Troeltsch?" 203.

178. Hollenbach, *Nuclear Ethics*, 25.

179. Ibid., 26.

180. Ibid., 28–29.

181. Gould, "Father J. Bryan Hehir," 198, 207. We shall return to a fuller examination of the U.S. Catholic bishops' advocacy efforts and the consistent ethic-of-life agenda in chapter 4.

182. Ibid.

183. Hehir, "The Consistent Ethic," 218.

184. Ibid., 233.

185. Baxter, "Dispelling the 'We' Fallacy from the Body of Christ," 370–71.

186. See Kristin Heyer, "U.S. Catholic Discipleship and Citizenship: Patriotism or Dissent?" *Political Theology* 4.2 (June 2003): 149–77 at 173.

187. David Schindler, *Heart of the World, Center of the Church: Communion Ecclesiology, Liberalism, and Liberation* (Grand Rapids, MI: Eerdmans, 1996).

188. Baxter, "Catholicism and Liberalism," 743–64 at 761.

189. Ibid., 761–62.

190. Gustafson, "The Sectarian Temptation," 84.

191. Ibid., 86. Gustafson rightly argues that "the theologian addressing many issues—nuclear, social justice, ecology, and so forth—must do so as an outcome of a theology that develops God's relations to all aspects of life in the world, and develops those relations in terms which are not exclusively Christian in a sectarian form." He controversially continues, "Jesus is not God," which I am certain would sound off alarms in the camps of those he is writing against, but I think his later phrasing puts his point more acceptably: "Theology has to be open to all the sources that help us to construe God's relations to the world; ethics has to deal with the interdependence of *all* things in relation to God. . . God is the God of Christians, but God is not a Christian God for Christians only." See Gustafson, "The Sectarian Temptation," 93–94. Hauerwas has responded to critiques such as Gustafson's with the defense that a model such as Baxter's and his own entails sufficient reality checks, for "one of the tests of the truthfulness of Christian convictions cannot help being the faithfulness of the church" (Stanley Hauerwas, *Christian Existence Today: Essays on Church, World, and Living in Between* [Grand Rapids, MI: Brazos, 1988], 11). The extent to which such assessment sufficiently ensues in groups that generally construe the influence between religious and nonreligious worlds unidirectionally or whose critiques typically focus on the outside world remains debatable.

192. Ibid., 84

193. Hehir, "Church-State and Church-World," 71.

194. Hehir, "Personal Faith," 5.

195. Ibid.

196. Ibid.

197. Hehir, "Response to Stephen Pope's 'Catholic Social Teaching and the American Experience.'"

198. Curran, *American Catholic Social Ethics*, 168.

199. Ibid., 159. This counters perhaps a typically Protestant conception of reason and its role vis-à-vis faith, particularly post-Fall, and it may be worth mentioning that some of Baxter's most formative influences (though not developed in detail here) include Protestant theologians Stanley Hauerwas and John Howard Yoder. Recall Komonchak's Thomistic and Augustinian distinctions outlined in chapter 2.

200. NCCB, "Economic Justice for All," no. 61 as cited in Hollenbach, *Justice, Peace and Human Rights: American Catholic Social Ethics in a Pluralistic Context* (New York: Crossroad, 1988), 75 (emphasis added by Hollenbach).

201. Curran, *American Catholic Social Ethics*, 158–59.

202. Robert Gascoigne, "Christian Identity and the Communication of Ethics," Annual Meeting of the Catholic Theological Society of America, San Jose, CA, (June 9, 2000).

203. David Hollenbach, "The Common Good in the Postmodern Epoch: What Role for Theology?" in James Donahue and M. Theresa Moser, eds., *Religion, Ethics and the Common Good, Annual Publication of the College Theology Society* 41 (Mystic, CT: Twenty-third Publications, 1996), 3–22 at 16.

204. As he puts it, "The God of Jesus Christ is always greater than anyone, even Christians, can comprehend" (ibid., 20).

205. Pope Paul VI, *Nostra Aetate* (*Declaration on the Relationship of the Church to Non-Christian Religions*), in Walter M. Abbot and Joseph Gallagher, 660–68; Pope John Paul II, *Centesimus annus*, no. 53 (in David J. O'Brien and Thomas A. Shannon, *Catholic Social Thought: The Documentary Heritage* [Maryknoll, NY: Orbis, 1998], 479).

206. Charles E. Curran, *Catholic Social Teaching 1891–Present: A Historical, Theological and Ethical Analysis*, Washington, D.C.: Georgetown University Press, 43.

207. J. Leon Hooper, S.J., "Religious Idolatries and Absolutist Claims," Woodstock Forum on the topic "Being Radically Religious in Public Life," *Woodstock Report* (June 2002): 8–9. Hooper is presently working on a related comparative study of Day and Murray.

208. Hooper implies this was perhaps easier for Day to do for the poor than for capitalist managers.

209. Hooper, "Religious Idolatries and Absolutist Claims," 8–9.

210. In a somewhat analogous critique of a Lindbeckian approach, David Tracy rightly fears that if theology does not engage critically and self-critically in the global, interdisciplinary conversation—which his own model embraces—it will not escape ideological distortion from within and without. Tracy notes that a self-enclosed model risks disregarding "religion's own suspicions on the existence of those fundamental distortions named sin, ignorance, or illusion" (David Tracy, *Plurality and Ambiguity: Hermeneutics, Religion, Hope* (Chicago: University of Chicago Press, 1987), 112.

211. I am not calling Baxter idolatrous here; instead, I am highlighting some of the risks entailed by the stance he represents and advocates.

212. Baxter, "A Sign of Peace," 35.

213. Ibid., 34.

214. Hehir, "The Implications of Structured Pluralism," 42.

215. Curran, *The Church and Morality*, 120–21. Curran borrows the phrase from Jacques Maritain, who used it to describe groups in civil society (Maritain, *Man and the State* [Chicago: University of Chicago Press, 1951]; Hehir, "A Catholic Troeltsch?" 202.

216. Ibid.

217. Ibid.

218. Hehir, "Church-State and Church-World," 71. Hehir has called the medieval model the moment where Troeltsch showed the wisdom of the Catholic Church's ability to incorporate both church and sect models within it. He notes that in the medieval period Innocent III governed the church and Saint Francis with his followers embodied a more sectarian approach (Hehir, "The Prophetic Voice of the Church").

219. Hollenbach calls this a "theological consequence of the incompleteness and partiality of *any* specification of the relation between the kingdom of God and the realities of history" (Hollenbach, *Nuclear Ethics*, 31–32).

220. O'Brien, *Public Catholicism*, 244–52.

221. NCCB, "The Harvest of Justice is Sown in Peace: A Reflection of the National Conference of Catholic Bishops on the Tenth Anniversary of the Challenge of Peace," (Washington, D.C.: USCC, 1993). They go on to insist that, "in the absence of a commitment of respect for life and culture of restraint, it will not be easy to apply the just-war tradition, not just as a set of ideas, but as a system of effective social constraints on the use of force" (ibid.).

222. Baxter would likely contest the success of the bishops' pastorals as combing the two approaches in a balanced manner. In Baxter's words, "'Public Catholicism' never seriously considers a scenario in which the United States of America proves incapable of adhering to the teachings of the gospel, or to the precepts of natural law, or even to the watered-down natural law principles regularly churned out by the N.C.C.B. in the form of public policy recommendations. This is because O'Brien's narrative is structured in such a way that its resolution can be found only in the marriage of Catholicism with the United States, and it is on this score that his narrative, like [John Tracy] Ellis' and [Jay] Dolan's narratives, should be read as a neo-Constantinian narrative." (Baxter, "Writing History in a World without Ends," 462.) Thus, Baxter finds O'Brien's attempt to allow the types to mutually inform one another questionable, because Baxter argues mainstream efforts to do so that rely on the typical paradigm of understanding public as accessible to and engaging national-level politics and discourse will necessarily privilege a public church model and fail to grant a radicalist, evangelical approach normative status.

223. See Curran, *American Catholic Social Ethics*, 167; Curran, *Catholic Social Teaching*, 45–47.

224. This seems to be a rising concern among the next generation of Catholic moral theologians. It was a theme repeatedly mentioned at the "New Wine, New Wineskins" conference that convened young Catholic moral theologians on topic of the vocation of the Catholic moral theologian, Notre Dame, Indiana, July 2002.

225. Baxter interview; Episodic lobbying alone ignores the role Catholic engagement plays in keeping normative questions alive in the public debates on an ongoing basis.

226. Even if every lay Catholic will not become involved in direct lobbying as such, such activism includes importance of becoming informed, advocating, engaging in public conversation about these issues that touch on human life and dignity—and voting.

227. Although his position sketched above on the dangers of Christian involvement with the nation-state led him to give a talk few years ago on the "Politics of Unholy Indifference," Baxter notes that his thinking has changed somewhat. Rather than indifference (or a Furfeyan nonparticipation), which, in my view, simply reinforces the status quo, John Cavadini has helped convince Baxter that indifference does not work. Cavadini points out that for Augustine, the virtue of apatheia is supplanted by the practice of forgiveness. Baxter now agrees that perhaps it is not enough to be apathetic (or stoic), but that rather we are called to actively seek the refuge of the forgiveness of sins for self and others, to actively

seek reconciliation by embodying the works of mercy (Baxter interview). Still, however, this does not supply a robust warrant for structural action.

228. William T. Cavanaugh, "Church," in *Blackwell Companion to Political Theology*, in Peter Scott and William Cavanaugh, eds., (Malden, MA: Blackwell, 2004), 393–405, at 404.

229. Hollenbach, "Response to Robert Gascoigne's 'Christian Identity and the Communication of Ethics,'" CTSA Convention, San Jose, CA, June 9, 2000.

230. He does, however, insist that this excludes the possibility of viewing the church as a self-contained narrative community, for it would bypass this necessary effort to discern and distinguish "cultural wheat from cultural chaff." Yet he admits uncritical appeals to natural law, the universal human community and reason are unacceptable as well. Hollenbach perceives this task as constitutive of life between the times (Hollenbach, "Response to Robert Gascoigne").

231. Ibid.

232. Baxter interview.

233. Baxter, "Catholic Americanism and Catholic Radicalism," 64–65.

234. Baxter, "Reintroducing Virgil Michel," 525.

235. See Walter J. Woods, "Liturgy and Social Issues," in Peter Fink, ed., *New Dictionary of Sacramental Worship* (Collegeville, MN: Liturgical Press, 1990) 1198–1201 at 1199. He suggests that when the liturgy's promotion of justice, peace, and charity through prayer and personal conversion predominate, they "can eclipse the historical and public dimensions that are also proper to liturgy." Further, the social teachings' natural law argumentation leads some to believe it is "tangential to the church's faith and worship," leading them to question the substance of such teachings and the legitimacy of public engagement.

236. As Hollenbach puts it, "Each of the sacraments has a social relevance that arises from the grace it bears. The sacramentalizing of God's grace that occurs in the church is not solely for the benefit of the internal life of the Christian community but also for the whole world. . . The Eucharist expresses not only the participation in the death and resurrection of Christ that is the source of Christian unity, but the radical source of the unity of the human race." See Hollenbach, *Justice, Peace and Human Rights*, 197. For an analysis of the potential contribution of the Catholic sacramental imagination to the church's prophetic and social mission, see Hollenbach's "A Prophetic Church and the Catholic Sacramental Imagination," in John C. Haughey, S.J., ed., *The Faith that Does Justice: Examining the Christian Sources for Social Change* (Woodstock Studies Vol. 2) (New York: Paulist Press, 1977), 234–63. The NETWORK case study in chapter 4 will serve to break down this false opposition and consequently challenge or bridge the theoretical divisions we encounter in Baxter and Hehir.

237. In fact, in a foreword to *Liturgy and Social Justice*, Hehir calls for a systematization and integration of the church's liturgical and social ministries: "For if, as John Paul II stated at Puebla, the Church's 'evangelizing mission has as an essential part action for justice,' then such action surely must be rooted in the liturgy that Vatican II called the summit and source of Christian life." See Searle, *Liturgy and Social Justice*, 9–11 at 10.

238. Hehir, "Personal Faith," 5.

239. Pope John Paul II, *Sollicitudo rei socialis*, no. 48, in O'Brien and Shannon, 431. In fact, in John Paul II's 2003 encyclical, *Ecclesia de Eucharistia*, in the course of his discussion of the relationship of the Eucharist to the church, he adds that those who are indifferent to the suffering of the poor are not worthy to partake in the Eucharist (see no. 20) (Pope John Paul II, "Ecclesia de Eucharistia." *Origins* 32, no. 46 [May 1, 2003]: 753–68 at 759).

240. Hollenbach, *Justice, Peace and Human Rights*, 201.

241. Searle, "Serving the Lord with Justice," 30.

242. Christine Firer Hinze has offered analogous proposals of a radical-transformationist ethics in her work bridging the approaches of liberals and liberationists. She applies this hybrid proposal to reformist and radicalist methodologies in Catholic social ethics in responding directly to Baxter's plenary address to the Catholic Theological Society of America. Firer Hinze notes that: "a radical-transformationist Catholic social ethic would seek, for example, to bring radicalist witness *into dialectical solidarity with* reformist policy initiatives; to hone a nuanced natural law language *overtly anchored in and accountable to* scripture and liturgy; insert Christians into secular society to serve their neighbors *in response to and as witnesses of* the love of Jesus Christ and the power of the Holy Spirit" (Christine Firer Hinze, "A Response to Michael J. Baxter," *Catholic Theological Society of America, Proceedings* 59 [2004]: 42–49, at 46). For her earlier proposals see Christine Firer Hinze, "Christian Feminists, James Luther Adams, and the Quest for a Radically Transformative Ethics," *Journal of Religious Ethics* 21 (Fall 1993): 275–302; and "James Luther Adams and U.S. Liberationists: Mutual Pedagogy for Transformative Christian Ethics," *American Journal of Philosophy and Theology* 17 (January 1996): 71–92.

# CHAPTER FOUR

# Catholic Political Advocacy in the Contemporary U.S. Context

The Catholic Church in the United States has maintained a presence in Washington since the National Catholic Welfare Conference was established just after World War I. Today, its successor, the United States Conference of Catholic Bishops (USCCB), works in part to advocate for the vulnerable and apply Catholic teaching to major social and political issues. Yet the Catholic lobby extends beyond this official arm of the U.S. church, including a variety of membership organizations, religious orders, and other associations. Although these groups, in most cases, do not directly oppose the work of the bishops' conference, there are a range of differences in emphasis and approach. The political patterns of Catholic advocacy generally defy typical partisan divisions, due to its progressive stances on social welfare and labor and conservative positions on abortion and education policy, yet various Catholic groups operate across the typical ideological spectrum. Those who tend to collaborate with more progressive secular groups include Catholic Charities USA, Jesuit Social Ministries, and the Campaign for Human Development. The more conservative Catholic League for Religious and Civil Rights works to fight anti-Catholic bias in the media and is generally opposed by groups such as the American Civil Liberties Union and Americans United for the Separation of Church and State.[1] Associations of Catholic hospitals and parochial schools lobby largely to protect their own financial interests. State Catholic conferences engage in legislative advocacy at more local levels. Finally, some groups are sustained by significant Catholic memberships although they are not chiefly Catholic organizations, such as National Right to Life (the oldest antiabortion group in the United States), JustLife (lobbies for the seamless garment agenda) and Bread for the World (the Christian hunger lobby).[2]

In their comprehensive study of religion and politics in the U.S. context, political scientists Fowler, Hertzke, and Olson name several strengths of the American Catholic lobby: "a theological comfort with politics, a scholastic tradition of serious reflection on issues, clear lines of leadership, and a potentially strategic position in broader political alignments."[3] The ways in which

Catholic groups approach public life are also shaped significantly by the fact that theirs is uniquely a world church, and by their connection to Catholic institutions (hospitals, schools, charities, and universities). The social and political issues taken up by Catholic lobbyists in general tend to defy strictly partisan boundaries, so Catholic advocacy frequently serves as a bridge between liberal Protestant and evangelical approaches and social issues, due to its positions on poverty and welfare on the one hand, and abortion and schools on the other.

Once again, for our purposes, NETWORK, Pax Christi USA, and the policy and advocacy arms of the USCCB will serve as illustrative cases that point to certain tensions that we have been examining. These three organizations are not intended to provide a comprehensive account of Catholic advocacy in the U.S. context. Rather, by exploring the activity, motivations, and self-understanding of these three Catholic advocacy groups, we will examine how the theological approaches we encountered in chapters 2 and 3 play out in the real world.[4] How do such groups consider their Catholic identity? What is the relationship of that identity to their political activity or how do they move from Christian values to the politics of Washington? What do some of their internal practices (such as their decision-making processes and coalition work) reveal about these differences in mission and practice? How do they measure their own effectiveness? An overview of each organization with an eye to these dimensions will shed further light on the appropriate possibilities for and limits to political advocacy.[5]

## NETWORK

In December 1971, 47 religious sisters from a variety of orders and 21 states convened in Washington, D.C., to discuss organizing a network of women religious concerned about public policy issues. There they decided to form a political action network for the communication of information, political education, and action, and with that step NETWORK became the first registered Catholic social justice lobby in the United States.[6] From its origins, the group set out to be "women-led, linked to the economically exploited, rooted in the social justice tradition of the church, reflective of experience, centered around working collaboratively, and dedicated to educating and organizing grassroots constituencies for political lobbying."[7] That description well fits the group thirty years later: Today, NETWORK's membership surpasses 12,000 and the group educates, lobbies, and organizes to influence the formation of federal legislation to promote economic and social justice.[8] In its own current mission and vision statements, NETWORK articulates its purpose and methodology in visionary terms: "NETWORK envisions a social, economic and political order that ensures human dignity and ecological justice, cele-brates racial, ethnic and cultural diversity, and promotes the common good. NETWORK supports and builds political will to develop a just, participatory and sustainable world community. Founded as a contemporary response to the ministry of Jesus, NETWORK uses Catholic Social Teaching and the life experience of people who are poor as lenses for viewing social reality. As a women-led membership organization, NETWORK values participation, mu-tuality, cooperation and stewardship."[9] In order to lobby for public policies that will enable all people's basic human needs to be met, NETWORK works in solidarity with the economically exploited.[10]

## Organizational Structure and Membership

To this day, NETWORK's staff consists of many women religious and layper-sons, with several lobbyists, field organizers, and staff who work on its edu-cational initiatives. Its membership comprises many congregations of women religious and laypersons, most of whom are very plugged in to contempo-rary policy issues and who "already perceive political advocacy as a man-date of faith and are waiting for NETWORK to tell them what to do."[11] Its membership includes more than 1,100 organizational memberships, more than 300 congregations of sisters, priests, and brothers, and about 800 parishes, dioceses, and other groups. NETWORK views itself as uniquely representing those at the bottom of the economic ladder (women, in particular, because they comprise 70 percent of the world's poor; immigrants; or those who fall between the cracks) as well as the middle class or those concerned about jus-tice issues. NETWORK addresses policy issues from the perspective of those living in poverty, but its own membership does not always reflect that demo-graphic. The group is trying to expand its membership beyond its current white, middle-class base to close the gap between its members and those it represents.[12] In a recent membership survey, one respondent notes, "If we advocate for people who are poor, we have a responsibility to be in relation-ship with people who are poor. We must continually strive to speak with rather than for the marginalized. 'Nothing about me, without me' as disabil-ity rights advocates wisely urge."[13]

NETWORK engages a variety of measures in the course of its advocacy work, from traditional lobbying; to activating its membership's advocacy via action alert alerts, a legislative hotline that allows members to e-mail their representatives on current legislation; sample letters to the editor and tele-phone scripts; and its bimonthly magazine, NETWORK Connection, with is-sue analysis, legislative news, and voting records. NETWORK's Education Program offers faith-based educational resources and training programs for its membership and other groups, providing "nonpartisan issues analysis, skills development for responsible citizenship, and faith reflection on political ministry."[14]

## Range of Issues

NETWORK's vision of a just world and its focus on Catholic social teaching requires that it make an option for the poor and create an environment of peace. Its lobbying work focuses on five issue areas: (1) housing; (2) the federal budget (military spending, taxes, campaign finance reform); (3) health care; (4) global trade, aid, and debt (sometimes includes ecological issues); and (5) economic equity or its antipoverty agenda.[15] NETWORK sends quarterly issue updates in each of these five areas to its members, with in-depth analysis and calls to action. National Coordinator Kathy Thornton, R.S.M., emphasizes that, because NETWORK focuses on people who are poor, its advocacy work remains attentive to issues that affect the poor the most, particularly around systems that make and keep people poor.[16] This is one reason NETWORK focuses so intensely on the federal budget, because the allocation of funds determines who gets what; throughout its history, NETWORK has continually worked for a better balance between military and domestic spending.[17] The organization has also focused on opposition to American military activity over the decades, due to its commitment to peace, (e.g., in the late 1970s and early 1980s it was particularly active on Central American issues, and it advocated against U.S. military involvement in Iraq beginning in 2003).

Every four years, leading up to presidential elections, NETWORK presents priority issues and then polls its membership to determine the issues on which the members would like NETWORK to focus its energies. This consultation-affirmation process is important both to ensure NETWORK represents the concerns of its members, as well as to live out its commitment to collaboration and participation more generally. The organization also works to get input from people who are poor, especially when it drafts statements. For instance, in 2000, NETWORK gathered economists, ethicists, and social workers, along with staff and participant representatives from four direct service agencies to generate its "Economic Equity Statement." NETWORK's connection to organizations operated by women religious and by service agencies helps to keep it in touch with those on the receiving end to facilitate such participation, as evidenced in its recent Welfare Reform Watch Program. In this program, NETWORK interviewed more than 3,000 patrons in various emergency facilities around the country (shelters, health clinics, soup kitchens) to examine the short- and long-term effects of the 1996 legislation. These connections also augment NETWORK's credibility in its lobbying work: When one of its lobbyists was called to testify on Temporary Assistance to Needy Families (TANF) reauthorization, she was able to bring with her a woman from Florida who gave first-hand experience of her attempt to move off welfare.[18]

A survey of NETWORK's agenda for 2005 (109th Congress, 1st session) conveys its most recent legislative priorities. This agenda includes working to

- establish and ensure a living wage for all workers;
- ensure the social safety net (the full funding of TANF, WIC, and food stamps);
- provide health care for all (including Medicare prescription coverage, the legalization of imported prescription drugs, and universal, comprehensive coverage);
- attain just treatment for immigrants, including affordable housing, and fair and just taxation;
- reorder budget priorities (by opposing increases in military spending for nuclear weapons, national missile defense, the Western Hemisphere Institute for Security Cooperation, and military aid to Colombia while supporting adequate investment in human needs domestically and globally);
- advocate for global peace and security (work to end war in Iraq, promote diplomatic efforts to resolve conflict and promote SMART security); and
- work toward fair and just trade and responsible investment (oppose CAFTA and Dominican Republic FTA and Trade Promotion Authority).[19]

NETWORK strives to bring Catholic social principles to bear on issues of economic equity, peace, and global justice with a perennial emphasis on issues it deems to have the most significant impact on the poor, such as federal budget priorities and social safety net legislation.

## Collaboration and Coalition Work

NETWORK often collaborates with other faith-based and secular groups, working in coalitions on various issues such as housing issues and tax cuts. It frequently works with other faith-based groups, and its members note that there is great respect across all groups for different faith traditions and a recognition of fundamental similarities undergirding major traditions (one staff member mentions resonance with Jewish and some Muslim groups on such Catholic social principles as human dignity and option for the poor, in particular).[20] With the Bush Administration's emphases on the faith-based initiative and compassionate conservatism, NETWORK has experienced more outreach to faith-based groups from the administration. NETWORK also works in coalition with secular organizations that share its goals, such as the Children's Defense Fund, the Coalition on Human Needs (a conglomerate of more than 100 agencies and service groups), the National Council of La Raza (Hispanic affairs), the National Association for the Advancement of Colored People, the American Federation of Labor and Congress of Industrial Organizations, and some national women's groups. Coalition members generally take a specific area (such as Medicaid or prescription drug coverage) and develop a plan together, and write both their own and joint letters to deliver to Congress and alert their field members. Thornton notes that "the processes of democracy and Catholic social teaching call us to be in collaboration with others," and NETWORK is also influenced by other faith traditions and other organizations that share the same vision as they collaborate together. She adds that NETWORK's mission is enhanced and promoted by working with others, consistent with its theological understanding that everything is sacred and nothing is profane; for if its mission of justice is to create right relationships, she notes, it needs to be in collaboration and dialogue without excluding other voices.[21]

## Catholic Identity and Theological Sources

Although NETWORK's mission and vision are deeply influenced by the gospel and Catholic social teaching, its Catholic identity has been somewhat distinct from that of the official hierarchy throughout its history. NETWORK staff describe its identity as informed not only by the Catholic tradition in general, but by the prophetic charism characteristic of congregations of women religious, in particular. Thornton characterizes the latter spirit as one calling NETWORK to a dynamic of continual growth and conversion and "to create in one's own structures what one believes should happen in the world."[22] NETWORK embodies a blend of "the justice vein of Catholicism" and the feminist perspective imbued in its founding and sustained by its connection with congregations of women religious.[23]

NETWORK describes three lenses it uses to select, critique, and construct legislation: (1) Catholic social principles and the gospel message (respect for human dignity, common good, dignity of work, option for the poor, dignity of all creation, and participation as basic human right); (2) the life experiences of people who are poor; and (3) a "feminist/womanist/mujerista perspective" that "promotes mutuality, equality, and collaboration" and values women as contributing members of society; respects "the diversity of women's experiences in moving from oppression to liberation," and that recognizes that the majority of people worldwide living in poverty are women.[24]

Throughout its written materials both for Congress and its members, NETWORK consistently integrates themes from Catholic social teaching, scripture, and U.S. bishops' pastorals into its analysis of policy issues. In NETWORK's education program, staffers also apply scripture and Catholic social principles to contemporary social problems, such as globalization, environmental destruction, and racism.[25] Thornton identifies three purposes that Catholic social teaching serves: it helps NETWORK staff to describe their vision of a just society; its principles help them analyze issues and articulate their position; and it influences how they construct lives together, or how they model within their organization what they want to see in the world. The final purpose is evidenced in NETWORK's participative decision making, its move to a collaborative management style that Thornton describes as "a new way of exercising power: power sharing rather than domination" (this aspect is also influenced by NETWORK's feminist perspective), and salary sharing to promote the value of work and equal human dignity.[26]

Because NETWORK is a women-led organization, founded amid the third wave of the feminist movement, a feminist perspective has always been another significant lens for interpretation. It emphasizes that respecting women as full moral agents and full human beings is basic to the dignity of each human person. At present, the organization's understanding of how its Catholic and feminist identities inform one another is evolving. Some staff view the organization as operating out of a feminist and justice strand of Catholicism that, in some ways, is able to remain prophetic precisely because this unique tradition remains outside of the official church hierarchy, and they perceive no tension. Other staff believe, however, that when NETWORK does educational outreach in mixed groups of Catholics at parish levels, for example, it is unfair (or unhelpful) to use that as a feminist Catholic forum when there are different levels of exposure to feminist and liberation theologies.[27]

At its thirtieth anniversary weekend of reflection in June 2002 in Washington, D.C., outside consultant and theologian Christine Gudorf reflected that the most significant question the organization needs to investigate is what the word Catholic means in Catholic Social Justice Lobby. She pointed out that, whereas the founders of NETWORK looked to Catholic social teaching and the bishops' statements as giving direction to their work, it is less clear today where NETWORK stands as a specifically Roman Catholic group. Gudorf noted the variety of rituals—Quaker, Buddhist, Native American—it included in its weekend retreat, and the fact that she did not hear words such as salvation, cross, or Jesus during the weekend.[28] When pushed on whether they consider NETWORK's primary identity to be Catholic or feminist, several staff members answered that they could not separate the two, one adding, "just like I cannot separate spirituality and justice."[29] The sources that inform NETWORK's vision and action are clearly defined, yet its Catholic identity may be evolving. The group's leadership understands the organization as situated within a prophetic vein of Catholicism, influenced by its social tradi-

tion and the experience of women religious, whereas other insiders and outsiders remain less clear about the Catholic character of NETWORK's identity.

## Catholic Values and the Politics of Washington

When they are explaining the unique presence of religious sisters on Capitol
Hill or how NETWORK moves from gospel and encyclical foundations to the
politics of Washington, NETWORK staff members insist that the call to be a
person of justice is implicit in the call to faith, and that working for justice entails working with government structures, which are human institutions. Several staff members refer to their work as a political ministry, because they perceive politics as a ministry of justice, not something evil or something to be
avoided.[30] Thornton believes that Jesus' message that "I've come that [you]
may have life and have it to the full" (John 10:10) is to begin in this life on
earth, so "NETWORK considers how to foster the fullness of life for all people in the here and now." She notes that the organization's founders viewed
their efforts at influencing society's structures and systems so they do not exclude as a new way to bring about God's reign here on earth, or a movement
toward that vision.[31]

Thornton characterizes NETWORK, as it enters its fourth decade, as still
transitioning from a movement to an organization, such that it continues to
pursue a prophetic vision approach, as the passion and energy that are part
of a movement remain present in this community of justice.[32] In an arena
where compromise is the name of the game, she contends, NETWORK's commitment to the poor means that "we will be on their side no matter what, even
if that means we are out there alone on some issues where others might
change, we stick with it if in our best analysis we cannot do anything differently."[33] Prophetic also describes the stance NETWORK wants to ensure it
maintains as it stands with the poorest who are affected by policies and who
are often left out. (For example, legislative measures often help the working
poor or persons with low incomes, but not persons at the very bottom, as evidenced in TANF debates, where sometimes it was deemed just too hard to
help people with multiple barriers.)

Although they agree NETWORK is more prophetic than pragmatic, its
lobbyists point out that a certain jockeying around is entailed in the political
process and that they must remain conscious of what is realistic in order to
make a difference. Even though politics is the art of compromise, they all emphasize that they do not compromise on principle. Reflecting on its mission
to bring gospel values to bear amid the American political climate, most NET-
WORK staff describe their approach as being open to incremental change
without compromising on their direction, or understanding that in a pluralistic society one might need to compromise on strategy, but not on one's goal.[34]

As an example of compromising in the sense of accepting incremental change, lobbyist Catherine Pinkerton, C.S.J., points to the fact that NETWORK believes that access to health care for all Americans is possible, but realizes that it will not achieve universal coverage overnight. As a result, the incremental changes it does achieve might entail compromise, but it remains firm on whether or not steps are leading toward its goal or fragmenting the effort.[35] One difference from other lobbying groups, however, is that it does not need to enter into trade-offs, such as supporting one bill at one point knowing others will perform another favor or guarantee a different vote at another time.[36]

Against those who would argue that prophetic voices must not engage the government, NETWORK views itself as having an important role to play by remaining at the table: nudging, expressing the need, although listening to others, and although its work sometimes entails compromise, it is important that it remain in the conversation so that undesirable policy does not go too far and to gain results that are "less bad."[37] In terms of distinguishing between the realms of purity and compromise that concern people when they bring Catholic principles to bear on political decisions, Thornton emphasizes her own view that poverty is evil. In Ignatian terms of the Kingdom of God and the Kingdom of Evil, she contends that "there is no way we can live on this earth and allow poverty to be what it is."[38] She says that, although some may warn of the corrupting nature of state, "if we want democracy to work, we need to be able to be in there and fight against what does corrupt, just as we must in our own struggle to be human beings."[39]

## Translation of Religious Language

One related issue for Catholic lobbyists is getting the lobbyists' religious message across amid a pluralistic context. Because NETWORK staff has found that religious language is often off-putting for people and that arguments framed solely in such language get dismissed, they find it important to be able to translate their vision into nuts and bolts language. Thornton notes that she herself is more comfortable in religious language: She talks about the vision of a just society, but when people ask what that entails, she translates her vision into concrete specifics such as "everyone has affordable housing, access to jobs, and resources for health care and welfare."[40] Religious values are desired by some members of Congress, however, and they want to hear the explicitly religious perspective or moral voice. Discussing TANF provisions with several religious organizations including NETWORK, Tom Daschle's legislative assistant notes that "there is an important role for faith-based communities in talking about these issues [related to TANF like provisions for immigrants, e.g.] on moral and individual levels, to counter the knee-jerk reaction that 'we shouldn't have to take care of these people.'"[41]

The language NETWORK uses also depends on its audience: On Capitol Hill, staff do not use the term *Catholic social teaching* as often, but in op-eds to diocesan papers they are more likely to do so. Furthermore, to some degree NETWORK is able to rest on its Catholic identity without having to explain it, for it is known as a Catholic lobby, and when lobbyists (all women religious) from NETWORK testify before Congress, they are introduced with the title "Sister." Others note that, although they may differ in language depending on the setting, they do not differ in the message. For example, they generally speak of justice in secular settings but social justice, or reign of God, in religious ones.[42] For NETWORK to be effective, it needs to remain at the table and communicate in accessible ways without compromising its values. These differences in language recall some of the methodological tensions we encountered in chapters 2 and 3.

## Measures of Effectiveness

NETWORK measures its own effectiveness in terms of its influence on Congress—how members vote, the information included in legislation—and how well and extensively it activates others to the work of justice by way of its educational and organizing efforts. It points to several relatively recent legislative successes on the Housing Trust Fund, the Family Medical Leave Act (FMLA), and campaign finance reform.[43] NETWORK's advocacy training sessions, online legislative action center, and "Making a Noise about the Need" welfare campaign have served to engage many people in connecting their faith to a responsibility to advocate for the common good and take action.[44] Throughout its history, thousands of people have been introduced to the concepts of Catholic social teaching and legislative advocacy, and have been moved to write letters to their representatives, write op-ed columns, and take action in a variety of ways. One staff member assesses NETWORK's effectiveness in this way: "On legislative victories, 'spotty,' on keeping worse things from happening, 'good,' and on keeping the conversation going and justice issues alive, year after year, no matter what administration is in power or what the issues of the day are, 'very good.'"[45]

## PAX CHRISTI USA

Founded in 1972, only one year after NETWORK was founded, Pax Christi USA (PCUSA) describes itself as "the national Catholic peace movement," working through nonviolence to transform U.S. society and to make peace-making a priority in the U.S. Catholic Church. The organization uses prayer, study, and action to raise awareness about peace and justice issues; its actions range from traditional lobbying efforts in Washington, D.C., to grassroots advocacy, and from Congressional briefings to prayer vigils and civil disobedience actions, all aiming to "bring a religious voice into the public sphere."[46] PCUSA is a chapter of Pax Christi International, a nonprofit, nongovernmental Catholic peace movement that began in France in 1945 in an effort to reconcile France and Germany, and which now operates in 34 countries.[47] As a national affiliate of Pax Christi International, PCUSA's work and mission are taken up in the context of political, social, and economic realities in the United States. Within the context of the Catholic Church in the United States, PCUSA was established at the initiative of a small group of mostly lay U.S. Catholics; today its membership surpasses 20,000 members. It works to educate and conscientize Catholics in the way of peace and to make the institutional church an instrument of peacemaking, drawing on the gospel and Catholic social teaching.[48] The organization itself articulates its purpose in this way: "Pax Christi USA strives to create a world that reflects the Peace of Christ by exploring, articulating, and witnessing to the call of Christian nonviolence. This work begins in personal life and extends to communities of reflection and action to transform structures of society. . . . Pax Christi USA commits itself to peace education and, with the help of its bishop members, promotes the gospel imperative of peacemaking as a priority in the Catholic Church in the United States. Through the efforts of all its members and in cooperation with other groups, Pax Christi USA works toward a more peaceful, just, and sustainable world."[49] PCUSA thus works for peace by means of a variety of educational, advocacy, and witnessing efforts.

## Organizational Structure and Membership

PCUSA describes its membership as Catholics who think critically and are politically active; many of its members are progressive on peace and justice issues but conservative on other issues, such as abortion.[50] Its members are typically active in parish life, serving on parish councils and in other parish ministries. Its membership has grown from 14,000 to more than 20,000 members nationwide since September 11, 2001, a rise due, in part, to increased interest in peacemaking efforts after the events of that day.[51] Its membership includes 120 U.S. Catholic bishops, 800 parish sponsors, 650 religious communities, 320 PCUSA local groups, and 100 college and universities.[52] A national executive director and bishop president lead PCUSA.[53] Members receive regular mailings, and its widely respected quarterly newspaper, the *Catholic Peace Voice*; parish and university members receive context-specific educational materials. Although it has had a strong and articulate pacifist membership from its founding, PCUSA explicitly embraces a pluralism of positions on peace issues such that espousing pacifism is not a condition of membership.[54] Membership in PCUSA requires only agreement with its statement of purpose.[55] Although pacifism is not a litmus test for membership, the group has sustained a commitment to teaching nonviolence as a way of engaging in conflict in "a way that flows from an adherence to values central to the life and teaching of Jesus."[56]

PCUSA employs its prayer, study, and action small group process for personal and social transformation within four priority areas: nonviolence; disarmament with justice; domestic economic and interracial justice; and human rights and global restoration. It engages a variety of methods to promote peace and justice in these areas, including issuing position papers; analyses by PCUSA bishops; press releases; convening prayer services; lobbying at local, regional, and national levels; and educating members about policy issues (e.g., it took part in the aforementioned Welfare Reform Watch program).[57] PCUSA has drafted a statement that its members can sign and submit to the members' district attorney and federal prosecutor (as well as elected officials), the "Declaration of Life and Vow of Nonviolence."[58] PCUSA also conducts national campaigns that combine education and policy advocacy, such as its "Bread not Stones" campaign, which offers analysis and action steps to redirect military spending to provide more funds for social needs such as health care, education, and job training.[59] PCUSA's Peace Studies Committee fosters interdisciplinary dialogue on peace and justice issues generally through its internet discussions, and its Haiti Task Force monitors the changing political situation in Haiti. PCUSA thus engages a variety of methods in the service of peace advocacy.

## Range of Issues

During its first two decades, PCUSA focused most of its energies on disarmament and arms trade issues amid the climate of the Cold War. In 1992, after the fall of the Berlin Wall, the organization conducted a membershipwide survey to poll its membership on what issues it should prioritize as it entered a new era. In response to the survey results, PCUSA broadened its scope to address the four issue areas it continues to prioritize today. In the area of "Disarmament, Demilitarization and Reconciliation with Justice," PCUSA promotes nuclear, conventional and domestic disarmament, an end to the international arms trade, economic conversion to a nonmilitary economy, conscientious objection, nonviolent alternatives to war, and the just reconciliation of enemies through the United Nations and other channels. Under "Economic and Interracial Justice in the U.S.," PCUSA works against economic injustice, militarism, and environmental destruction, which are particularly harmful to those who are poor, minorities, children, and women. In addition, it works toward eliminating racist structures in the Catholic Church and the country, working toward equality of all people.[60] Under its "Human Rights and Global Restoration" rubric, the organization promotes universal human rights, both at home and abroad, through solidarity with oppressed and marginalized people struggling for dignity. The group rejects political and economic domination over others and fosters a reverence for all creation by working to end the death penalty and promote peace between Israelis and Palestinians, for example. Finally, in the realm of "Spirituality of Nonviolence and Peacemaking," PCUSA promotes Christian nonviolence on the personal, communal, national, and international levels, denouncing and resisting the evils of violence although striving to reflect the Peace of Christ.[61]

The emphasis on different issues varies at the different levels of operation (local, regional, national, and international), but PCUSA also emphasizes the interrelatedness of the issues it addresses, such as poverty and violence. Although war and peace issues remain a major emphasis, particularly leading up to the war in Iraq, at its March 2003 lobby day in conjunction with its national gathering, PCUSA members from around the country lobbied on the federal budget and TANF reauthorization. It links domestic issues such as welfare to the war and its consequences and uses issues such as immigration and globalization as lenses through which to examine peace issues. One staff member framed PCUSA's activities and commitment from 2001–3 as countering the Bush Administration's new paradigm of global domination.[62] Its efforts then focused on opposing military action in Afghanistan and Iraq. At a congressional briefing at the time, PCUSA partnered with the National Council of Churches, bringing in international religious leaders from security council countries to speak out against U.S. military action in Iraq.

In an event leading up to its March 2003 national gathering that gained significant media attention, PCUSA organized an act of civil disobedience to protest the war in Iraq. Sixty-eight participants were arrested for violating a U.S. Park Police ban on large gatherings in Lafayette Square, across the street from the White House. The demonstrators met to send the message that the current war in Iraq is immoral, unjust, and unnecessary. Among those arrested with the group were Bishop Gumbleton of Detroit (a founding member of PCUSA); Daniel Ellsberg, the former State and Defense Department official who leaked the Pentagon Papers to reporters during the Vietnam War; Nobel Prize winners Mairead Corrigan Maguire (the 1976 award winner for her work to bring peace to Northern Ireland) and Jody Williams (1997 awardee for her work to eradicate land mines). They remained for about two hours, praying and speaking against the war before being arrested.[63] In this way, PCUSA has expanded its range of issues over the past decade, yet continues to understand the peace and justice issues it addresses as inherently connected.

## Collaboration and Coalition Work

PCUSA frequently partners with outside organizations. Executive director Dave Robinson finds such exchanges mutually enriching, because from the richness of the Catholic tradition PCUSA "offers a perspective on the dignity of individual human person and the cultivation of the common good that resonates with others who do not share its religious beliefs, but do share its hope for a world that is more peaceful, just and sustainable."[64] PCUSA often serves as a bridge between secular and faith-based groups in much of its collaborative work, for it remains active in secular peace and justice circles as well as in religious circles. It is often called on to link these different groups. For example, PCUSA's policy director Jean Stokan relies on the research done by the NGO Education for Peace in Iraq Center (who, in her view, did some of the best Iraq lobbying prior to U.S. intervention in 2003). She has invited this NGO to meetings of faith-based groups as a resource with which other religious organizations might not be in touch otherwise. Secular groups view PCUSA as bringing a moral voice and elevating issues on which they collaborate.[65]

Although it is rooted in the Catholic tradition, PCUSA is committed to working ecumenically and interreligiously with other groups toward common objectives. It has most recently partnered with the National Council of Churches (NCC; when the USCCB decided against collaborating with NCC), Winning without War, United for Peace and Justice, and Churches for Middle East Peace in its advocacy against military intervention in Iraq. PCUSA's membership in Pax Christi International provides it with opportunities to collaborate on larger scales and gives it clout, due to its connection to international bishops and the president of the international organization, Michel Sabbah, Latin Patriarch of Jerusalem. Sabbah helped PCUSA gain access to the State Department in its efforts to oppose the war in Iraq, for example.

## Catholic Identity and Theological Sources

PCUSA grounds its commitment to social change, world peace, justice and reconciliation in its understanding of God, relationship with Christ, and proclamation of the kingdom of God. In addition to Catholic social teaching and scripture, its religious sources include papal encyclicals, U.S. bishops' pastorals, the spirituality of nonviolence that has been articulated from Jesus to St. Francis to Dorothy Day, and the stories of saints and holy people, from St. Martin of Tours to Oscar Romero and beyond.[66] The Gospel call to conversion found in the Sermon on the Mount, in particular, drives PCUSA's peacemaking efforts. PCUSA leadership view the organization's role, in part, as promulgating Catholic social teaching which, the leaders believe, is not as widely known in the United States as it could be. Robinson names the life and dignity of every human person, solidarity, and the option for the poor as particularly expressed in PCUSA's work.[67] Pax Christi International adopted *Pacem in terris* as its charter in 1963 to provide a broad framework for peace based on the pillars of truth, love, justice, and reconciliation.[68]

PCUSA's role also includes needling the Vatican and U.S. church to take even stronger stances than they do on social issues; the church's just-war stance persists as the organization's biggest object of criticism. PCUSA has entered the early stages of beginning a "People's Peace Pastoral Process," trying to help move the church from just-war theory to a just-peace theory. It believes itself to be vindicated by recent pronouncements from the Vatican such as Renato Martino's statement that perhaps church teaching on the war is going the way of the death penalty, from reluctant toleration to quasiabolition.[69]

PCUSA members describe themselves as firmly rooted in the heart of the Catholic tradition, their work grounded in scripture and Catholic social teaching. At the same time, they are bringing to bear the imperatives for justice and peace not only on structures and actions of wider society, but also on the church itself. In terms of its strategies in particular, PCUSA documents cite Martin Luther King, Jr., on theological roots of civil disobedience, and Daniel Berrigan and John Dear on "civil disobedience as sacrament."[70] Of the impact of its distinctive integration of prayer and action, theologian and former vice president of Pax Christi International, Mary Evelyn Jegen, S.N.D., writes that, unlike many movements, "Pax Christi has the strength that comes from fostering the spiritual and theological development of its own members along with its work on social issues."[71]

## Catholic Values and the Politics of Washington

In his address at PCUSA's annual meeting in 2002, Bishop Gumbleton juxtaposed the pax Americana with the pax Christi, highlighting the inevitable tensions inherent in the organization's efforts to advocate for values that might contradict those prioritized by the American way or a particular administration. PCUSA communications director Johnny Zokovitch notes that, although it does not want to be completely anti- or countercultural, it remains attentive to the significant differences between those Christian and American paradigms. In the course of its critical engagement through a variety of methods, PCUSA strives to be in the world but not of it. The tensions between the American and the Christian approaches may be more pronounced in the organization's growing legislative advocacy efforts, rather than its prayer and education models. Robinson insists, however, that engagement in politics, economics, and society more generally is mandated by Christian faith.[72] Stokan echoes this inextricable link, noting that the church is already inserted into the polity; given that we are in the world, we must consider how we are going to speak to it. She cites *Justitia in mundo* regarding such action as constitutive of preaching the gospel. Although she allows that there is room at the local level for diversity in terms of approaches, she insists that political involvement of some sort is necessary.[73]

Some PCUSA staff members, however, highlight the long-standing challenge Catholics face regarding where to firmly place their loyalties, in the gospel or with the United States, adding that with the Bush administration in particular there exists "a real cleave between what it means to be American and what it means to be Catholic."[74] In line with some of Baxter's concerns, PCUSA staff worry that, especially in times of war, accomodationist tendencies that justify war or place patriotic loyalties above Catholic ones point to a scriptural and theological illiteracy within the church. For example, Zokovitch laments, "American Catholics have learned much more about what it means to be American than what it means to be Catholic."[75] This attitude is reminiscent of a popular saying among some PCUSA members: "We are called to be faithful, not effective." Yet as Ron Pagnucco points out in his comparative study of faith-based and secular peace groups, "For many PCUSA members, this saying does not mean that they should not use tactics that might change government policies. Rather, it means that they must work for peace and justice even if they are not at the moment 'winning.'"[76]

Whereas PCUSA's method of prayer, study, and action has been its hallmark, some segments of its membership are more comfortable with certain strategies than others, and the local chapters sometimes take on different characteristics as a result of different emphases. The national staff note that PCUSA has consistently tried to use whatever strategies are open to it and stress that action can play itself out in very different ways, from lobbying (which has grown in recent years) to civil disobedience.[77] In terms of attitudes toward the U.S. government in particular, the membership of PCUSA falls along a spectrum, some wanting to engage the government via lobbying and others preferring resistance through demonstrations or civil disobedience, the former retaining faith in the possibility of reforming the system and the latter believing only revolution can effect genuine justice. Zokovitch notes that "out of respect for the different ways members want to engage the system, PCUSA retains a variety of strategies from pouring blood on weapons to lobbying Congress."[78]

Although Zokovitch himself professes some skepticism about engaging the system, he points to the concrete positive impact such efforts have sometimes had, citing the recent success achieved by Catholics working against the death penalty in Illinois in affecting the lives of sixty-five death row inmates. He also notes that, resulting from its experiences working with those who come from vastly different backgrounds than most of its middle-class membership, PCUSA has come to see that engaging the system can be important. Many with whom it works, such as farm workers or inmates on death row, have concrete political agendas that they want to achieve; getting PCUSA's support will make a difference in getting legislative gains that make major differences in their lives. For example, in March 2005, PCUSA helped the Coalition of Immokalee Workers reach a groundbreaking agreement with Taco Bell Corporation to raise the wages and improve the working conditions of farm workers in the Florida tomato industry.[79] Nevertheless, Zokovitch emphasizes that the group must always stand in a position of strong critique of the system even as it engages the system.[80] One staff member warns, "If we become a part of the system, then we've lost."[81]

Even within its organizational leadership, PCUSA exhibits some of the tensions explored at the theoretical level. According to Robinson, it is crucial to continually attend to fidelity and effectiveness. He notes that PCUSA appreciates the fact that the policies and decisions made in Washington affect the lives of people all across the world, and that "symbolic stands, while they may make us feel good about our 'rightness,' don't necessarily help put food into the mouths of hungry children, keep inmates from being executed, or assure healthcare for those who are sick."[82]

## Translation of Religious Language

PCUSA at once reveres its undiluted Catholic identity as central to its identity and work, and values diverse expressions of others' contributions to the common good amid religious pluralism. The organization understands its primary responsibility as empowering Catholics to act for peace and justice in the world, because it is a constituent part of their faith. Yet, according to Robinson, when dealing with political issues PCUSA must recognize that, whereas our religious values might motivate its own involvement, PCUSA must seek intersections between Catholic religious values, the values of other people of faith, and those values held by people who are not part of any specific faith tradition.[83]

Stokan maintains that translating Catholic identity in collaborating with non-Catholics or in lobbying to a pluralistic legislature has not been a problem for PCUSA. Much of what the organization undertakes deals with human realities that cut across traditions, she notes, such that using the language of life, or of civilian deaths, needs no translation. In fact, she finds instead that others welcome PCUSA to the table and that the underlying principles are so basic and common that regardless of language those principles have an impact.[84] PCUSA speaks a particular language from a particular perspective, yet understands that, at times, it can gain ground by way of incremental changes or it may at times adjust its language, yet never compromise its values or principles.[85] PCUSA collaborates with other groups on one issue even if it disagrees on another issue (e.g., it might partner with a group that differs from PCUSA on its official opposition to abortion to jointly oppose the death penalty), because it can speak from the practical as well as the religious perspective.[86]

Although the desire to be at once visionary and effective means PCUSA must strike a delicate balance, overall the organization "errs more on the prophetic and less on the practical," in the view of its leadership. As an example, Stokan points to its continual demand that aid to Israel be frozen and occupation end in the Middle East even if it "doesn't have a snowball's chance in hell" to work.[87] From another's perspective, "We don't only want to make a symbolic protest, but rather want to see change for those whose lives depend on it, so we have to be politically astute and strategic in our work. That said, there may come points where the only avenue we have left is to raise our voices in (symbolic) protest."[88] Again, the tensions between Catholic and American paradigms affect the ways PCUSA advocates, including the language it uses and the battles and coalition partners it chooses.

### Measures of Effectiveness

PCUSA measures its own effectiveness by the extent to which local groups at the grassroots level are empowered to participate in the political process and believes that its own efforts are making a difference. For PCUSA as a whole, effectiveness depends not on whether its positions are always adopted, but rather whether its concerns are heard, and the fact that it continues to raise the religious dimensions of issues and moral voice—"especially now that [the Bush] Administration is overtly religious in ways that contradict our own religious values," as Zokovitch puts it.[89] Zokovitch measures PCUSA's success by how much access it has to the American public through its materials or press coverage, rather than whether it has as much access to legislators as big money lobbyists.[90] PCUSA also serves as a resource for other religious groups who, because of the present circumstances, want to do peace work but usually have not researched or staffed that topic. Like NETWORK, PCUSA points not only to legislative successes, but also to grassroots participation; as we shall see below, like the USCCB, PCUSA measures whether and how it affects the larger public conversation.

## UNITED STATES CONFERENCE OF CATHOLIC BISHOPS

The United States Conference of Catholic Bishops (USCCB) is an assembly of the hierarchy of the United States who jointly exercise pastoral functions on behalf of U.S. Catholics. Its various offices and committees include several dedicated to public policy formation and lobbying. When the American bish-ops gathered in council at Baltimore during the nineteenth century, they ig-nored social and economic problems, for the most part, and were silent on political issues.[91] By the beginning of the twentieth century, however, some church leaders discerned a need for a national organization to protect Catholic interests.[92] Msgr. John J. Burke, C.S.P., initiated the National Catholic War Council during World War I, its expressed purpose to coordinate the Catholic war effort and serve as a liaison with the federal government.[93] After the war ended Burke argued forcefully for a permanent organization to protect the church's interests in Washington, and the bishops approved an organization, renamed the National Catholic Welfare Council (NCWC), that would convene an annual meeting and have a Washington-based staff. Burke served as its first general secretary.[94] For the most part, the NCWC operated as an information clearinghouse, defending the church's interests and issuing statements on so-cial issues. In these early decades, Thomas Reese, S.J., notes, the bishops' views coincided with those of the U.S. government on most issues, but "as Catholics became more acceptable to American society, however, the bishops became braver in challenging American culture."[95] In 1922, the National Catholic Wel-fare Conference (NCWC) was created to address such concerns as education, immigration, and social action, the word "conference" replacing "council" to underline the fact that it was consultative rather than legislative.[96]

When the American bishops returned home after the Second Vatican Council (Vatican II), they immediately reorganized their own national confer-ence to conform to the new conciliar principles. They dissolved the NCWC in 1966 based on a Vatican Council decree calling for national councils through which bishops would jointly exercise their pastoral office for the greater good.[97] The bishops met in November 1966 at the Catholic University of America, and erected the National Conference of Catholic Bishops (NCCB) as the canonical body to attend to ecclesial matters and the United States Catholic Conference (USCC) to attend to public policy matters.[98] On July 1, 2001, the NCCB and the USCC were combined to form the USCCB. The USCCB con-tinues all of the work formerly done by the NCCB and the USCC with the same staff. The bishops themselves form approximately fifty committees, each with its own particular responsibility.[99] Today, the USCCB's mission is to pro-mote "the greater good which the Church offers humankind, especially through forms and programs of the apostolate fittingly adapted to the cir-cumstances of time and place."[100]

## Organizational Structure and Membership

The U.S. bishops themselves constitute the membership of the USCCB. They are joined by the USCCB's staff of more than 350 laypersons, priests, and religious, all trained experts who aid the bishops in researching problems, drafting policy statements, and communicating their concerns to the greater public and to the government.[101] The USCCB staff is headed by the general secretary who is responsible for directing the bishops' staff and ensuring that the bishops' will is served.[102] The Conference supports and assists local bishops, enables the hierarchy to deal in a united way with national issues, and structures the U.S. church's relationship with Rome.[103] For our purposes, the Office of Social Development and World Peace (SDWP), Office of Government Liaison (OGL), and Committee for Pro-Life Activities are most pertinent with respect to the bishops' political advocacy.[104] As noted, the conference's original legislative concerns were limited to issues that directly affected its own institutional interests, but by the mid-1970s the Conference began to take a more activist role on Capitol Hill on a wider range of issues. The OGL's mission is to represent the Bishops' positions before Congress on a wide variety of public policy issues.[105] The office has four lobbyists and a director, each covering an interest area within the conference's legislative agenda (e.g., international justice and peace issues, immigration and refugee issues). Experts from other offices who conduct the actual policy analysis and monitor issues coordinate closely with the lobbyists so that the USCCB staff all speak with one voice on the Hill.[106]

SDWP, headed by its long-time secretary John Carr, is the national public policy agency of the U.S. Catholic bishops that helps bishops devise policies and programs on economic development, justice, and peace issues. SDWP includes two permanent offices, the committees for domestic social development and international justice and peace, which work on behalf of the bishops to share and apply Catholic social teaching on domestic and international issues.[107] The Office's stated purpose is to "advocate effectively for the poor and vulnerable and for genuine justice and peace in the public policy arena; and build the capacity of the Church (national and diocesan) to act effectively in defense of human life, human dignity, human rights, and the pursuit of justice and peace."[108] Finally, the Secretariat for Pro-Life Activities, under the guidance and direction of the Committee for Pro-Life Activities, works to protect all human life from conception to natural death by developing education programs on life issues, as well as by conducting educational campaigns in the public square, disseminating information on critical issues, and advising on public policy efforts concerning life issues.[109]

The U.S. bishops convene every June and November to discuss pastoral, political, and social issues, and SDWP, OGL, and Pro-Life activities and priorities flow from the policies adopted by the bishops.[110] An extensive and detailed process for reviewing any testimony or letters to government officials exists to ensure that the staff represents what the bishops want and that various offices coordinate their operations, including assessments of impact and specific sources for each conference policy or position.[111] Hehir emphasizes that this structured process of accountability makes the USCCB different from most other advocacy organizations, noting that "because the USCCB has to satisfy the concerns of over 200 bishops, they must have a very clear paper trail to point to in order to explain why they took each position and which committees it went through before approval."[112] Carr echoes Hehir's assessment, noting, "I've never been in a more accountable position," because the Conference's clout and agenda comes from the bishops alone.[113] These measures complicate the Conference's ability to react quickly to changing political events. In Carr's mind, however, "that's the price you pay for being a strong entity—an entity that really reflects what the bishops want."[114] When lobbying on the Hill or to other bodies, it is clear to everyone that the USCCB represents the bishops. Also, the USCCB staff and members work simultaneously at many levels on a particular issue: Cardinals might call the White House, bishops might contact congresspersons, parishioners might contact representatives and then have experts testify and people with experiences (such as recipients at Catholic service agencies affected by legislation on welfare) share their stories.[115]

Although a common criticism over the decades has been that the staff at the USCCB has set the direction of the bishops' advocacy, most agree that, while the staff completes much of the work of the Conference, the bishops themselves set the direction of the Conference and decide policy.[116] The staff clearly play a major role in developing the bishops' positions, yet the majority of policy positions taken by the USCCB have a long history rooted in the pastoral letters and statements issued by the conference and its committees over the years, and "the staff could not lobby for a position that contradicted conference policy without inviting criticism from their proponents and getting in trouble with the bishops."[117] Although from the outside it may seem that USCCB policy stances span unusual divisions or that the bishops have two sets of friends (with conservatives on abortion and liberals on social welfare), Conference members believe that the Conference's positions on issues are internally consistent, because they are based on a consistent ethic grounded in Catholic teaching.[118] Whereas the USCCB's origins reach back to the NCWC during World War I, its offices have come to have an activist presence and to address a wider range of issues only since the approximate time of the origin of NETWORK and PCUSA, in the early 1970s.

## Range of Issues

At its founding the episcopal conference's purpose was mainly to protect Catholic interests and to deal with specific government officials. Since that time, the concerns of the USCCB have expanded to include not only institutional interests (such as aid to Catholic schools, tax exemptions for church entities, and funding for Catholic social services), but also a broader array of social issues. In recent decades, the USCCB has addressed abortion, welfare reform, housing, communications policy, immigration policy, civil rights matters, criminal law, family policy, farm policy, labor legislation, and military and foreign policy. At its Annual Social Ministry Gathering in Washington, D.C., in February 2003, Carr's plenary address highlighted the range of concerns on the USCCB's radar at that time. Carr asked, "Who are sharing the burden or are left behind as we seek greater security, at a time when some go to war and others get tax cuts?" He discussed military action in Iraq, domestic poverty, tax cuts, the Israeli-Palestinian peace process, a culture of violence, abortion, the death penalty, and the economy, stressing "every life is precious, whether in the World Trade Center or Baghdad, a fetus or a person on death row, rich or poor."[119]

The SDWP office's 2003–4 legislative priorities centered around issues on Iraq, domestic budget priorities, CAFTA, TANF, tax relief (earned income tax credit and child tax credit) and debt relief.[120] Their ongoing campaigns include reducing global poverty, working to achieve peace in the Holy Land and universal health care in the United States; in March 2005 the bishops launched a campaign to end the use of the death penalty. The bishops' document, *A Place at the Table: A Catholic Recommitment to Overcome Poverty and to Respect the Dignity of All God's Children*, brings new focus and urgency to overcoming poverty at home and abroad as a religious duty and moral imperative. The international office also plays a significant role in representing the views of other local churches around the world in the course of its justice and peace advocacy; recent examples include advocacy on concerns facing those in Timor-Leste (formerly East Timor), Haiti, and Central America.

Carr describes Catholics as "politically homeless" and the Annual Social Ministry Gatherings reveal the USCCB's commitment to unambiguous nonpartisanship. The USCCB staff leadership repeatedly confer criticism and praise alike to different aspects of each party platform as judged against a Catholic ethic, its annual inclusion of a congressperson from each party and member from the current administration, and Carr's own language in introducing these guests, both thanking and strongly challenging each.[121] In 2003 Carr explicitly criticized both sides of the aisle from a Catholic perspective: Republicans for their treatment of the poor (citing John DiIulio's comment that the compassion agenda got lost when the Republicans won both houses of Congress) and Democrats for standing for nothing but abortion on demand ("they call Catholics single-issue oriented," he noted, but Democrats have become single-issue oriented regarding their pro-choice stance, "when extreme views have come to mean putting any restrictions on abortion whatsoever").[122] For this reason, Carr has stated, the USCCB stances do not fit easily into the conventional political framework, and its agenda does not often make sense to people who think only in terms of how Democrats and Republicans typically divide. The bishops support universal health care and oppose abortion, for example, and Carr notes that few follow a consistent life ethic in either party, so often the bishops' range of issues is perceived as a "mismatch."[123]

In its recent history, however, the relative attention given to different issues—such as the bishops' conference's treatment of abortion as opposed to its approach to other domestic and international social issues—has raised criticisms of the conference from many inside and outside of the church.[124] The bishops' shift to the now-famous consistent ethic of life under the leadership of Cardinal Bernardin remains evident in their rhetoric and actions today, and yet their positions remain open to criticism. As noted, Hehir himself was instrumental in helping the bishops broaden the focus of their agenda to consider life issues beyond abortion alone and to link such concerns.[125] In his 1983 speech at Fordham University, Bernardin first presented what has become known as the seamless garment or consistent ethic of life, his philosophical and theological integration of the bishops' stance on war, peace, human rights and abortion.[126] Whereas some critics call Bernardin's efforts a new Americanism, because his argument "includes an appeal for a more pluralist attempt to build consensus within American society, rather than reliance on uncompromising pronouncements (on abortion, especially)," many agree that over the past two decades the bishops' advocacy has changed for the better in adopting a multi-issue approach.[127] Partly in response to criticisms that the Conference's focus on abortion indicated a single-issue approach, in 1975 the USCCB administrative board began issuing the quadrennial political responsibility statements before every presidential election year summarizing the bishops' positions on a range of political and social issues.[128] The bishops' agenda in the past decade seems to give more even attention and resources to a wider range of social and political issues, according to those both who have worked at USCCB and those on the outside.[129]

Sharon Daly, former director of the Domestic Social Development Office at USCC, and current vice president for social policy at Catholic Charities USA, insists that when she worked at the USCCB during the 1980s social justice issues received just as much time and attention as did the pro-life agenda. In recent years, too, she maintains, the bishops remain very involved in questions surrounding U.S. policy toward Iraq and they were very involved in the debate over welfare reform in 1995–96 and the reauthorization debates of 2002–3. She notes that any organization engaging in legislative advocacy must look at "which issues are thrust upon you, which are targets of opposition, and which are perennial issues that you work to improve the boundaries on" (such as the universal health insurance push, driven by bishops' preferential option for the poor and vulnerable). Daly maintains that it is difficult to describe the

USCCB's priorities to outside observers, and that the secular press generally does not report when the bishops' staff lobbies on social justice issues rather than abortion. She points out that abortion is an institutional issue that the church cannot neglect, that the church's stance is proactive or defensive depending on the administration, but that overall the committee structure of the USCCB ensures that it develops a wide range of priorities and polices.[130] Daly adds that comparing USCCB approaches to abortion and other social and economic issues is like comparing apples and oranges, because pro-life issues tend to be very stark and that is rarely the case with other social issues. As an example, she calls the 2003 vote on whether to ban partial birth abortion a life or death issue, and asserts "few public policy issues have that kind of starkness or seldom do they depend on voting something up or down."[131]

## Collaboration and Coalition Work

Whereas tension existed in the past within the conference about coalition building with groups that have positions that the conference opposes, today, in general, the USCCB often collaborates with others but tends to work in coalition much less frequently than other groups, and then only on an ad hoc basis. The bishops have recently worked in coalition with others on the reauthorization of TANF and debt relief, and their more permanent coalition partners include their civil rights allies and labor unions. The bishops tend to work closely with others without joining in coalitions, as was the case with their recent work with others on issues of capital punishment and land mines. The USCCB is not an easy coalition partner, given its extensive mechanisms for review and the pace at which it must work by committee. Smaller organizations tend to work often in coalitions and to let the coalition speak for them, because they do not have large staffs to specialize on issues. A larger organization such as the USCCB deals with coalitions largely as working groups where they share specific concerns, developing complementary tactics and strategies, but it seldom signs on to group letters or has coalition partners speak on its behalf.[132] Carr adds that "coalitions sometimes involve the bringing together of weakness rather than strength," noting that in some cases it makes a more powerful impact for the White House to receive similar letters separately from the U.S. bishops and other major religious leaders on a certain issue than to receive one letter cosigned by many religious groups.[133]

The bishops' unique stance that crosses typical political divisions does give them greater access to dissimilar collaboration partners than most groups enjoy. Although the uncompromising nature of some of their positions sometimes cost them allies on certain issues (such as their abortion stance precluding their direct cooperation with some feminist groups), at times their ethic gives them unique access to allies.[134] For example, Daly notes "other advocates in town of children and poor people don't have access to the kinds of Republicans and conservative Democrats that [the USCCB] has access to because of its pro-life agenda."[135] Although the USCCB engages in coalition work less frequently than smaller organizations, its cooperation and lobbying span the entire spectrum due to its comprehensive ethic.

## Catholic Identity and Theological Sources

Unique among other Catholic advocacy groups within the United States, the Catholic identity of the USCCB stems from its very identity as the official voice of the U.S. hierarchy. USCCB statements and advocacy rely on scripture, the Catholic social tradition, and official church teaching in more explicit and systematic ways than most organizations' materials or advocacy. Documents from the bishops' conference tend to use scripture more thoroughly and often, and draw on the whole range of church teaching in the USCCB's efforts to apply Catholic insights to social problems. In the bishops' recent *A Place at the Table*, the bishops integrate a biblical vision that draws on the Hebrew scriptures and the New Testament, insights from the Catholic social tradition, the experiences of people living in poverty, and concrete socioeconomic data.[136] Whereas the USCCB is more likely to use theology and scripture more systematically in its dual audience documents that address intra- and extra-ecclesial contexts, it uses theological concepts in its lobbying efforts, as well. For example, in a February 2003 letter to members of the House of Representatives regarding TANF reauthorization, it grounded its concerns about the bill under consideration in the fact that work is the means by which individuals participate in God's creation.[137] In USCCB advocacy on food and nutrition programs, it bases its commitment to combating hunger on "the Lord's command to feed the hungry" and "the Eucharist we celebrate as the Bread of Life."[138]

Amid this depth and breadth of Catholic resources, Carr names three theological cornerstones at the heart of the USCCB's efforts: defense of the life and dignity of the human person, the option for the poor, and solidarity. He notes that the first one grounds its chief priorities in defending human life, whether in lobbying on capital punishment, abortion, war and peace, or poverty issues. The option for the poor affects its method of looking at economic and foreign policy from the bottom up, through the lives of the most poor and vulnerable. Finally, a notion that we are all in this together shapes its approach, and this principle of solidarity leads USCCB to consider political policies and agendas in terms of its impact on the common good, so that the bishops are not asking, "Are you better off today than you were four years ago," as the typical election slogan goes, but rather "Are *we* better off? Are the poor better off?"[139] In introducing *A Place at the Table* at the 2003 plenary,

Carr noted that "the moral measure of our society and Catholic witness is how the least of these are doing. A defining measure of our being Christian is how we treat the poor, and while other issues are often hotter, poverty is central."[140] Thus, the USCCB's Catholic identity is perhaps more explicitly evident and clearly defined than are PCUSA's or NETWORK's identities, yet, like the other two organizations, the USCCB relies most heavily on Catholic social principles to guide its advocacy work.

## Catholic Values and the Politics of Washington

Objections persist that the bishops should not give such attention, staff, and resources to political affairs lest they give the impression that improving the structuring of human society is more important than faith or holiness.[141] Critics on the right and left have published counterpastorals, challenged the bishops' authority to speak on sociopolitical issues, and otherwise voiced dissatisfaction with the bishops' actions in the national arena. Some argue that these actions have led to the proliferation of new Catholic lobbying and advocacy organizations to advance views that differ from the bishops' views.[142] To the question of whether the bishops should meddle in politics, Daly responds, "If the followers of Jesus do not stand with the poor, we have been given a foretaste in the gospel of what will happen to us—and Catholics believe we must not just do this as individuals but together and at the public policy level as well." As Formicola explains, we have Catholic Campaign for Human Development that helps the poor to speak for themselves, Catholic agencies to meet direct needs, and then lobbying arms of USCCB or other Catholic groups (such as Catholic Charities USA) to ensure that the interests of the poor are not neglected in policy.[143] Nevertheless, some Catholics fear that the bishops' social actions risk a "dangerous deviation from Catholic tradition, a secularization that transforms the otherworldly transcendent Gospel into an immanent Catholic Social Gospel."[144]

To those who suggest the bishops should not spend their time lobbying on so many issues beyond strictly institutional Catholic concerns, Daly replies that such types mistakenly believe that some things are religious and some things are not, and that the bishops should concern themselves with internal issues alone, such as the placement of the sign of peace in the liturgy. She insists, however, that the bishops are critically important in staking out ground as the official church, and she welcomes lay contributions, too, "but if there is no voice of the [institutional] church defending the poor in the public square or those on death row, how can they be defended?"[145] She also emphasizes the independence that the bishops uniquely enjoy, warning that most think tanks are rarely independent from financial sponsors, such that we should always ask "Who is paying for this public policy analysis and what are their priorities?"[146]

Although some have criticized religious organizations in general for getting involved in policy recommendations, others criticize the USCCB for not going far enough or not being prophetic enough. Carr reminds those who criticize USCCB for a dearth of prophecy that bishops are pastors not prophets, and that they represent a diverse community that "extends from Opus Dei to Pax Christi."[147] He adds that as a big church we are better off for having PCUSA and the Right to Life and other prophetic and particular interest groups operate within the American Catholic landscape, but that none of those groups (nor the bishops' conference) constitutes the whole church.[148] Many within the church remain suspicious of the bishops' advocacy endeavors and are frustrated by their often measured approach. In Carr's view, however, amid such a broad community as the U.S. Catholic one, the USCCB appropriately lifts up a central set of values that consistently elicits objections from either end of the spectrum to the effect that it has not gone far enough to one side or the other. Carr's response to these equal opportunity critiques gets to the heart of some of the differences we encountered between Baxter and Hehir in chapter 3. He reflects, "People assume that nuance, restraint in language, and willingness to compromise indicate a lack of passion or lack of courage. That can be the case. They can also be a sign of wisdom and of making a difference for poor people."[149]

Baxter's apprehensions regarding the very origins of the USCCB reflect a concern shared by others that involvement with the government in advisory or advocacy capacities necessarily risks crass accommodation. For such critics, the bishops' record on the issue of American use of force, in particular, points to such tendencies. Prior to issuing "The Challenge of Peace," the American bishops had not systematically applied the just-war tradition to the American context, but rather had "traditionally offered unquestioning support for the foreign policy and war aims of the American state from the revolution to the Vietnam War. World War I and World War II served to reinforce American Catholic patriotism."[150] Although Carr admits that power and politics are potentially seductive or dangerous, he insists that this is certainly not a problem for the Roman Catholic Church at present: "We're not getting any invitations to the Lincoln Bedroom these days!"[151] The USCCB sent four letters to the Administration in the five months prior to the war condemning the pursuit of military action in Iraq, Carr reminds those who worry that the bishops capitulate on issues of force, in particular.[152] In the USCCB's efforts to work out of a consistent life ethic that defies partisan categories on the whole, it believes that it is in less danger of co-optation by one party because it always has major disagreements with the party or administration in power.

The USCCB encounters challenges posed by the fact that compromise is the name of the game in Washington, but it perhaps bears an even greater responsibility to guard against complicity in aspects of legislation that contradict its articulated values. "Sometimes you don't get everything you want in a given piece of legislation," Daly concedes, and you must decide whether to support the compromise and "hold your nose" or let the amendment go down. At the same time, the USCCB must ensure that it is never complicit in something it knows is wrong. As an example, she notes that the bishops opposed the Hyde Amendment to restrict the number of abortions because it included some exceptions, but that in most cases similar to that one, the bill passes anyway.[153] Admitting that legislation really is sausage making, that most legislation has a million provisions, and that issues of compromise are rarely clear, Daly notes that such decisions depend on the situation and are made at the tactical and strategic level. In the end, however, the church cannot stand with the poor alone, because the magnitude of the problems that the poor face requires the government's help. She asserts that the Catholic theological understanding supports this approach, that we are inescapably in the world, and that "we do not get dirty or sinful by working in the world."[154]

### Translation of Religious Language

Although the USCCB's first audience is the church itself, when dialoguing with society it often relies on the more widely accessible approaches a public church model advocates.[155] Bishops' pastorals use theological language as well as Catholic social teaching, natural law–argumentation, and concrete examples of how the principles they hold up might play out. The operating assumption in USCCB advocacy efforts is that people of goodwill can disagree on social issues, and that the USCCB can then persuade them that the Catholic wisdom offers the right way.[156] Reminiscent of Hehir's valuing of the empirical together with the theological, Carr states that although the USCCB uses the language of religious values, it believes that "faith is not a substitute for facts or data."[157] USCCB letters to Congress and action alerts to Catholics around the country integrate Catholic principles with concrete data about the impact of legislation, and in lobbying the USCCB uses examples of such impact from contact with those served by Catholic agencies.[158]

As we noted above, however, by its very nature and identity the USCCB lobbyists are more likely to be explicitly Catholic and theological in their efforts than any other group. When asked about translating Catholic identity into more accessible modes amid the pluralism of the legislature and secular policy debates, Daly simply responds that "there are plenty of other people to be accessible!" She thinks that many secular groups and governmental groups can make the case on more accessible terms (e.g., the Children's Defense Fund on children's issues), so that although working at the USCCB and Catholic Charities she has not tried to mute the specific Catholic identity or language. She adds that the secular arguments are already familiar, but that the Catholic groups such as USCCB add the moral dimension that often makes the difference on undecided legislators' positions. That said, she also mentions using experience from Catholic service agencies in advocacy efforts (e.g., the impact legislation or budget priorities will have on children of single mothers from data from Catholic Charities agencies' experiences). Overall, however, she thinks that it is the proper role of faith-based groups to make the religious or moral case, adding, "the State Department can make the practical arguments about how certain measures are in line with our national security, for example, but the church must make the moral and religious argument—the fact that God connects us all to one another, or that we have a common responsibility for all children."[159]

Although the particularly Catholic character of their lobbying will be clear from the bishops' identity and some of their language, Bernardin's and Hehir's emphases on civility and accessible arguments continue to influence USCCB advocacy today. In pastorals, action alerts, and letters to Congress, the USCCB uses arguments and examples that are available (and potentially persuasive) to those who do not necessarily share in the fullness of the Catholic vision. Bernardin urges a style governed by the following rule: "We should maintain and clearly articulate our religious convictions but also maintain our civil courtesy. We should be vigorous in stating a case and attentive in hearing another's case; we should test everyone's logic but not question his or her motive."[160] Carr's approach reflects this style, and he notes that amid controversies over the involvement of the church in political questions, "there is a temptation to think that we just need to get the words right, or that proclamation and prophecy are the central task; but in public life the USCCB wants to be principled but we also must be persuasive and respectful of others," mentioning the lines in most bishops' pastorals and statements alluding to the fact that people of goodwill may apply the same principles in different ways when we descend to the particulars.[161]

## Measures of Effectiveness

Carr notes that the USCCB staff measure effectiveness based on how much impact their efforts have, how faithful they remain to church teaching, how they contribute to the public discussion, and whether they are viewed with respect or as "just another interest group."[162] He points to the USCCB's involvement with the Jubilee 2000 campaign for debt relief as an example of the bishops making a significant difference recently.[163] He adds that sometimes the impact and effectiveness come through in the ways USCCB is able to shape the debate rather than the final outcome, reminiscent of Hehir's perspective. As an example, Carr identifies how Catholic just-war terminology had pervaded and framed public debates about whether the United States should go to war in

Iraq in early 2003.[164] Furthermore, the connection of the USCCB's advocacy efforts to the Catholic institutional presence around the country contributes to its effectiveness (from its own perspective). Carr notes, "We are significant because of whom we represent, the fact that we have experience, and that part of our contribution to the social welfare of this country is not just the pastorals we adopt, but the schools we run and the shelters we run."[165]

Daly, who has worked at the Children's Defense Fund and Catholic Charities and on local levels in addition to her time with the USCC, ranks the USCCB as one of the top organizations in the country in its ability to make an impact at institutional levels. "I've spent my whole life doing things for poor people and trying to move bureaucracies, trying to move institutions, and this is a great fulcrum to move institutions. It may be one of the best you can work from in Washington if you're trying to move the administration of the Congress or get other folks, other organizations mobilized. Once the Catholic conference is moving on something, it really does make a difference."[166] This is the case because the Roman Catholic Church is such a major social actor both nationally and internationally, it has enormous prestige, clout, and attention-getting potential, and because of its attachment to every diocese.[167] Daly adds that another asset is the fact that the USCCB's letters and lobbying efforts are rooted in a long history of moral tradition as well as in the lived experience of the church and its agencies' experiences with those in need, in particular.[168]

Carr names three major sets of assets that the USCCB brings to its advocacy efforts: ideas, institutional experience, and the Catholic political presence in the United States. These recall the assets articulated in the bishops' political responsibility documents. Under ideas, he points to the Catholic social principles, such as respect for human life, the common good, option for the poor, solidarity, and subsidiarity. Under institutional experience, he highlights the work Catholic educational and service institutions perform as the largest nongovernmental organization (NGO) that provides education, health care, and human services in the country. Furthermore, with 60 million Catholics in the country as 25 percent of the population, in 20,000 parishes, the bishops lead a fairly large constituency (not a voting bloc).[169] Finally, he notes, "The U.S. bishops have been leaders on life issues as well as on war and economic justice in ways that are not politically correct but not entirely countercultural either. Catholicism is not a 'head for the hills' religion, we are involved in the world."[170] Thus, like NETWORK and PCUSA, the USCCB measures its own effectiveness not only in terms of the direct legislative impact of its efforts, but also in terms of its ability to shape the debate with its distinctive framework and the expertise it brings from connections to a more institutional presence. Beyond the USCCB's own advocacy efforts per se, the antipoverty and empowerment efforts of the Catholic Campaign for Human Development, the international relief and development work of Catholic Relief Services, and the social services provided by Catholic Charities USA constitute substantive, quality contributions to the USCCB's overall effectiveness.

The clergy sexual abuse scandal that came to light in January 2003 raised doubts regarding the effectiveness of the bishops' social advocacy.[171] In the fall of 2002, it was then-prelate of Boston, Cardinal Bernard Law, who took the lead in voicing the bishops' opposition to American use of force in Iraq— serving as a symbol for many of the compromised moral credibility and public witness the bishops both individually and collectively faced in the wake of that crisis. Yet, according to Hehir and Carr, among others, the church's social witness and advocacy have become more crucial to the church's mission and to its ability to regain trust in U.S. society (Hehir interview; Carr plenary).[172] Due to their relative institutional independence, NETWORK and PCUSA have not suffered any discernible impact on their credibility or effectiveness as a result of the scandal.[173]

Several events unfolded leading up to the 2004 presidential election that bear on the analysis of USCCB advocacy efforts. Following the 2004 sanctioning of several Catholic politicians on local levels, beginning in April several archbishops announced that they would deny communion to the presumed Democratic presidential nominee, John Kerry, because the Catholic candidate's voting record in the Senate had been unambiguously prochoice.[174] Another bishop issued a pastoral letter warning that American Catholic voters should not receive communion if they vote for politicians who support abortion rights, same-sex marriage, euthanasia, or embryonic stem cell research.[175] According to proponents, Catholic politicians and voters who support such issues were placing themselves outside of full Communion with the church and jeopardizing their salvation.

In light of some bishops' calls for such sanctions, others of their brother bishops decried the refusal of Communion to politicians and voters as canonically problematic, pastorally inappropriate, and counterproductive.[176] Amid the intra-Catholic debates that resulted, the USCCB's "Task Force on Catholic Bishops and Catholic Politicians" convened. Headed by Cardinal Theodore McCarrick, the ad hoc committee was appointed in 2003 to review the relationship of the church to Catholics in political life, considering how bishops should respond to Catholic politicians who publicly disagree with church teachings. The bishops' task force presented an interim report at the bishops' June meeting in Englewood, Colorado, with the body approving a brief statement, "Catholics in Political Life," by a vote of 183 to 6. In response to the looming question of denying communion to politicians who depart from church teachings, the task force concluded that bishops may legitimately make different judgments on the most prudent course of practical action.[177] Although the bishops disagreed over the merits and dangers of a single issue approach in general and over sanctions for politicians in particular, among those who expressed their views, the majority oppose refusing communion by a margin of roughly three to one. At its November plenary session, the task force's final statement largely rehearsed the interim report's findings without new analysis of the divisive issues raised at the time and intensified by subsequent events, reflecting the task force's desire to at once express unity in teaching and respect diversity in pastoral practice.[178]

Although the bishops issued their standard "Faithful Citizenship" document and affirmed its overall approach in their corporate statements, the statements of individual bishops calling for sanctions gained far more attention and media coverage. Although the Catholic vote in November's election remained divided (52 to 47 percent), the bishops' individual and corporate statements raised questions about the responsibilities of voters with respect to weighing issues of human life and dignity, about which tactics best serve fidelity and effectiveness while living up to the bishops' own challenge to remain political but not partisan, and about the lasting effects of the Congregation for the Doctrine of Faith's (CDF's) "Doctrinal Note" on Catholic public participation for future relationships between Catholic politicians and their bishops.

## COMPARATIVE ANALYSIS OF ORGANIZATIONS

In the work of NETWORK, PCUSA, and the USCCB we encounter valuable and tireless efforts to bring the vision and values of the Catholic social tradition to bear on social and political issues in the U.S. context. The three reflect many similarities in sources, approach, and agenda, but each operates with a distinctive identity and mission that lead to significant differences.

These distinct organizations collaborate with one another to varying degrees and have distinct understandings of one another's work. PCUSA and NETWORK have begun to work closely together, especially as PCUSA expands its efforts into the legislative arena; NETWORK's political savvy on legislative strategies has been particularly valuable to PCUSA. The two organizations have partnered on welfare reform, military spending, and opposing military retaliation in the aftermath of September 11. PCUSA has assisted NETWORK, in turn, by lending its membership base to joint initiatives and working on the educative end.[179] Both Dave Robinson and Kathy Thornton participated in the Iraq Peace Journey in December 2002.[180]

Although PCUSA supports "efforts of the USCCB to use their authority and power to address those issues which are at the heart of Catholic social and political thought," it notes regretfully that its working relationship with the

SDWP office has not been very positive.[181] Zokovitch remarks that the bishops' conference has not accepted its partnership efforts, but that PCUSA is always trying to build a better relationship.[182] Carr points to a difference in approach between the two organizations that may, in part, explain their lack of collaboration. He reflects that, unlike bishops' pastorals and advocacy, PCUSA tends to deemphasize respectful dialogue and to avoid concessions along the familiar lines of acknowledging that people of goodwill potentially disagree with various positions. Rather, in Carr's view, PCUSA attempts to define clearly what "true believers" should think and do, and then call those who disagree morally suspect or people who are not thinking right. The USCCB, conversely, places an emphasis on civil and mutual exchange, and in Carr's words, "we are less likely to engage in shrill, partisan rhetoric, and that sometimes disappoints Catholics on both the right and the left."[183]

NETWORK collaborates with the USCCB more frequently than does PCUSA, cooperating on some peace and justice issues (including welfare reform, affordable housing, land mine legislation, some aspects of health care reform). As Thornton puts it, the USCCB is much more engaged in promoting the totality of the Catholic reality and NETWORK is focused on a smaller portion of the peace and justice agenda of the church: "There is not an antithesis, we are moving together, but the USCCB has a much bigger agenda than NETWORK's."[184] Even when NETWORK and USCCB have not conducted any formal conversation on certain issues, Daly notes, "it is remarkable that their positions will come out 100% the same." The two organizations may collaborate to discuss timing, strategy, and tactics alone, yet because both start from Catholic social teaching and the lived experience of the church as their framework, they repeatedly come out at the same place on poverty issues.[185]

Although they have been united on some peace issues, NETWORK differs from the bishops in its response to the events of September 11. NETWORK and PCUSA opposed military retaliation in Afghanistan, whereas the bishops expressed the opinion that force was justifiable. As Thornton puts it, "NETWORK responded to the bishops' invitation to dialogue" in its contributions to the statement following September 11, "A Catholic Community Responds to War, Living with Faith and Hope."[186] The statement, signed by many members of religious orders, took issue with the bishops' justification of antiterrorist use of force. "We take seriously the dialogic nature of the church and so we understand our responsibility as individuals and a group to reflect on the gospel and our life experience and offer our interpretation to the church," Thornton adds. Whether critique of society or the church is needed, NETWORK engages in each, but it is not about being in disagreement for the sake of disagreement. Another major difference between NETWORK and the USCCB is that the former does not take up the abortion issue. Overall, Carr summarizes, the three groups share common Catholic values and act on them in Catholic and American ways, and "it is important not to challenge motives in politics."[187]

Despite the organizations' differing degrees of cooperation with one another, significant similarities exist among their priorities and methods. All three organizations approach political issues from the perspective of people who are poor or from the bottom up. Each relies on Catholic social teaching to a significant extent, and draws on scripture and the experiences of people who are poor to varying degrees. There exists much overlap in the domestic peace and justice agendas of each organization; for example, each has been very involved recently in advocating for TANF reauthorization more in line with Catholic social and economic priorities and against U.S. military intervention in Iraq. All of the groups decry the Catholic social teaching illiteracy among most U.S. Catholics and understand their own missions, in part, as promulgating the church's social teaching.

Although they are all working out of the Catholic tradition, the identity of the USCCB is more aligned with that of the official and universal church, whereas NETWORK and PCUSA work out of more prophetic strains of the Catholic tradition and understand part of their mission as calling the church itself to justice and accountability.[188] NETWORK presents its mission and advocacy in visionary terms, although the USCCB frames its priorities in terms of the protection of all life. PCUSA, in part due to its focus on peace issues, tends to frame its stance as standing in stark opposition to the secular national paradigm. Unlike the other groups, the bishops do not mention empowering others to action, but they do uniquely mention fidelity to the tradition as a measure of their own effectiveness.

## Impact of Leadership

The nature of the leadership and staff of each organization, whether composed of women religious, bishops, or a mix of laity and clergy, has a unique influence on the style and stance of each group. The approach and voice of congregations of women religious affect the priorities and methods that NETWORK embraces, as we have seen, and, similar to PCUSA, it enjoys the freedom to be perhaps more prophetic by virtue of its independence from the official church hierarchy. One NETWORK lobbyist notes that her organization is able to be less cautious about how it appears and that it operates with more of a sense of abandon than the official church, without worrying about protecting institutions or risking the forfeiture of funding.[189] When members were asked to name NETWORK's strengths in a recent survey, one respondent alluded to this distinct location, noting that the organization's credibility stems from its "ability to remain Catholic without being 'USCC Catholic.'"[190]

Unlike the USCCB who, in PCUSA's view, must deal with all sides of the Catholic population on a given issue, PCUSA is free to move more easily with its critiques, and it can be a more prophetic resource or a reference point different from the (bishops') consensual position that must be more moderated.[191] (PCUSA generally has two bishops on its national council). PCUSA involves the collaboration of clergy and laity, it has always elected a bishop as international president and most national presidents, and laypersons make up the majority of its membership and are the majority of the international executive committee, which is democratically elected. As a result, PCUSA is not dominated by any one voice and there is an equal voice at all levels, including leadership, for laity, priests, women and men religious, and bishops.

What the USCCB does bring to the table uniquely, however, is the voice of the official church and immediately recognizable clarity about whom it represents. It is clear whom the staff speak for and so "decisions are not made lightly, and when they are made they tend to stick." As Carr notes in general, and as might be charged of NETWORK and PCUSA in particular, "Some other church bodies have a problem in that 'Whom do you speak for?' is a confusing question and the answer is even more confusing."[192] The clear organizational structure allows the bishops to speak with authority for the church.[193] When the bishops speak out on issues, they are guaranteed media attention, as contrasted with many smaller advocacy groups whose constituency is less clear—whether the publicity is positive or negative. The USCCB does have to contend with the internal politics of the bishops' conference, of course, and with which bishops happen to serve as various committee chairs at particular historical moments. Yet Carr insists that, for the most part, his office receives substantial support from bishops across the ideological spectrum, rooted in its common commitment to Catholic social teaching.[194] The structure of the USCCB restrains its language, which is less polemical, less overtly partisan, and often lacks a certain prophetic edge, as statements written by committee tend to do.[195] Archbishop Rembert Weakland once told reporters that the bishops could afford to take a long-range view on various issues because "we don't run for office." Some have argued, however, that this same fact (of papal appointment rather than election) challenges the bishops' accountability within a culture that prizes elected and representative leadership.[196] Thus, stability and clarity of presence may sacrifice a prophetic edge, although the independence that enables such an edge can sometimes coincide with less clarity or clout.

## Coalition Work

With respect to coalition building and collaborative work, the three organizations diverge somewhat. PCUSA seems compelled to work in coalition due to its size and its relative inexperience in the legislative arena. Although it possesses some clout by virtue of its international affiliation, it gains numbers, legislative expertise (via NETWORK) and clout (via NCC) by working in coalition. NETWORK is also a smaller organization, but it is well respected on Capitol Hill for the quality of its research and its moral voice. It has an adequate staff size and sufficient expertise in advocacy work such that its coalition work seems to be due more to a commitment to mutual exchange, participation, and dialogue than to practical necessity. Finally, the USCCB does not need to work in coalition for reasons of size, staff, clout, or expertise, and in fact staff members report finding that cosigning letters or otherwise working in coalition weakens the impact of its advocacy. NETWORK and PCUSA lobbyists both note that in the course of their collaboration with others they repeatedly encounter a basic similarity among different religious groups on underlying principles. Furthermore, NETWORK and the USCCB emphasize the importance of meeting with offices and members who are not natural allies, noting that it is still important to make the connections for members even when they disagree.[197] Although some similarities surface among the groups' collaborative efforts, they diverge on what drives each to work (or not to work) in coalition with others. The different motivations of each raises the question of what constitute the USCCB's and PCUSA's mechanisms for learning from or allowing public activity to enrich each's own stance. NETWORK seems to value collaborative work, in and of itself, more than the others.

### Partisanship

My impression from representatives from each group is that, at least in recent years, the bishops' conference has been most successful in retaining a nonpartisan approach. That said, the aforementioned events of 2004 threatened to upset the delicate balance of politically homeless engagement. Reports in the Catholic press on the bishops' November 2004 meeting suggest polarizing divisions between the social justice and the pro-life sides of the church in the bishops' elections and deliberations. Some individual bishops' statements that warned about candidates' and voters' complicity in moral evil risked de facto politicization by their language, restricted range of issues, and failure to treat prominent pro-choice Catholic Republicans with the same severity as pro-choice Democrats.[198]

Some of the comments made by staff at NETWORK and PCUSA indicate that an explicitly nonpartisan approach does not rank as high a priority for these groups as for the bishops' conference, although this may be due, in part, to the recent realities of budget cuts for social services, delays in TANF reauthorization, and the war in Iraq. One NETWORK staff member admits that the organization struggles to present a nonpartisan perspective and is not always successful in doing so.[199] The great importance of the church witnessing to transcendent values and remaining independent demands its nonpartisanship in intent as well as in effect.

## Abortion

The 1973 U.S. Supreme Court decision legalizing abortion catalyzed the church's active involvement in antiabortion politics on the national level. Since then, the bishops' conference has employed a variety of methods to work against abortion, from lobbying, to participating in mass demonstrations, to acting as amicus curiae in almost every abortion case heard by the Supreme Court since *Roe v. Wade*.[200] In 1975 the NCCB/USCC adopted the "Pastoral Plan for Pro-Life Activities," that called for the development of well-organized pro-life units in every congressional district. They also engendered the National Committee for a Human Life Amendment, which works through grassroots lobbying and political action toward the passage of a human life amendment to the U.S. Constitution.[201] Through their lobbying efforts, the bishops have negotiated conscience clauses to protect Catholic institutions and most recently the USCCB lobbied in support of the Partial-Birth Abortion Ban Act of 2003. Many have charged that, although the bishops have broadened their range of issues under the umbrella of the consistent life ethic, they have effectively put abortion first in election politics and have addressed abortion differently than they have other issues.[202]

The bishops have also faced criticism on their approach to the abortion question on moral and procedural levels.[203] Sociologist José Casanova contends that the bishops' actions against abortion are inconsistent with their pastoral letters on other social issues which undermines the public credibility of their teaching.[204] Beyond his challenges to Catholic doctrine on abortion (fundamentalistic absolutization of human life over personhood and denial of moral ambiguities in different circumstances), he charges that what is particularly problematic is that the different level of authority that bishops ascribe to the abortion issue stands in contrast to norms concerning military and economic practices (where there can exist legitimate disagreement). Furthermore, he challenges the bishops' difference in tactics and approach, seeking to translate its recommendations into law directly in the case of abortion and not the others, grassroots mobilization and committing substantial financial and institutional resources on abortion alone, and screening political officials and candidates by their abortion stance alone. Finally, he adds that "the bishops refuse to acknowledge one of the most evident and significant 'signs of the times,' the universal-historical movement of the liberation of women from patriarchy and all its consequences," in affecting the abortion question or consulting women ("women are deprived of moral agency") in composing binding normative decisions on abortion.[205] Gudorf similarly contrasts the bishops' approach to legislation on war and abortion:

> When the church recognizes that abortion is as complex, as social, and as conflictive of rights as the issues of war or hunger, then perhaps we, the Church, can address abortion with more evenhanded compassion and war and hunger with even more rigor. I second Cardinal Bernardin's call for a consistent ethic of life, a "seamless garment." But . . . [we] will never convince those involved in taking the one and a half million aborted lives a year to consider the life of the unborn reverently if we do not evince reverence for the mothers of those unborn, for the starving millions of our world, the hundreds of thousands of innocent civilians threatened by death in war.[206]

Catholic teaching on abortion and Vatican directives on its political implications are unambiguous, however. As we have seen above in Daly's comments, the abortion issue is a stark one with the U.S. bishops ranking among the major defenders of unborn life in the United States. Many in the USCCB today would probably respond to Gudorf's objections that they are, in fact, evincing reverence for life across the spectrum, with relatively equal concern and fervor if not the level of binding moral authority.

Although Thornton believes that the USCCB would prefer that NETWORK work on the abortion issue, she and most of her staff believe that it is inappropriate for their organization to lobby on abortion due to its size, focus, and the urgency of work for the poor in this country. She calls the bishops' focus on respect for life a great service to society, but she thinks that, given the cultural attitudes toward and the need for more work on care for the poor, NETWORK should remain focused on the poverty issues that it currently addresses.[207] Other staff name other reasons such as the difficulty of organizationally taking a stand on such a polarizing issue ("it would rip our staff, board and membership apart") and that the impact any stance on abortion would have on all of the other work the organization does (standing up against church teaching would sacrifice its Catholic credibility and a strong antiabortion stance would forfeit some of its progressive support). Still others believe that NETWORK should remain silent on abortion until "we face a situation where women's voices are actually heard and represented and discrimination ceases."[208] Some both inside and outside NETWORK perceive its avoidance of the issue as being a hindrance, some staff say that they encounter members or parishioners who do not understand why NETWORK excludes abortion from its voting record publications or who think that it undermines the positions that it does take. Daly indicates that some dioceses' bishops have not welcomed NETWORK in to do training on legislative advocacy because of objections regarding this issue.[209]

For its part, PCUSA has issued an official position paper on abortion stating its antiabortion stance that was written in 1980 and then reaffirmed in 1989, 1998, and 2001. PCUSA was one of the founding organizations of the seamless garment initiative. Although there may exist a variety of private positions on abortion among its membership, Zokovitch notes, its official position remains "pro-life from the womb to the tomb."[210] Although its official opposition to abortion is based on "a total commitment to the principle of unwavering reverence for human life" and rejection of "the claim of any individual, any group or organization, any nation to the 'right' to destroy human life, whether singly or as entire populations," it connects its opposition to concern for the well-being of children, social conditions that limit women's options and the treatment of women who undergo abortions, and its stance on the spectrum of life issues, including the death penalty, war, the nuclear arms race, and anything that threatens life.[211] PCUSA does not lobby on abortion, however, explaining there are enough people filling that niche.

Thus, the organizations diverge on some of their particular approaches and the issues they take up. These differences affect their overall stances on how to understand the interaction of faith and political advocacy and how to resolve the tensions inherent in religious lobbying amid pluralism. In some respects, the groups seem to face these tensions similarly, as each group understands political compromise mostly in terms of adopting incrementalism and each guards against compromising principles or end goals in the course of the advocacy process. The normative dimensions of the range of issues taken up, their collaborative work, and the implications of one's position on abortion advocacy also affect how the groups resolve such tensions.

The mission and strategies of each organization raise further questions about the theoretical maps we have encountered. On the one hand, each of our cases presents some degree of engagement with the federal government, whereas on the other hand, Baxter harbors deep suspicions about any such endeavors. Nevertheless, PCUSA's basic approach and some of its strategies resonate with Baxter's stance, whereas the USCCB embodies Hehir's public church model to a great extent, due in no small part to his influence at the conference during his tenure there. Although NETWORK understands itself as a prophetic community of justice, its staff raise significant objections to the type of paradigm Baxter's evangelical stance promotes. We shall probe these connections and divergences in our next and final chapter to at last establish a better understanding of what constitutes an authentic and responsible social ethic in the U.S. Catholic context.

## NOTES

1. The Catholic Family and Human Rights Institute is another conservative advocacy group that focuses on international issues.

2. Robert Booth Fowler, Allen D. Hertzke, and Laura R. Olson, *Religion and Politics in America: Faith, Culture and Strategic Choices*, 2nd ed. (Boulder, CO: Westview Press, 1999, 1995), 69–71. In addition, the Family Research Council and Focus on the Family count a number of conservative Catholics among its members and staff.

3. Ibid., 71.

4. These three organizations do not comprehensively account for the full spectrum of Catholic advocacy, but they represent a range of constituencies and leadership models (such as the institutional hierarchy, congregations of women religious, a lay Catholic movement with some clergy involvement) and exemplify the tensions exhibited in Catholic social ethics discussed thus far. It was important to select explicitly Catholic advocacy groups rather than ecumenical lobbies or think tanks to adhere to this study's parameters, although the lobbies and think tanks claim significant Catholic membership and influence in the contemporary U.S. context. Finally, each of the organizations selected addresses a reasonable range of issues, and does not serve as a single-issue lobby. This is a significant characteristic for the sake of comparative analysis.

5. This chapter is based on a review of the documents they have made public about their work, interviews with current and former staff at the organizations, and in some cases, observations of their advocacy work. All of the information, then, is largely internal in source (secondary sources published on the USCCB constituting the only exception), and the focus remains on their self-perceived identity and impact.

6. Patrick Connor, SVD, "NETWORK, A Politician's Nightmare," *Word* (publication of the Divine Missionary Brothers) 50, no. 1 (January 2001): 24–25 at 24.

7. Ibid., 25.

8. The total number represented by individual and institutional memberships surpasses 100,000. See www.networklobby.org/about/(accessed May 12, 2005).

9. Ibid.

10. 1998 NETWORK membership survey, archives available at NETWORK's national office, Washington, D.C. We shall encounter concrete examples of this below.

11. Interview with NETWORK staff member, July 2002. See the bibliography for details regarding NETWORK staff interviews, which all took place at NETWORK's national office in Washington, D.C.

12. As NETWORK attempts to shift its membership away from predominantly well-educated women religious, its mission may expand to include educating members to help those members to connect faith to action.

13. 1998 NETWORK membership survey. NETWORK staff emphasize that NETWORK does not represent or speak for the poor, but rather it is in solidarity with those living in poverty. "No one is voiceless," the staff note, "it's just that people in power are not listening" (interview with NETWORK staff member).

14. www.networklobby.org/about (accessed May 26, 2005).

15. NETWORK uses the visionary language of economic equity, or articulating what it would like to see in a more humane world, rather than negative terminology such as antipoverty. To view its official Economic Equity Statement, go to www.networklobby.org/about/eequity.html (accessed May 26, 2005).

16. Thornton's 11-year term as national coordinator of NETWORK ended in June 2003. She went on to serve as president of her religious community in Cedar Rapids, Iowa. Simone Campbell, S.S.S., began serving as national coordinator in late 2004. Maureen Fenlon, O.P., served as national coordinator in the interim.

17. Interview with Kathy Thornton, R.S.M., Washington, D.C., July 26, 2002.

18. Although testifying or lobbying with those most affected by legislation does not happen with regularity, several staff mentioned it is a direction in which the organization is moving, in its efforts to speak with, and not simply for, those in poverty.

19. The Western Hemisphere Institute for Security Cooperation was formerly referred to as the School of the Americas.

20. One NETWORK staff member mentions that groups from different faith traditions do not always agree on particular policies (e.g., abortion), but that, more often than not, general principles are essentially agreed on (interview with NETWORK staff member).

21. Thornton interview. She cites Mircea Eliade and Teilhard de Chardin on the sacredness of all things and a cosmology of the interconnectedness of all reality and potential for all reality to reflect God.

22. Ibid.

23. Similar to PCUSA leadership, NETWORK staff point to the Synod of Bishops' "action on behalf of justice and participation in the transformation of the world fully appear to us as a constitutive dimension of preaching the gospel, or, in other words, of the church's mission for the redemption of the human race and its liberation from every oppressive structure" (Synod of Bishops, *Justice in the World*, in David O'Brien and Thomas A. Shannon, eds., *Catholic Social Thought: The Documentary Heritage* [Maryknoll, NY: Orbis Books, 1998], 289, introduction). NETWORK staff characterize themselves as practitioners of justice interested in transforming the world (Interview with NETWORK staff members).

24. www.networklobby.org/issues/background.html#analyze (accessed May 26, 2005).

25. See NETWORK's "Shaping a New World, A Challenge for the 21st Century," 6th ed., (updated and revised by Mary Ann Smith, M.M., NETWORK education coordinator, 1998), where it integrates themes gleaned from papal encyclicals, synodal documents and Bishops' Conference statements (along with some scripture) with what it takes to be pressing signs of the times: the globalization of the economy, sexism, racism and ecological devastation.

26. Every NETWORK employee earns the same salary, regardless of length of service, education or experience, or position, in an effort to emphasize that the work that everyone does enhances the achievement of the mission. Because NETWORK works to create structures of equity, it attempts to begin at home. Thornton notes that the collaborative management style takes considerably more time and work, but that the result is a greater ownership of the organization by all of the

staff and a better working environment. This approach originally drew her to the position as national coordinator.

27. NETWORK also understands itself as steeped in white feminist culture, and although the board has worked on antiracism initiatives and it is working hard to broaden its membership base, NETWORK acknowledges that there exist major differences even among women who do not want to be labeled feminist but womanist or mujerista. As a result, one staff member noted, "NETWORK wants to meet people where they are at, yet there exist varied ideas about justice and Catholicism." Its staff and membership may not represent the group that NETWORK is reaching out to (such as the Latino community, for example), and it still needs to determine "what does it say about who we say we are and how to we express that to a population speaking in a different language?" (interview with NETWORK staff member).

28. Interview with NETWORK staff member; confirmed with Gudorf via email correspondence, May 25, 2005. Gudorf also mentions that there are a variety of post-Christian expressions, but that it is up to NETWORK to determine and articulate how it perceives itself.

29. Interview with NETWORK staff member.

30. Ibid.

31. Thornton interview.

32. Ibid. She contrasts this sense to the dulling effects evident in organizations that have transitioned beyond the movement stage and become more bureaucratic.

33. Ibid.

34. Interview with NETWORK staff member. Thornton adds that this entails "being open to the idea that there is more than one way to accomplish something."

35. Interview with Catherine Pinkerton, C.S.J., July 23, 2002. Lobbyist Anne Curtis, R.S.M., describes a similar approach to the issue of campaign finance reform: "NETWORK's position is for public financing with a ban on PAC's and soft money, but the bill that was passed bans soft money, so NETWORK's position was to support the bill, but call it only a step and decide to continue to work toward comprehensive campaign finance reform, for our position is more comprehensive than that passed" (interview with Anne Curtis, R.S.M., July 25, 2002, Washington, D.C.).

36. Ibid.

37. Interview with Mary Elizabeth Clark, S.S.J., NETWORK lobbyist, July 24, 2002.

38. Thornton interview.

39. Ibid.

40. Ibid.

41. Joan Huffer, legislative assistant to then-majority leader Senator Tom Daschle (D-SD), in a meeting with representatives from NETWORK, Bread for the World, Call to Renewal, and a Reformed Jewish group regarding TANF reauthorization, July 24, 2002.

42. Interview with NETWORK staff member.

43. Following the passage of the Bipartisan Campaign Finance Reform Act in March 2002, the bill's sponsor Senator Russ Feingold (D-Wisc.) named NETWORK as one of four groups that played a major role in moving the legislation forward. Some have charged that NETWORK's activity on campaign finance reform was

several steps removed from direct action on behalf of poor, but this was an issue its membership urged the organization to take up, and as an organization it believes that campaigns controlled by money skew democracy and influence in ways that negatively affect those it seeks to protect.

44. The "Making a Noise about the Need" campaign run by the NETWORK education program involved workshops across the country and an interactive website to coordinate advocacy efforts leading up to (what were thought to be) TANF reauthorization votes. (These have continued to be pushed back from their expected September 2002 date due to delays caused by other pressing business. As part of the relief package for Hurricane Katrina, the House and Senate passed the eleventh temporary extension of TANF continuing its services through the end of 2005.) The efforts sought to provide participants with skills and information to advocate for welfare policies that would help people achieve a better quality of life rather than simply to reduce welfare rolls. NETWORK organized a lobby day in May 2002 that empowered many participants and led to further actions and some changes on TANF. (A delegation from Ohio that participated in NETWORK's lobby day convinced Sherrod Brown [D-13] to change his position and vote for the Democratic amendment that NETWORK supported.)

45. Interview with NETWORK staff member.

46. Jean Stokan, PCUSA policy director, telephone interview, April 7, 2003.

47. Today, Pax Christi International comprises autonomous national sections, local groups, and affiliated organizations spread over thirty countries and five continents, with more than 60,000 members worldwide. The movement works in all areas of peace but has a specific focus on demilitarization, security and arms trade, development and human rights, and environmental protection. PCUSA has consultative status as a nongovernmental organization at the United Nations.

48. Marvin L. Krier Mich, *Catholic Social Teaching and Movements*, (Mystic, CT: Twenty-third Publications, 1998), 300.

49. www.paxchristiusa.org/aboutus.html (accessed April 13, 2003).

50. Johnny Zokovitch, PCUSA communications director, telephone interview, April 7, 2003.

51. Zokovitch attributes some of PCUSA's recent, unprecedented rise in membership to both the U.S. military response in Afghanistan and now Iraq following the events of September 11, as well as the clergy sexual abuse scandal. He surmises that, in part, Catholics are looking for alternate routes for expending their time and effort (to that of the institutional church).

52. Local groups consist of three or more persons registered as PCUSA members with the national office who come together to pray, study, and act for peace with justice. A PCUSA region consists of six or more PCUSA registered local groups or two hundred registered PCUSA members in a specific geographic area. (Membership numbers updated May 5, 2005, thanks to Johnny Zokovitch).

53. In 2003, Bishop Gabino Zavala succeeded Bishop Walter Sullivan and Bishop Thomas J. Gumbleton to become PCUSA's third bishop president.

54. A perennial question remains whether the Catholic peace movement broadly considered can embrace both pacifist and just-war approaches—or the theoretical methodologies of a Baxter as well as a Hehir. One relatively recent contribution to the debate has been theologians' and bishops' turn to constructive

peacemaking as a common call of both approaches. See, for example, USCCB, "The Harvest of Justice is Sown in Peace," Glen Stassen, ed., *Just Peacemaking: Ten Practices for Abolishing War* (Cleveland: Pilgrim Press, 1998; rev. ed., 2004); and *Journal of the Society of Christian Ethics* 23, no. 1, (Spring/Summer) which features six theologians' articles on just peacemaking and an annotated bibliography on the subject.

55. PCUSA's statement of purpose is, "Pax Christi USA strives to create a world that reflects the peace of Christ by exploring, articulating, and witnessing to the call of Christian nonviolence. This work begins in personal life and extends to communities of reflection and action to transform structures of society. Pax Christi USA rejects war, preparations for war, and every form of violence and domination. It advocates primacy of conscience, economic and social justice, and respect for creation. Pax Christi USA commits itself to peace education, and, with the help of all its members and in cooperation with other groups, Pax Christi USA works toward a more peaceful, just, and sustainable world" (PCUSA promotional brochure).

56. Mary Evelyn Jegen, S.N.D., "Peace and Pluralism: Church and Churches," John A. Coleman, S.J., ed., *One Hundred Years of Catholic Social Thought: Celebration and Challenge*, (Maryknoll, NY: Orbis, 1991), 286–302 at 293.

57. Concerned about the effects that the 1996 Personal Responsibility and Work Opportunity Reconciliation Act (also known as the Welfare Reform Act) which abolished the federal welfare system, PCUSA joined with NETWORK, the Daughters of Charity, Sisters of St. Joseph, and the Sisters of Mercy to monitor the effects of the Welfare Reform Act and advocate for just welfare reform. For more information, see www.paxchristiusa.org/news_events_more.asp?id=40 (accessed April 11, 2003).

58. The Declaration of Life states an affirmation of life and requests that in the case of homicide the district attorney or prosecutor not file or prosecute an action for capital punishment against the perpetrator. See www.paxchristiusa.org/news_events_more.asp?id=56 for the full text of the Declaration of Life (accessed April 11, 2003).

59. PCUSA initiated the campaign in response to a statement by its bishop members in which it declared, "In a time of unprecedented economic prosperity and budget surpluses, our political leaders cannot find the resources to provide a good education and reliable health care for tens of millions of our nation's children. . . . We view the federal budget as a moral document that must reflect our degree of compassion for those who are poor and suffering in our own society. . . . We must marshal our resources and summon our moral courage to say 'no' to a bloated military budget which robs those who are poor and vulnerable and 'yes' to a budget which helps lift people out of poverty." See www.paxchristiusa.org/pc_bread_stones.asp?DBNUM=1&DBNAME=pc_disarmament (accessed May 26, 2005). Other recent campaigns include PCUSA's antiracism effort, Brothers and Sisters All, campaign for conscientious objection, and the People's Peace Initiative. See www.paxchristiusa.org/pc_con_object.asp (accessed May 20, 2005).

60. PCUSA is undertaking a major, twenty-year initiative on racism, developing a structural analysis of racism and prejudice, offering training programs for how to take people of color into account and become accountable to them. As one

staff member put it, "PCUSA is an organization that is 95% white in a church that is not 95% white, and we want to investigate how we can become the way the Body of Christ looks" (interview with PCUSA staff member). According to executive director Dave Robinson, "In our particular context in the U.S., racial reconciliation is also a core value. This commitment is best expressed through our desire to dismantle racism within our own organization and to transform our movement into a truly diverse organization shaped by the agendas, stories and experiences of all segments of the U.S. Catholic Church" (telephone interview with Dave Robinson, May 5, 2005).

61. Descriptions of PCUSA's issue areas are adapted from the organization's own self-descriptions, available at www.paxchristiusa.org (accessed May 20, 2005).

62. Interview with PCUSA staff member, April 7, 2003.

63. See Debbi Wilgoren, "Peaceful Protest Ends in Peaceful Arrests, Nobel Winners Among 68 Detained Activists," Washington Post (March 27, 2003), B01. Bishop Gumbleton remarked, "As people of faith and conscience, we proclaim that it is a grave sin to support this war. We cannot stand silent while the Bush administration murders innocent men, women and children." See PCUSA press release available at www.paxchristiusa.org/news_events_more.asp?id=517 (accessed May 27, 2005).

64. Robinson interview.

65. Stokan interview.

66. Robinson interview.

67. Ibid.

68. Although PCUSA seems more inclined to use scriptural points of departure and the radical teachings of Jesus than the other groups, *Pacem in terris* is a largely natural law–based document.

69. Stokan interview.

70. For an analysis of PCUSA's nonviolent direct action tactics, see Ron Pagnucco, "A Comparison of the Political Behavior of Faith-Based and Secular Peace Groups," in Christian Smith, ed., *Disruptive Religion: The Force of Faith in Social Movement Activism* (New York: Routledge, 1996), 205–22.

71. Jegen, "Peace and Pluralism," 293.

72. Robinson concludes, "Any serious study of Scripture and the teachings of the Church lead to the understanding that it is the responsibility of every follower of Jesus to be engaged in the issues of our time" (Robinson interview).

73. Stokan interview.

74. Interview with PCUSA staff member.

75. Zokovitch interview.

76. Pagnucco, "Comparison of the Political Behavior," 218.

77. Ibid., 210–19, for a historical overview and sociological analysis of PCUSA's use of both citizen action and unruly tactics.

78. Zokovitch interview.

79. Taco Bell Corporation, a division of Yum! Brands, agreed to raise tomato farmers' wages by one penny per pound, and to work on several fronts to improve working conditions. In return, the Coalition of Immokalee Workers agreed to end its three-year boycott of Taco Bell. Full press release available at www.paxchristiusa.org/news_events_more.asp?id=538 (accessed May 19, 2005).

80. Zokovitch adds that it is one thing to dismiss or denounce the political system and its importance from a middle-class perspective, but that it is a matter of authenticity to listen to the voices of those whose lives may be affected by those legislative successes and failures (Zokovitch interview).

81. Interview with PCUSA staff member.

82. Robinston interview.

83. Ibid.

84. Stokan interview.

85. Zokovitch interview.

86. Ibid.

87. Stokan interview.

88. Zokovitch interview.

89. Ibid.

90. Ibid.

91. The Baltimore councils focused on internal church issues such as a national catechism, training for clergy, and the discouragement of mixed marriages. See Thomas J. Reese, S.J., *A Flock of Shepherds: The National Conference of Catholic Bishops* (Kansas City, MO: Sheed & Ward, 1992), 22.

92. Some have argued that this was instigated by Catholic desires to prove themselves as patriotic and genuinely American rather than Roman. The USCCB website describes the move as a response to Pope Benedict XV's urging the hierarchy to join him in working for peace and social justice; still others suggest that it simply coincided with the increasing significance of the federal government at the time.

93. Reese, *A Flock of Shepherds*, 23. As a result, public officials courted members of the Catholic hierarchy to encourage Catholics to participate in the war effort, (in contrast to the anti-Catholic sentiment that was prevalent at the time). Reese notes that both church and state found the NCWC a useful tool. Elizabeth McKeown adds that Catholic leaders "were also aware that anything less than full support of the war could lead to reprisals against American Catholics by zealous patriots." See Elizabeth McKeown, "The National Bishops' Conference: An Analysis of its *Origins*," Catholic Historical Review 66 (October 1980): 565–83 at 567.

94. Reese, *A Flock of Shepherds*, 23–24.

95. Ibid., 24–27.

96. www.usccb.org/whoweare.htm (accessed May 26, 2005).

97. Mary Hanna, "Bishops as Political Leaders," in Charles W. Dunn, ed., *Religion in American Politics* (Washington, D.C.: Congressional Quarterly Press, 1989), 75–86 at 77; Pope Paul VI, *Decree Concerning the Pastoral Office of Bishops in the Church, Christus Dominus*, #38, October 28, 1965. Available at www.vatican.va/ archive/hist_councils/ii_vatican_council/documents/vat-ii_decree_19651028_ christus-dominus_en.html (accessed June 14, 2003). At Vatican II, the Council determined episcopal conferences to be a useful vehicle for dealing with church issues and implementing conciliar reforms. Although the theological status and teaching authority were debated at the Council, participants recognized their practical necessity. See Reese, *A Flock of Shepherds*, 28–29.

98. "The NCCB operated through committees made up exclusively of bishops, many of which had full-time staff organized in secretariats. In the USCC the

bishops collaborate with other Catholics to address issues that concern the church as part of the larger society. Its committees included laypeople, clergy and religious in addition to the bishops." See www.usccb.org/whoweare.htm (accessed April 19, 2003). Several new committees were added to the NCWC structure. Several bishops remarked at the time that the major difference between the new and old structures were that social issues had become increasingly researched and staffed, the arena of interest had been broadened, and deference to issues particular cardinals raised had been diminished, with bishops voting on the merits of the issues alone no matter who raised them. See Reese, *A Flock of Shepherds*, 31–32.

99. This merger was an attempt to combine perceived authorities. When the USCC was separate, the fear was that its more liberal statements and actions appeared to come from a voice of professionals that was independent of the bishops and did not reflect the bishops' authority.

100. www.usccb.org/whoweare.htm (accessed March 22, 2003).

101. See also Hanna, "Bishops as Political Leaders," 77. The USCCB is organized as a corporation in the District of Columbia and its purposes under civil law are: "To unify, coordinate, encourage, promote and carry on Catholic activities in the United States; to organize and conduct religious, charitable and social welfare work at home and abroad; to aid in education; to care for immigrants; and generally to enter into and promote by education, publication and direction the objects of its being." See www.usccb.org/whoweare.htm (accessed April 18, 2003).

102. Reese, *A Flock of Shepherds*, 77. Reverend Monsignor William P. Fay currently serves as general secretary. The bishops elect their president and other officers by secret ballot, and a network of committees convene regularly encompassing internal and religious as well as social and political issues.

103. For a discussion of the USCCB's relationship with Rome, see Reese, *A Flock of Shepherds*, chapter 8 ("The Shepherds and the Chief Shepherd"). Some observers note that since the mid-1980s, following the bishops' pastorals on the economy and peace, the bishops have tended to reduce their national voice on justice and peace issues and to understand the relationship with Rome as essentially unidirectional. For example, Peter Steinfels writes that the 1980s pastorals were not followed by others because their public character "made Rome nervous." He adds, "The Vatican began choosing a new kind of bishop, oriented more toward assuring internal church order than embarking on controversial political initiatives." See Peter Steinfels, *A People Adrift: The Crisis of the Roman Catholic Church in America* (New York: Simon & Schuster, 2003), 84.

104. Since its founding, the Conference has also had an office dealing with legislation. Soon after the NCWC was founded, it dealt with proposed federal regulations for obtaining altar wine during Prohibition. See Reese, *A Flock of Shepherds*, 196.

105. The USCCB's legislative concerns fall under the areas of communications, domestic social development, education, international justice and peace, migration and refugees, pro-life, and tax policies, and church and state issues. See www.usccb.org/ogl/whoweare.htm (accessed April 18, 2003).

106. Reese, *A Flock of Shepherds*, 199.

107. Currently, Most Reverend Nicholas DiMarzio of the Diocese of Brooklyn serves as chairman of the Domestic Policy Committee and Most Reverend

John H. Ricard, S.S.J., Bishop of Pensacola-Tallahassee, serves as chairman of the International Policy Committee. Rev. J. Bryan Hehir formerly directed this division.

108. www.usccb.org/sdwp/greetings.htm (accessed March 29, 2003).

109. Recent activity includes lobbying and letters regarding the partial birth abortion ban; cloning ban; the Abortion Non-Discrimination Act; USCCB statements, "Light and Shadows: Our Nation 25 years after *Roe v. Wade*" (1997); statements on euthanasia; "Faithful for Life: A Moral Reflection" (1995). See www .usccb.org/prolife/whatsnew.htm (accessed April 18, 2003). The other departments and offices at the USCCB that deal with social issues include the Catholic Campaign for Human Development, Faithful Citizenship, Migration and Refugee Services, and, to a certain extent, the Committee on Science and Human Values.

110. Telephone interview with John Carr, director, SDWP, USCCB, April 15, 2003.

111. Final approval is granted by the general secretary, and committee chairs' testimony must be cleared by the USCCB president. For a copy of the consultation form for presentation and letters to Congress that details the levels of review, see Reese, *A Flock of Shepherds*, 202.

112. Hehir interview, July 13, 2002.

113. Reese, *A Flock of Shepherds*, 200.

114. Ibid., 203. Reese notes that "when absolutely necessary, the conference can move quickly," citing the example of the six Jesuits who were murdered in El Salvador: a letter from the NCCB/USCC president was faxed to the White House National Security Office and testimony before a Senate subcommittee was approved with great speed. An executive committee of bishops serves to take action on time-sensitive issues or to resolve disagreements among the USCCB staff or general secretary. See Reese, *A Flock of Shepherds*, 200–201.

115. Carr interview, April 2003.

116. Reese, *A Flock of Shepherds*, 104. Some have noted that John Carr has attempted to counterbalance the bishops' post-1980s hesitation to speak out forcefully on social issues. After the USCCB's November 2004 meeting, others criticized the "leftism" of the staff at the USCCB, charging that their "equation of life issues with the minimum wage" ill befits the bishops' policy arm.

117. Ibid., 200; telephone interview with Carr, April 2003.

118. Hehir interview; Carr interview.

119. John Carr plenary, Annual Catholic Social Ministry Gathering, "Catholic Social Mission: Seeking Justice, Overcoming Poverty, Building Peace," Washington, D.C., February 9–12, 2003.

120. Additional action alert areas in recent history include the national housing trust fund, minimum wage, the faith-based initiative, food stamps, farm aid, environmental justice measures, in 2000 social security and Medicare, substance abuse and women, child care and children's health, and the uninsured. Beyond the SDWP, OGL advocated on issues relating to Federal Marriage Amendments, education legislation, the Sudan, immigration reforms; Pro-Life Activities was active on issues of abortion and assisted suicide.

121. Senator Sam Brownback (R-KS), Sen. Kent Conrad (D-SD) and Michael Gerson were invited to the 2003 gathering, and Carr lamented that "for Democrats

culture trumps economics and for Republicans conservatism trumps compassion." When introducing the speaker from the Bush Administration (Michael Gerson) at the 2003 gathering, Carr praised the work of the administration on abortion, the faith-based initiative, and foreign aid promised for fighting AIDS, and strongly criticized the administration's positions on responding to the threat in Iraq and its approach to reauthorizing TANF. Annual Catholic Social Ministry Gathering, February 11, 2003, Washington, D.C.

122. Carr plenary. At its social ministry gathering in 2000, the SDWP scheduled Senator Patrick Leahy (D-VT) and White House Senior Advisor Karl Rove to speak back-to-back, which is probably a unique combination in Washington.

123. Carr interview.

124. "Abortion has often been the centerpiece of the bishops' political activities not only because of the strong antiabortion position of the universal Church and clarity of the Vatican's directives on the political implications of such opposition, but also because of the particular way their position on that issue has intersected with the political process. The bishops' position on abortion is clearer and more politically accessible than their positions on other issues. 'Right-to-life' has been a political rallying cry and powerful tool of partisan mobilization." See Timothy A. Byrnes, *Catholic Bishops in American Politics*, (Princeton, NJ: Princeton University Press, 1991), 144–45. See CDF, "Vatican Declaration on Abortion," *Origins* 4, no. 25 (December 12, 1974), 385–92 at 390. Much has been written on the bishops' approach to abortion in comparison to their approach to other social issues. See, for example, Timothy Byrnes and Mary Segers, eds., *The Catholic Church and the Politics of Abortion: A View from the States* (Boulder, CO: Westview Press, 1992). We shall turn to a further discussion of the USCCB's abortion advocacy in the final section of this chapter. In terms of the bishops' policy agenda, many have argued that "abortion is not simply one issue among many for the bishops. It is rather the bedrock, non-negotiable starting point from which the rest of their agenda has developed. The bishops' positions on other issues have led to political action and political controversy, but abortion . . . has been a consistently central feature of the Catholic hierarchy's participation in American politics" (Byrnes, *Catholic Bishops in American Politics*, 143). "Bishops can be found who do not agree with all of the conclusions and implications of 'The Challenge of Peace' or 'Economic Justice for All.' But you will not find, either now or in the foreseeable future, a bishop who is not strongly opposed to abortion." Even Bernardin never backed off from an aggressive stance regarding abortion (ibid., 144).

125. William Gould argues that Hehir's role in expanding bishops' concerns to the consistent ethic of life, "by publicizing Catholicism's rich, broad social vision, did a great deal to alter the misperception that the Catholic Church is a single-issue church engaged in an unholy alliance with the political Right. Instead, many in the policy community and the academic world began to realize what they should have known all along: that Catholicism is the repository of a long, complex, and extremely distinguished tradition of moral reasoning that has much to offer our pluralistic society." See William J. Gould, "Father J. Bryan Hehir: Priest, Policy Analyst, and Theologian of Dialogue," in Jo Renee Formicola and Hubert Morken, eds., *Religious Leaders and Faith-Based Politics: Ten Profiles* (Lanham, MD: Rowman & Littlefield Publishers, Inc., 2001), 197–223 at 216.

126. Joseph Cardinal Bernardin, "A Consistent Ethic of Life: An American-Catholic Dialogue," in Thomas G. Fuechtmann ed. *Consistent Ethic of Life* (Kansas City, MO: Sheed & Ward, 1988), 1–11.

127. Gene Burns, *The Frontiers of Catholicism: The Politics of Ideology in a Liberal World* (Berkeley: University of California Press, 1992), 124. Mary Segers criticizes the bishops, nevertheless, for their coercive treatment of pro-choice Catholic office-holders (indicating their "failure to understand the dilemma of being a lawmaker in a pluralist society with traditions of religious freedom and church-state separation"); their failure to consult feminists about proper abortion policy "in any serious, systematic way"; and their emphasis of abortion to the relative neglect of other significant life issues (noting grassroots mobilization and parish-based education campaigns have remained limited to abortion and not on other life issues). See Mary Segers, "Where Are We Now? The 'Catholic Moment' in American Politics," in R. Bruce Douglass and Joshua Mitchell, eds., *A Nation Under God? Essays on the Future of Religion in American Public Life* (Lanham, MD: Rowman & Littlefield, 2000), 111–34 at 126–27. We shall return to the bishops' treatment of abortion in their electoral politics as compared with their abortion lobbying efforts below. Segers notes that over the past two decades the Catholic bishops have learned several lessons as a result of their abortion advocacy, namely, "the importance of not being partisan, the necessity of a multi-issue approach to American politics, and the necessity of presenting a rational and convincing case for their position rather than appealing to scriptural or papal authority for their justification" (126).

128. Reese notes that although the statements themselves have been fairly non-controversial and widely supported, controversy has arisen over what issues should be given priority. As a result, the bishops decided to list the issues in alphabetical order to reduce conflict over priorities, which at least avoided the appearance that abortion was more important than other issues. Yet, the terminology of issues over the years has sometimes been carefully adjusted to reflect implicit emphases, such as in 1980, when those interested in peace issues changed the title of their topic from military expenditures to arms control and disarmament, moving it from last to second place, and agricultural issues were always listed under food lest they outrank arms control. See Reese, *A Flock of Shepherds*, 191–92. Since the 1970s, the conference has also sent a bishop or staff member to make presentations on this range of issues to the platform committees of each national party in each election year. Ibid., 192.

129. This sentiment was repeated in my interviews with Hehir, Carr, and Sharon Daly, and was offered by Thornton. Although it is beyond of the scope of this study, many rich insights might emerge from a more extensive survey of outsiders to better gauge the impression of those on Capitol Hill or in the press of the bishops' consistency in their approach to abortion as opposed to other social justice issues, because they have remained open to this critique in varying degrees. Nevertheless, outside perception of this consistency is not as essential to my purpose here, because I am focusing on the bishops' own statements and actions on a broad range of issues in the recent years and their own perception of their approach.

130. Telephone interview with Catholic Charities vice president for social policy, Sharon Daly (former director, Domestic Social Development Office), April 1, 2003.

131. Ibid. Daly notes that perhaps issues such as the entitlement of poor children to assistance or state votes on the death penalty are analogous to the starkness of the abortion issue, but that the bishops are moral teachers and their position on the abortion question is not one that is shared by many other mainstream religious groups in the United States.

132. Ibid.

133. Carr interview.

134. Even on issues of great interest or sympathy to the conference, ensuring legislation is abortion-neutral has been a priority. Abortion might relate to other issues such as health insurance, foreign aid, school-based clinics, etc. Daly has said, "The policy of the conference, at least where abortion is concerned, is to not say you are for a bill until it's fixed." See Reese, *A Flock of Shepherds*, 204.

135. Reese, *A Flock of Shepherds*, 205–6. Daly recounts the story of her persistent lobbying of Henry Hyde (with Mark Gallagher of OGL) on the FMLA legislation in the mid-1980s. In the beginning, she recounts, the only defenders were the National Organization of Women (NOW) and labor groups, and when the NCCB decided to support the bill it was able, over time, to convince Republicans such as Hyde that the bill was actually pro-life and pro-family, and of the importance from an antiabortion perspective of protecting the jobs of workers after illness or child bearing. The USCCB lobbied Hyde for seven years; when it finally convinced him that women will have abortions if they cannot stay home from work without losing their jobs after delivery, he brought twenty Republicans with him. Hyde made a speech on the floor saying he is not a regular supporter of restrictions on corporations, but that in this case he had pro-life and profamily reasons for doing so. This serves as an example of the USCCB's unique ability to convince pro-life and pro-family congresspersons that this was important (not just on the terms of NOW, which Republicans rejected; Daly interview).

136. USCCB, *A Place at the Table: A Catholic Recommitment to Overcome Poverty and to Respect the Dignity of All God's Children*, (Washington, D.C.: USCC, 2002). In his analysis of the bishops' peace and economics pastorals of the 1980s, Philip Berryman notes that the bishops take a salvation-history approach to their subject, following the sequence of Creation, Exodus/Covenant, formation of Israel, the prophets, Jesus Christ, the Church, to the final consummation of the kingdom." See Philip Berryman, *Our Unfinished Business: The U.S. Catholic Bishops' Letters on Peace and the Economy* (New York: Pantheon Books, 1989), 13–15. The pastorals also use Catholic social principles and natural law–argumentation, but I would hold that USCCB documents and advocacy remain more overtly and thoroughly theological than do the other organizations' methods. We have encountered this methodological tension in the social tradition more broadly in chapter 2.

137. Joint letter from USCCB and Catholic Charities USA (signed by Theodore E. Cardinal McCarrick, archbishop of Washington, chairman, Domestic Policy Committee, and J. Bryan Hehir, president, Catholic Charities USA) to members of the U.S. House of Representatives, dated February 11, 2003. The letter was distributed to all participants at the USCCB's Annual Catholic Social Ministry Gathering for the participants' lobby day visits. The letter also grounds opposition to the pending bill in more natural law–arguments, such as the dignity of the human person, the common good of society, subsidiarity, option for the poor, and solidarity.

138. USCCB, Domestic Social Development Office, "Food and Nutrition Programs," Position Paper, February 2003.

139. Carr interview.

140. Carr plenary.

141. See, e.g., Avery Dulles, S.J., "Gospel, Church, and Politics" in Richard John Neuhaus, ed., *American Apostasy: The Triumph of "Other" Gospels* (Grand Rapids, MI: Eerdmans Publishing Company, 1989), 29–55, esp. 47–49. Such objections rest upon the assumptions that the two efforts are not connected, that bishops are not qualified to make policy recommendations, and that such activity neglects pastoral responsibilities. These debates also relate to broader, ongoing debates regarding the role of justice and peace efforts in the life of the church.

142. Jo Renee Formicola, *Pope John Paul II, Prophetic Politician* (Washington, D.C.: Georgetown University Press, 2002), 124. For example, a group of Catholics issued an eighty-page counterstatement five days prior to the release of "Economic Justice for All," hoping to undercut the bishops' stance by contending (alternatively) that American capitalism was the most effective solution to problems of poverty and tyranny. See Lay Commission on Catholic Social Teaching and the U.S. Economy, *Toward the Future: Catholic Social Thought and the U.S. Economy: A Lay Letter* (New York: American Catholic Committee, 1984). Another group including Michael Novak and William F. Buckley published *Moral Clarity in the Nuclear Age*, a "Letter from Catholic Clergy and Laity," arguing that the just-war doctrine supports nuclear deterrence as an ethical imperative to ensure justice and freedom in our world. See Michael Novak, *Moral Clarity in the Nuclear Age* (Nashville, TN: Thomas Nelson, 1983).

143. Daly interview.

144. José Casanova, *Public Religions in the Modern World* (Chicago: University of Chicago Press, 1994), 186. Criticisms arise not only from those who think the bishops should refrain from entering into such discussions or such moral teaching should not be binding, but also from those who reject the idea that bishops' statements could constitute one idea among others in public debate (like the applications portions of the pastorals or some policy statements are intended as). According to then-Cardinal Ratzinger, for example, "It is wrong to propose the teaching of the bishops merely as the basis for debate; the teaching ministry of the bishops means that they lead the people of God and therefore their teaching should not be obscured or reduced to one element among several in a free debate." See Peter Hebblethwaite, *Synod Extraordinary: The Inside Story of the Rome Synod*, November-December 1985 (Garden City, NY: Doubleday, 1986), 59, as cited in Casanova, *Public Religions in the Modern World*, 188. For example, in "Economic Justice for All," the bishops state "there is certainly room for diversity of opinion in the Church and in the U.S. society on how to protect the human dignity and economic rights of all our brothers and sisters. In our view, however, there can be no legitimate disagreement on the basic moral objectives" ("Economic Justice for All: A Pastoral Letter on Catholic Social Teaching and the U.S. Economy," [Washington, D.C.: USCC, 1986], no. 84).

145. Daly interview.

146. Ibid. Daly notes that many who criticize the bishops for speaking out on social issues are lay Catholics who work out of conservative think tanks. For ex-

ample, she points to the Heritage Foundation and the American Enterprise Institute and wonders, "If their priority is cutting taxes, then how much emphasis will they necessarily have on defending the poor?"

147. Carr plenary.

148. Carr interview.

149. Ibid. We shall take up the ways in which this assessment and other insights from these case studies shed light on and inform and challenge various approaches in chapter 5.

150. Casanova, *Public Religions in the Modern World*, 189. Mary Hanna notes that "World War I produced only one American Catholic conscientious objector," although the two hundred Catholic conscientious objectors of World War II were nearly all members of the Catholic Worker movement. She adds, "throughout American history the Catholic Church and its bishops were probably the biggest hawks in our skies." Mary Hanna, *Catholics and American Politics* (Cambridge: Harvard University Press, 1979) 40–42. We reviewed in chapter 3 how Baxter points to this characteristic as part of the Americanist tradition in Catholic ethics and history of accommodation to the nation-state.

151. Carr interview.

152. Bishop Wilton Gregory to President George W. Bush (September 13, 2002); Statement on Iraq by USCCB (November 13, 2002); statements of Bishop Gregory (February 26 and March 19, 2003). Subsequently, the bishops have also issued multiple statements on the moral responsibilities of the United States in Iraq, the abuse of Iraqi prisoners, and on torture and human rights.

153. Daly concedes that most of the time, certain legislation is able to pass anyway even if the bishops make a protest on principle, and that she is not sure if she (or the USCCB) would always feel the same way if its support would be affecting swing votes (Daly interview).

154. Daly interview.

155. As Carr put it in 2000, "Much more of our work is directed to the community of faith than to Washington. . . . The most widely used statements of the bishops over the last decade have focused on the social mission of the parish, the opportunities to share Catholic social teaching in elementary schools and seminaries, and higher education—in the everyday responsibilities of lay men and women to carry forth that mission and how they act at work, how they raise their kids, what kinds of citizens they are." (Carr interview). See discussion following Stephen Pope's "Catholic Social Teaching and the American Experience," at the Spring 2000 Joint Consultation, "American Catholics in the Public Square" initiative, Commonweal Foundation and Faith & Reason Institute (Annapolis, MD: June 2–4, 2000). Available at www.catholicsinpublicsquare.org/papers/spring2000 joint/pope/popepaper1.htm (accessed May 26, 2005).

156. Carr plenary.

157. Carr interview.

158. At the 2003 Annual Social Ministry Gathering during a panel discussion on legislative office visits, Mark Gallagher (associate director, OGL, USCCB) and Kathy Curran (policy advisor, SDWP, USCCB) urged those attending to use personal examples and stories from their experiences in Catholic dioceses and service agencies around the world in making their case as they lobbied congresspersons

later that day. Gallagher and Curran urged the lobbyists to include in their meetings someone whose life is affected by the issue on which they were lobbying—a TANF recipient, for instance—reflecting how the USCCB values and uses data from personal experience in its lobbying efforts. Annual Catholic Social Ministry Gathering, "Catholic Social Mission: Seeking Justice, Overcoming Poverty, Building Peace" (Washington, D.C.: February 9–12, 2003).

159. Daly interview.

160. Bernardin, "A Consistent Ethic of Life," 10.

161. Carr interview.

162. Ibid.

163. Ibid.

164. Ibid. Some would argue that these criteria have been subsumed by international law theory and that its contemporary use is not directly connected to Catholic or Christian origins.

165. Reese, *A Flock of Shepherds*, 220.

166. Ibid., 218.

167. Daly interview.

168. Ibid.

169. Carr interview.

170. Ibid.

171. Starting in January 2002, *The Boston Globe* reported on a widespread pattern of sexual abuse by priests that was covered up by the Archdiocese of Boston. The scandal led to the resignation of Bernard Cardinal Law in December 2002. As documents started flowing from the church in 2002 and more alleged victims came forward, it became clear that clergy abuse was, in fact, a systemic problem in the Boston Archdiocese (and others), involving scores of priests and hundreds of victims across the metropolitan area and throughout the country. For the U.S. bishops' document, "Restoring Trust, Response to Clergy Sexual Abuse," including its "Charter for the Protection of Children and Young People," see www.usccb.org/comm/restoretrust.shtml (accessed May 26, 2005).

172. At his 2003 plenary, Carr stressed the fact that "the church exists not for itself but to preach the gospel and serve the least of these," and that therefore it must fix the problems and damage done amid the current scandals and get back to its mission. This institutional recovery does not just entail internal focus but a renewed commitment to social ministry, for if the church loses its prophetic voice and withdraws, there would be a great loss; "this is a time for solidarity and mission" (Carr plenary). As Cardinal Theodore McCarrick noted at a press conference when asked about the scandal, "We're more than our mistakes. We care for the weak. We stand up for life. We serve the sick. We welcome the stranger. And we try to help people live their lives with dignity and with faith so that they can help shape a better world." Comments cited by Carr in his 2005 plenary address, "The Church in the Modern World: Learning Lessons, Making a Difference and Keeping Hope," Annual Catholic Social Ministry Gathering, February 21, 2005. Available at http://usccb.org/sdwp/carrspeech.htm (accessed May 21, 2005).

173. According to a lobbyist at NETWORK, if, as a result of recent scandals, the Catholic Church becomes more democratic and therefore galvanizes a rise in the laity's voice and participation, and people's faith in the gospel rather than

(ecclesiastical) structures, then it will coincide with some the strengths and values of NETWORK's own approach (interview with NETWORK staff member).

174. Archbishop Raymond Burke of St. Louis, Archbishop Alfred Hughes of New Orleans, and Archbishop John Vlazny of Portland, Oregon.

175. Bishop Michael Sheridan of Colorado Springs in his May 1 pastoral letter, "The Duties of Catholic Politicians and Voters," *Origins* 34, no. 1 (May 20, 2004): 5–7.

176. For example, then-Archbishop William Levada of San Francisco, Cardinal Roger Mahoney of Los Angeles, Cardinal Theodore McCarrick of Washington, D.C., and Bishop Anthony Pilla of Cleveland.

177. USCCB, "Catholics in Political Life," *Origins* 34, no. 7 (July 1, 2004): 98–109.

178. For a discussion of the task force's origins and deliberations by its chair, see Cardinal Theodore McCarrick, "The Call to Serve in a Divided Society," *Origins* 34, no. 40 (March 24, 2005): 634–40.

179. Zokovitch interview.

180. The Iraq Peace Journey included a group of Roman Catholic laypersons, sisters, and priests describing themselves as committed to active nonviolence as a means to reconciliation and healing of the conflicts that grip our world today. From December 8–21, 2002, they traveled in Iraq, to stand with their sisters and brothers who daily live under the threat of violence and war. Robinson went on a speaking tour for PCUSA in the spring of 2003, drawing on that experience ("Eyewitness from Iraq: War, Conscience and Faith").

181. Robinson interview. PCUSA staff single out the Catholic Campaign for Human Development and USCCB's ministry work, in particular, for praise.

182. Zokovitch interview.

183. Carr interview. I have not had occasion to ask John Carr if he agrees with Zokovitch's characterization of the relationship between his office and PCUSA. Carr's perception of PCUSA is that it does not engage in domestic policy issues, so that misunderstanding may also be a contributing factor.

184. Thornton interview.

185. Daly interview.

186. Catholics for a Peaceful End to Terrorism, "A Catholic Community Responds to the War, Living with Faith and Hope." Statement available along with a list of signatories at http://web.sbu.edu/fcsc/a_catholic_community_responds _to.htm (accessed May 26, 2005).

187. Carr interview.

188. This latter role is more explicitly clear in PCUSA's mission, but NETWORK is committed to dialogue with the official church on matters of disagreement and a prophetic stance on such issues, where warranted.

189. She fears that the bishops cannot afford to be strong enough in their own pastorals and efforts for fear they have to pay for and protect Catholic institutions, and she worries that this is not truly being the church of the poor. Some point to NETWORK's ability to take a prophetic stance post–September 11th that departed from the USCCB position on Afghanistan as an example of the prophetic independence they enjoy (interview with NETWORK staff member).

190. 1998 NETWORK membership survey.

191. Stokan interview.

192. Reese, *A Flock of Shepherds*, 203.

193. Fowler, Hertzke and Olson add that "this is a distinct political advantage. Thus, even if lay opinion is divided on an issue, the 'official' Church position can be articulated clearly." See *Religion and Politics in America*, 69.

194. There were only 14 no votes in the November 2002 meeting on their statement on war with Iraq. Carr said all of the bishops begin with the same values, and sometimes they differ on priorities or emphases (Carr interview).

195. Ibid.

196. Hanna, "Bishops as Political Leaders," 83. Archbishop Weakland chaired the bishops' committee that drafted "Economic Justice for All"; he made this comment in 1986.

197. NETWORK lobbyist Anne Curtis, R.S.M., adds that she does not want members of the administration to be able to say that "we didn't hear from faith-based groups on this issue" (Curtis interview).

198. As Sheridan ("The Duties of Catholic Politicians and Voters," 7) puts it, "It is by your prayers and by your votes that the politicians who are unconditionally pro-life and pro-family will serve our country."

199. Interview with NETWORK staff member.

200. Formicola, *Pope John Paul II*, 120–21.

201. For example, Reese, *A Flock of Shepherds*, 191, although the committee does not explicitly endorse political candidates, it distributes literature showing how congresspersons have voted on pro-life issues.

202. See, for example, Reese's 1992 study of the NCCB, *A Flock of Shepherds*, esp. 223–24. In his conclusions, he highlights that "for no other issue, except the tuition tax credit, have the bishops developed and implemented a detailed blueprint for grass-roots education and action" (224). Perhaps most famously, John Cardinal O'Connor openly disapproved of Catholic candidates who tolerated or supported abortion in the 1984 elections (presidential, state, and local). Just before the 1984 election, the NCCB released a statement that indicated that "the Church does not take positions for or against particular parties or individual candidates. . . . We are constitutionally committed to the separation of Church and State, but not to the separation of religious and moral values from public life." NCCB, "Text Statement by Bishops on Church Role in Politics," *New York Times*, October 14, 1984, A30. He was speaking out against Geraldine Ferraro in her bid that year for the vice presidency, and condemning her for suggesting the Catholic pro-life stance was not monolithic. That year, Bernard Cardinal Law also designated abortion as the critical issue of the election. In addition, in 1990 O'Connor warned pro-choice Catholic politicians that they risked excommunication. Ari I. Goldman, "O'Connor Warns Politicians Risk Excommunication over Abortion," *New York Times*, June 15, 1990, A1.

203. As Segers ("Where Are We Now?" 128–29) writes, "In style and manner, the bishops recognize subtlety, nuance, the importance of listening, and the need for compromise in public policy in these complex issues [economic and peace pastorals and their political responsibility statements]—whereas on abortion they tend to display an absolutistic moral-political method that leaves no room for maneuver or compromise." In her view, "the church can better witness to the transcendent by witnessing Gospel norms of charity and compassion in assisting in-

voluntarily pregnant women than by lobbying legislators or using church services as occasions for grassroots political mobilization."

204. See Casanova, *Public Religions in the Modern World*, 193–201 for a full discussion of his charges that the bishops' antiabortion efforts contain semantic, performative, and procedural inconsistencies.

205. Ibid., 200–201.

206. Christine Gudorf, "To Make a Seamless Garment, Use a Single Piece of Cloth," *Cross Currents* 34, no. 4 (Winter 1984–85): 473–91 at 490.

207. As a result, NETWORK sticks to "economic equity, peace and environmental issues," and because it does not deal with abortion, it also does not deal with capital punishment or end-of-life issues (interview with NETWORK staff member). This staff member regrets the fact that NETWORK does not take up capital punishment, because so many prisoners on death row are poor. In contrast to Thornton's praise of the USCCB's witness, another staff member objects that the "USCCB has done a disservice in how it has framed the election issue—that is, that no Catholic can vote for a pro-choice candidate without losing Eternal Life."

208. Interview with NETWORK staff members. One NETWORK lobbyist suggests there is often more at stake (personally) for suburban Catholics to vote with the stance of the official church on socioeconomic issues than on life issues alone (the abortion issue alone).

209. Daly interview.

210. Zokovitch interview.

211. See www.paxchristiusa.org/news_events_more.asp?id=71 for PCUSA's 2001 statement (accessed May 27, 2005). PCUSA's online campaign during the 2004 presidential election reflected this integrated approach to life issues. In its *Called to Embrace All Life*, PCUSA underscores the fact that the Christian faith is an integral unity and warns Catholic voters that neither candidate was completely pro-life and that voters are called to assess candidates in light of the full range of their positions. Its statement and web resources referred to "Faithful Citizenship" and the CDF's "Doctrinal Note" and opposed what it refers to as a minority of Catholic voices who claimed that there was only one pro-life candidate and that Catholics who voted against (Bush) were committing mortal sin. See Dave Robinson, "The November Presidential Election," *The Catholic Peace Voice*, 29, no. 6 (September-October 2004) available at www.paxchristiusa.org/the_cpv/sept_oct_04/news_thecatholic_pv_story2.asp (accessed May 21, 2005).

# CHAPTER FIVE

# Catholic Public Theology for the Twenty-first Century

We have already alluded to some of the ways in which these case studies of Catholic political advocacy organizations shed light upon the theological foundations and theoretical distinctions that have emerged. In some instances, the cases serve to exemplify theological conceptions of church-society engagement, and in other instances the organization's practices pose challenges to the classic typological divisions we have explored. Putting theory and praxis into conversation will help to determine what finally constitute the possibilities for and limits to public theology and political advocacy in the U.S. Catholic context. The normative conclusions that result highlight the ways in which different theories and practices exhibit different strands of the tradition, and suggest that fidelity to the fullness of the tradition calls for mutual clarification of the different strands by one another.

Several specific methodological directives emerge from our investigation to help guide public theology and political advocacy, in particular: (1) strengthen the connection between embodiment and advocacy, (2) install mechanisms for self-critique, and (3) address a comprehensive range of issues. In the end, a theoretical approach that is fully theological and fully public holds most promise for achieving an authentic and responsible social ethic.

## THEORY AND PRAXIS

Now that we have completed our investigation into theoretical understandings and practical expressions of public theology in the contemporary U.S. context, we are better able to discern ways in which Catholic political engagement on the ground both corroborates theological tensions and challenges standard typological categories.

## Corroborations

On the whole, the case studies exemplify the perennial tensions intrinsic to relating faith and tradition to contemporary social and political issues. In particular, the ambivalence inherent in the fullness of the Christian tradition highlighted in chapter 2 and embodied by J. Bryan Hehir's and Michael Baxter's approaches plays out concretely in some of our case studies. For example, whereas Pax Christi USA's (PCUSA's) mission is particularly enlivened by the Sermon on the Mount, *Pacem in terris* serves as its charter and framework, perhaps the quintessential natural law encyclical in the Catholic social tradition, reflecting the tensions between the scripture's hard sayings and natural law—arguments that we have encountered. Although its work for peace often places PCUSA in opposition to mainstream patriotism or militarism and it remains very attentive to the divergences between the pax Americana and pax Christi, the organization uses Catholic social teaching and empirical arguments in its witness and advocacy work. The political advocacy groups surveyed also reflect the outlooks of Hehir and Baxter in more decisive and particular ways.

Perhaps most apparent are the ways in which the work and outlook of the United States Conference of Catholic Bishops (USCCB) distinctly reflects the theology and strategies of J. Bryan Hehir. As noted, Hehir's influence at the bishops' conference has been considerable, and the continued impact of his work there remains evident. Both Hehir and the USCCB combine a positive conception of the state with an equally sanguine view of the need for contributions from other agencies in the social arena, including religious organizations. Each similarly operates with the assumption that the church's role among people of goodwill is a persuasive one, and each opposes an approach that would impose the church's views amid legitimate pluralism or retreat amid an unfriendly environment. John Carr's characterization of the USCCB's efforts to take empirical information seriously ("faith is not a substitute for facts or data") also reflects Hehir's methodology. The bishops' nuance and restraint in language reflect Hehir's own approach, which, he admits, sacrifices prophetic edge for pastoral and public responsibility.

Hehir himself has explicitly characterized the advocacy activity of the USCCB as fitting squarely within Troeltsch's church type: "From the bishops' arguments in defense of the rights of the unborn, to their human rights analysis of U.S. policy in Central America, to their just-war critique of nuclear policy, the Catholic leadership has tried to play this mediating role between faith and culture, between church and society. On all these issues there has been a conscious effort by the bishops not to adopt a sectarian posture. They have maintained this position in spite of criticism from quarters within the church who want a 'stronger' or more 'evangelical' emphasis, less open to the balancing of various claims and less concerned about shaping the teaching in a manner accessible to those outside the community of faith."[1]

Hence, Hehir's impact resulting from his work at the Conference, including his influence on Cardinal Bernardin and Bishop James Malone in helping them draft speeches and letters, remains evident.[2] Bernardin's conception of the substance and communication of the consistent ethic of life also reflect Hehir's influence. Bernardin noted that although the substance of the consistent ethic is rooted in a religious vision, Catholics need to state their case to wider society in nonreligious terms that members of different faiths or those who are not members of a faith can find morally persuasive, given the moral and religious pluralism characterizing American society. He urged a public church style in light of the often emotional and divisive nature of life issues.[3]

Carr's implicit comparison of the USCCB's and PCUSA's approaches mirrors differences in the respective stances of Hehir and Baxter. Carr contrasts the bishops' commitment to respectful dialogue and allowance for disagreement among people of goodwill in particular applications of principles to other groups' prioritiziation of prophecy and proclamation in an uncompromising manner. Carr also explicitly characterizes PCUSA's approach in dividing true believers from the morally suspect in ways that reflect Baxter's stance. Conversely, he describes the bishops' centrist approach that promotes civil and mutual exchange (that disappoints those on the right and the left) in a manner reminiscent of Hehir's approach. PCUSA echoes Baxter's outlook and approach on its own terms, as well. The organization's consistent attentiveness to the gulf between American and Catholic values, its work for peace, and its concern about accomodationist tendencies especially in times of war recall Baxter's concerns. Baxter and PCUSA leadership also similarly lament the scriptural and theological illiteracy within the church, the fact that, "American Catholics have learned much more about what it means to be American than what it means to be Catholic."[4]

In terms of the sources on which the advocacy organizations rely, they seem to defy categorization under either Baxter's scriptural or Hehir's strictly philosophical method. All three organizations—NETWORK, PCUSA, and USCCB—rely most heavily on Catholic social teaching, which in part reflects Hehir's bias. Yet the USCCB, the group most closely identified with Hehir's public church, is the group that most thoroughly uses scripture in addition to social principles.[5] On the whole, however, the organizations surveyed take for granted or underplay the use of scripture. Whereas we might expect to find PCUSA using scripture the most, it seems to depend on Catholic social principles and natural law–argumentation more exclusively than do the bishops. Staff at all three organizations name the role of experience (e.g., of the poor) as a key source in communicating amid pluralism. Using such experience as a source is somewhat analogous to the role empirical evidence plays in Hehir's approach, but the experience (as a source) of the poor or marginalized is generally overlooked in both Hehir and Baxter's strategies as articulated. Hence, on the whole, the sources on which these advocacy organizations rely reflect Hehir's preference for Catholic social principles, and the groups supplement sources advocated by both theoretical models with the importance of experience.

## Challenges

Although the approaches of each political advocacy group in some ways corroborate the theoretical stances explored, the cases also serve to challenge some typological distinctions. For example, the activity of these organizations calls into question Baxter's insistence that a dialogical stance necessarily leads to accommodation or assimilation. In their pastorals of the 1980s, the bishops challenged deeply held American values such as the free enterprise system, individualism, patriotism, and anticommunism. They argued that such values should be examined in light of moral principles, but the perception among the public, the media, and Catholics was often that they were challenging basic American tenets.[6] The bishops' more recent advocacy, as well as the work undertaken by NETWORK and PCUSA, confirms my argument that, depending on the issue, the church's structural engagement with the world may be understood as countercultural rather than risking co-optation (particularly on such issues as abortion, military intervention, and capital punishment). Baxter is correct to warn that engagement in a culture that contradicts Christian values in many ways risks corruption, if one does not continually guard against co-optation and form oneself in the Christian tradition. Yet the cases demonstrate that structural advocacy on behalf of the poor or unborn can provide ways of responding to the gospel's call, rather than assimilating to an American or liberal paradigm.

NETWORK Director Kathy Thornton's general perception of government falls somewhere between Hehir's optimism and Baxter's pessimism. Her view of government as a preeminently human institution, with all of the limits and possibilities that entails, compels her to work to influence structures so that those structures do not exclude, and to understand such work as one way of helping establish the fullness of life that Jesus inaugurated, rather than as co-optation. Thornton roots NETWORK's engagement with the state in Catholic anthropology: "Humans are social, relational, made for community, and we must promote the common good." She notes that as a result, "limiting work for justice to *ad hoc*, community-based efforts or non-cooperation with the state discounts our social nature," or the ways in which we are tied to one another beyond discrete local communities.[7] As Thornton puts it, "We are not angels, we interact, we live with one another, so our call is to create avenues for us to be in harmony with one another and nature."[8] Sharon Daly's reflections that the magnitude of today's problems requires government assistance ("the church cannot stand with the poor alone") similarly reflect a desire to collaborate with human institutions in service of the poor rather than to gain mainstream clout per se.

In contrast to Baxter's claim that the USCCB spends the majority of its time lobbying Congress when its primary task should be the formation of the faithful, Carr reports that he spends half of his time on the road talking to pastors, school principals, and parish staff about Catholic values and their own needs, and the other half of his time in Washington, D.C., advocating for the implementation of those values. He does not view his efforts in Washington as competing with or detracting from other important Catholic tasks and agrees that "work in D.C. is only a small part of the social mission of the church."[9] Carr adds, "Catholicism combines deep prayer and spirituality with action, we do not check our faith at the door when we act as citizens. Only a few are called to the monastery."[10]

Baxter would likely challenge this last statement, in line with a more evangelical emphasis on the universal call to holiness and counsels of perfection, and would charge that putting our discipleship and citizenship on equal footing is part of the problem. Yet, in line with efforts to bring together Baxter's focus on discipleship and liturgy with social outreach and action, most of those interviewed in the case studies strongly connected these two aspects of their faith and mission of the church. In the words of Mark Gallagher, associate director, Office of Government Liaison (OGL), USCCB: "Catholics go to church so that we can leave church and have the grace to respond to the needs of our brothers and sisters."[11]

PCUSA's work also challenges some of the theoretical divisions we have encountered. Although its attentiveness to the considerable disparities between Christian and American paradigms and work for peace reflect Baxter's concerns, its expansion beyond education and civil disobedience into lobbying and coalition work challenges the approach he advocates. PCUSA's collaboration with others suggests that evangelical and public church models of engagement approach one another more than typological divisions imply. PCUSA and NETWORK have begun to collaborate frequently as PCUSA expands its efforts into the legislative arena. They have partnered recently on welfare reform, military spending, and opposing military action in Iraq.[12] Similarly, John Coleman's studies of paradenominational groups engaged in citizen activism have shown that PCUSA members conceive of its engagement as at once involved and critical—again in ways that challenge standard typological divisions or Baxter's assumptions. When asked about tensions between their discipleship and citizenship, some members named "consumerism, individualism and militarism as anti-Christian values" and that in any real or imagined conflict between the two roles they would want discipleship to trump.[13] Nevertheless, Coleman has documented a strong association between such activists' faith and their work for various civic causes and has encountered a healthy critical patriotism even among those who engage in civil disobedience. He notes that one PCUSA member demonstrating at Ritsmouth Air Force Base compared her actions to parenting: similarly, "criticizing children doesn't mean you don't love them."[14]

The activities and attitudes of some PCUSA members challenge Baxter's blanket opposition to engagement with the state in the pursuit of social change. Conversely, the use of theological language attested to by those interviewed in conveying the impact of Catholic values amid lobbying and other advocacy efforts casts doubt on Hehir's insistence that only mediated, philosophical arguments are appropriate given the situation of pluralism in the United States. It is interesting to note that the USCCB uses theological language in its lobbying efforts most explicitly out of the three organizations. We encounter the examples of the USCCB grounding its Temporary Assistance to Needy Families (TANF) and antihunger lobbying in Creation, Eucharist, and Jesus' examples, yet the bishops' conference also remains heavily influenced by Hehir's contributions and reflects his approach in other significant ways.

Again, the fullness of the Catholic call requires both charitable and structural justice efforts. The case studies reaffirm this conclusion and challenge a one-sided focus that either Baxter's or Hehir's approach alone might promote. The range of NETWORK and PCUSA's activities also reveals the importance of both charitable and justice-oriented efforts. As NETWORK lobbyist Anne Curtis, RSM, emphasizes, the scriptures do not call us to meet immediate needs alone, for we must attend to both the parable of the Good Samaritan and Exodus. She notes that "we always need people like Moses to liberate us from structures of enslavement as well as Samaritans to respond to people on sides of the road," and it is insufficient for the church to approach the problems of injustice by one method alone.[15] In Curtis's words, "We need the menu of strategies; NETWORK doesn't offer the only way of putting one's faith into practice; yet to stand balanced, we need to have 'the two feet of justice,' direct service and systemic change. We need to respond to immediate needs as well as continually ask, 'Why do we need shelters and food pantries?' Therefore we must also look at structures and policies that keep people from living with their full dignity and must attend to both. Our faith and social teaching promote and call us to both [direct service and work toward structural change], and as a community we need both to remain balanced."[16] Although NETWORK staff members believe that different strategies come together for change at some point, they maintain that if you do not have some way of engaging with the state, "you'll always be protesting war, and not preventing it or engaging other ways of dealing with conflict." Curtis adds, "If we only go to the streets it may, at some point, create change in structures, but short of anarchy I don't understand how else the state will be[come] less than a tool of violence." She notes that pitting one strategy against another is not helpful as it risks the danger of engaging in some of the very behaviors against which one is protesting.[17] NETWORK's institutional outlook challenges the adequacy and effectiveness of approaches that Baxter would endorse, but it also confirms the caveat that we should avoid a false choice between the strategies that Baxter and Hehir favor.

Similarly, PCUSA engages in a variety of strategies that reflect both Baxter and Hehir's different approaches, from prayer vigils and pouring blood on weapons to lobbying Congress, evidencing the prophetic potential for a range of strategies, including legislative advocacy. Although some PCUSA members would prefer that the organization not engage the state legislatively, the organization as a whole has moved in a direction that is more inclusive of strategies that both Hehir and Baxter would advocate. As Johnny Zokovitch's comments convey, although PCUSA retains a strong commitment to critiquing the system and attending to the divergences between the Christian and American paradigms, PCUSA staff have become convinced—in part by the substantial concrete impact legislative advocacy has had on the lives and concrete political agendas of those they serve and defend—that working within the system has a place in their work for peace and justice.

Given these various confirmations of and challenges to theory by praxis, what are we to conclude about the possibilities for and limits to public theological engagement? What constitutes a responsible and authentic approach given the insights of contemporary theologians and activists?

## CONCLUSIONS ON PUBLIC THEOLOGY AND POLITICAL ADVOCACY

These challenges posed to typical theoretical divisions by the advocacy groups' practices underscore the inadequacy of any one typological approach on its own. On theoretical grounds alone, we encounter potential for mutual clarification of Hehir's and Baxter's approaches by their discrete insights, and we can now recognize ways in which concrete cases of political advocacy shed further light on our comprehensive understanding of Catholic public engagement. Given this mutual clarification of theory by praxis, what may we conclude about the possibilities and limits for public theology in its fullest sense? Of course, in one sense the pluralism of approaches and understandings that have emerged remains appropriate and inevitable, sociologically and theologically, as we have seen. The transcendence of God and God's reign relativizes any historical efforts to relate church and society. Any historical action will inevitably fall short of the fullness of the Kingdom of God, so any one political or theological agenda cannot encompass the fullness of God's agenda.

This eschatological tension has resurfaced throughout our explorations of theological foundations for Catholic engagement, the methodological emphases of Baxter and Hehir, and the advocacy groups' strategies for bringing Catholic values to bear amid the realities of Washington politics. As a result of the inherent incompleteness of any historical attempts, then, we might identify two tactics. One tactic is for us to do as much as we can (to help the poor, work for peace and justice in this world) with the understanding that such efforts will inevitably entail some compromises. The other tactic is for us to avoid sinful interactions and compromise at all costs, given the ambiguities of our situation in this life. This distinction characterizes (if exaggerates) the stances of Hehir and Baxter, or the bishops' conference as opposed to PCUSA, to some degree. What, then, are we to conclude amid the inherent limits of any one approach?

Theoretical and practical analyses indicate that public theological or religiopolitical engagement is possible on the civil societal level, within limits. In terms of limits, the theories and praxes together suggest that such engagement must guard against politicization, against co-optation with the state, partisanship, total withdrawal, relativism, and must acknowledge the complex character of the church and world (acknowledge the presence of sin and activity of the Spirit in both). Within those limits, we have encountered a range of forms of legitimate public engagement, in contrast to charges that (1) bishops have no business descending to public policy matters, (2) any engagement with the state is unchristian accommodation, (3) modes of witness as resistance ignore the plight of the oppressed, or (4) debates about the specificity and binding nature of social teaching related to public policies will be interminable and indeterminate. We have seen how, rather than inherently posing dangers to our pluralist context or religion itself, respectful, critical religiopolitical engagement can, in fact, contribute to wider society, from generating social capital and civic skills to consistently raising the normative dimensions of social issues in public debate. A Catholic understanding of public theology will inherently encompass some pluralism of modes and strategies, because as the U.S. bishops assert in *A Place at the Table*, government and business, faith-based organizations and families and individuals all have important roles to play in countering poverty and working for a more just society.[18] This capacious norm encompasses approaches that must navigate between the dual dangers of the opposition and identification of faith with work for justice. Just as Hehir describes a public church as working to avoid both co-optation and conflict, or as the bishops characterize appropriate Catholic political engagement as being involved but not used, distinct approaches should work to ensure that they avoid opposing fidelity to the tradition with work for justice or unduly deemphasizing the former in pursuit of the latter.[19]

On balance, Baxter too starkly separates discipleship and citizenship and Hehir does not allow discipleship to be sufficiently normative. Other shortcomings and limitations of each theory and organization we have reviewed indicate the need for a framework for attending to the comprehensive scope of what the Catholic tradition requires. Although NETWORK draws on Catholic social teaching, the life experiences of people who are poor, and a feminist perspective in significant and valuable ways, its lack of explicit attention to thick theological symbols (e.g., the cross, Jesus Christ, the resurrection) reveals a lacuna and the need for a model encompassing the ambivalence and tensions we have encountered. A Catholic approach should strive to be informed by the fullness of the tradition—both scripture and natural law, or in this case, the thickness of theological categories and mediated principles—as well as by signs of the times. One recommendation arising from these observations and analyses is that NETWORK's approach should continue to include experiences of the poor and of women as a source, but should be continually critiqued and informed by other emphases, in its case the more evangelical strand that Christine Gudorf identified as lacking.[20]

Our investigation calls for a framework that incorporates insights, emphases, and strategies from both of the two outlined general approaches. From our investigation into Hehir and Baxter and in light of the cases, it has become clear that something valuable and significant is at work that any one approach on its own fails to capture adequately. This reality demands the dynamic, mutual correction of each rather than mere coexistence. Just as David Hollenbach argues that only the simultaneous presence of distinct approaches ensures the full content of Christian hope is made visible in history, we might add that only the mutual clarification of one stance by the other—ensuring simultaneous attentiveness to the fullness of the tradition and to the demands of the social context—will ensure that closer approximations of Christian hope and the Reign of God are made ever more present in history.[21]

## Attending to the Fullness of the Tradition

The two basic postures explored fundamentally reflect different strands within the Christian tradition, and bear on social and political questions. As noted above, Baxter and Hehir diverge on the segregation of theology and politics, each accusing the other's stance of falsely separating the two.[22] Baxter's supernatural view does not separate the two at all, in his own view, whereas Hehir's supernatural concerns compel attention to natural, temporal matters, which in his view remain implicitly supernatural. Hehir's and the USCCB's approach reflect the Thomistic understanding that the Christian is at home in the political order and that the gradual sanctification by the Spirit in Christ takes place *within* it, rather than over and against it. On this view, political authority and law do not exist merely due to the reality of sin, as Baxter's more Augustinian approach implies, but rather government corresponds to needs and purposes inherent in human nature itself and helps establish and maintain conditions that allow citizens to live the good life. Tensions also emerge from the understanding of human reason present in each stance. One strand generally stems from an appreciation of our ability to reason and to understand as reflecting the *imago Dei* and a Thomistic commitment to reasonable moral order knowable in principle by all humans. An Augustinian approach, however, focuses on the divine basis of order and its disruption by sin.[23] Finally, we recall the more specific ways in which divergent theological emphases lead to distinct stances, emphasizing, for example, creation, resurrection and neighbor love or the suffering servant and love of enemies.

These tensions or somewhat complementary strands, of course, reflect longstanding theological differences. Yet our emphasis here focuses on ways to bridge and mutually inform both strands, because Catholics are committed to such propositions as these: Faith and reason are complementary, not contradictory; the church is the Body of Christ and a human community; and the Incarnation neither merely confirms human nature nor destroys nature, but rather transforms nature. For our destiny, union with God through knowledge and love, fulfills natural human capacities while elevating those capacities to a qualitatively different level.[24] Amid life between the times, then, while inherent tensions persist, we must seek ways to temper Hehir's optimistic "already" with the complexity and hesitancy appropriate to Baxter's "not yet." We must find ways to allow Hehir's integrated understanding of believer and citizen to challenge the potential dualism of Baxter's outlook.

### Framework for Mutual Clarification

In light of these epistemological and eschatological tensions, Catholic public theology and political advocacy should employ a framework for the mutual clarification of these two strands of thought. Hence, beyond guarding against the aforementioned risks to any religiopolitical engagement, a particularly appropriate ethical paradigm for engaging in public theology and political advocacy entails holding in creative and dynamic tension these distinct strands we have revisited. An overall framework for such mutual clarification should encompass two aspects or movements whereby (1) the distinct strands of the tradition correct one another's opposing emphases in order to attend to the *fullness* of the tradition, and (2) fidelity to that tradition is held in dynamic tension with responsibility to our shared reality. In this two-step dynamic, the models we have explored interact in ongoing ways, moving beyond the mere coexistence of divergent typologies and achieving a more authentic and responsible social ethic.

In terms of the first step, whether an approach reflects a public church or a more evangelical stance, the practitioner must continually work to allow such tendencies to be critiqued and advanced by the contributions of the opposite pole by means of this framework for mutual clarification. Whatever the particular preferred emphasis or pole—whether it reflects the gospel's hard sayings or efforts to discover a common human morality—one must allow the other pole or strand within the tradition to move the stance forward by letting the opposing tendency challenge one's motives and actions. In this way, one is always examining what one is too ready to accept or dismiss because of one's own particular emphasis.

Beyond this first dynamic, the second step entails a dynamic reciprocity between fidelity to this full sense of the tradition and responsibility to signs of the times. This involves bringing Catholic theological resources to bear on the realities of the world and allowing those realities to inform one's theological outlook. The signs of our times indicate multiple phenomena that are not easily reducible to a single directive that implies a standard typological stance. For example, we encounter at once global injustice and human suffering on a scale that beggars localist approaches, violence that contradicts Christian values, and other phenomena that call for resistance. We face genocide in the Sudan and ubiquitous commodification in the United States. The signs of our times also include a situation of de facto pluralism with which we must contend; as a result we must find ways to cooperate—but not to assimilate—in our common life. The case studies also reveal the incompleteness of any one emphasis or approach, underscoring our need to account for both the thickness of the tradition (scripture, theological symbols, and Catholic social teaching) and empirical data, including the experiences of people who are poor.

Thus, in the end, the insights of theory and praxis taken together suggest that a fitting normative framework for guarding against the dual dangers of the identity and dichotomy of faith and temporal efforts requires this two-phased process: (1) holding in a creative and dynamic tension the fullness of what our tradition imparts—mercy and rigor, creation and crucifixion, justice and peace, nature and grace; and then (2) holding in creative and dynamic tension the fullness of that tradition with responsibility to the demands of our shared life together.

Beyond this rather abstract normative framework, the mutual clarification of our theological categories by the practices of our case studies suggest several principles that will serve to help navigate between these poles and advance these dynamics of mutual clarification.

## METHODOLOGICAL DIRECTIVES

We turn now to an exploration of three such directives: (1) to strengthen the connection between embodiment and advocacy; (2) to install mechanisms for self-critique to guard against distortion; and (3) to address a comprehensive range of issues.

### 1. Strengthen the Connection between Embodiment and Advocacy

*Catholic public engagement should both embody and advocate the values it advances.*

The first directive that my study suggests is that joining embodiment to advocacy efforts will bridge theoretical divisions, strengthen credibility, and aid in the mutual correction of each strand. Baxter's and Hehir's approaches focus on modeling and communicating Christian norms, respectively. Baxter's appropriation of the work of Virgil Michel and his insistence that faith and justice are not to be applied to social problems, but rather embodied, falsely opposes embodiment and application in concrete social circumstances. My conclusions regarding the role liturgy and Christian formation might play in aiding discernment for public engagement and in bridging Baxter's and Hehir's approaches highlight the intrinsic connection between embodiment and application or advocacy. The case studies serve to substantiate further the importance of this link between embodiment and communication. This connection between how the church models justice, peace, and Christian discipleship and how it communicates the implications of those values to wider society and brings them to bear upon our shared life together serves as this first directive to help navigate between the poles within our framework for mutual clarification.

NETWORK's internal practices challenge a theoretical or typological opposition of embodiment and advocacy and illustrate the importance of modeling *and* advocating in the spirit of *Justitia in mundo*. The organization understands itself as a prophetic community of justice, and as such it works to embody the very values that it advocates in its lobbying work. NETWORK's collaborative management style with participative decision making promotes the value of equal human dignity, and its uniform salaries emphasize the fact that the work that everyone does enhances the achievement of the mission. Because NETWORK works to create structures of equity, it attempts to begin at home. NETWORK consciously strives to model within its organization what it wants to see in the world. This link, reminiscent of *Justitia in mundo*'s maxim that those who venture to speak about justice must first be just, underscores efforts to bring together approaches such as Baxter's that focus on performative witness with Hehir's stress on communication and advocacy. Reinforcing this connection would also enhance the credibility of the church's teaching and advocacy efforts.

Others have pointed out the challenges that a need for internal reform poses to the church's public witness. The fact that women are excluded from positions of ecclesial leadership, for example, has caused many to charge that the church's credibility on issues such as abortion remains compromised. Similarly, Thomas Massaro, S.J., cites sexism, clericalism, and authoritarianism as a particularly vexing trio of internal challenges to the Catholic Church's public advocacy efforts. He cites what many Americans detect as a "dissonance between the public face of the Church (especially in its social teachings which espouse the values of equal human dignity, participatory democracy and collegiality) and what they consider to be lamentable internal Church praxis," calling that dissonance a serious instance of hypocrisy and an obstacle to social witness.[25] From his own perspective, Bishop Raymond Lucker of New Ulm, Minnesota, highlights the church's shortcomings with respect to salaries and benefits for lay employees; racism and sexism; the stipends and retirement of religious; due process; and the ordination of women among the internal challenges to the church's public witness. Lucker emphasizes the human nature of the church (in the face of tendencies to divinize it) and cites Rahner's call for its ongoing growth and reform.[26] *Justitia in mundo* itself underscores the need to safeguard rights within the church (women's participation, a living wage for church employees, the freedom of expression and thought) and admonishes believers that their use of material goods should bear witness to the gospel.[27] Hence failures to embody justice in the way a church organization operates internally will significantly compromise its promotion of human rights, participation, or social justice.

The clergy abuse scandal has at least posed challenges to the institutional church's ability to communicate its social message persuasively, with the bishops' full attention. Although the internal practices of the church (failures of just embodiment) have impaired its advocacy efforts, the scandal also highlights the limits of a method that relies on modeling or witness alone. Several of the individuals interviewed indicated that the church's advocacy work is more important now than ever—both in continuing to stand for the poor and vulnerable and in helping the church to regain credibility. Certainly, amid times of internal strife, its social system serves as another face of the church, but these observations also suggest ways that the church as advocate may help heal the church as model. The scandal serves as a reminder of the ways in which secular insights can, in some cases, inform ecclesial practices in valuable ways unavailable to an enclosed or embodiment model alone. For example, many have called for the church to become more informed by secular standards of accountability, transparency, and participation in light of the way that the church protected and reassigned priests who abused minors.

This internal-external link also relates to the idea of the church as teacher and learner from society, and the impact that collaboration and coalition work can have on Catholic organizations themselves. Hehir's theological outlook reflects this two-way street of church-society engagement, and is reflected to varying degrees in the case studies.[28] The case studies also convey ways in which the church's advocacy work can directly affect its internal practices in positive ways, strengthening its credibility and this internal-external link. Daly notes that because of the USCCB's campaign for a living wage, local churches have been called on to inspect their own internal practices. She reports that about a half dozen dioceses' participation in the campaign generated internal examinations of its own pay scales, and that in many cases changes were made.[29] Both collaboration with outsiders and particular advocacy campaigns may affect internal practices and bolster this internal-external link in ways reminiscent of the relation of formation and liturgy to social action or of a dynamic of mutual clarification between Hehir's and Baxter's approaches.

An embodiment approach severed from any external communication or advocacy limits its witness efforts in the face of internal challenges, just as advocacy severed from embodiment of the norms and practices one promotes significantly undermines credibility. A unidirectional mode of witness (church as teacher but not learner) also disregards the interreligious and ecumenical cooperation to which the post–Vatican II tradition calls Catholics. Taken together, Catholic theory and praxis indicate ways in which joining embodiment to advocacy strengthens credibility and facilitates the mutual correction of each strand. A commitment to strengthening the connection between embodiment and engagement of Christian norms, principles, and practices will enhance the integrity of public theology and political advocacy.

### 2. Install Mechanisms for Self–Critique to Guard against Distortion

> *Catholic public theology should be dialogical and discerning in its*
> *method, in order to avoid distortion both from within and without.*

Our next directive indicates the importance of installing mechanisms for self-critique to guard against distortion, both from within and from without. This guidepost marks a path for avoiding distortion from within, or the risks of remaining self-enclosed, as well as distortion from without, a risk posed to advocacy divorced from embodiment. The theologies and practices of public engagement explored underscore the significance of different dialogical practices to guard against internal distortion and proper formation and discernment to guard against external distortion. As we have seen, each of the theoretical and practical models is subject to particular risks, whether co-optation, an exclusivist idolatry, or watered down principles. My investigation suggests that another important directive for such engagement involves maintaining mechanisms for self-critique that guard against both distortion from within—mechanisms for internal self-critique, understanding the church as learning as well as teaching, and structures of participation—as well as distortion from without—mechanisms for discerning what types of engagement or resistance are called for and practices of formation.

Although Baxter's reservations about the sinful character of the state and secular society leave him well positioned to critique Hehir and others on grounds of accommodation, an approach such as Baxter's that focuses on ecclesial formation as witness conversely entails risks of its own. A self-contained model risks vulnerability to a type of distortion from within by virtue of remaining isolated from critique on the part of other modes of construing reality. In James Gustafson's terms, doctrine becomes idolatry, and, as discussed, such a model may be inattentive to limits or sin within the church and God's activity in the wider world. Mutual engagement with others provides one important tool to guard against such distortion from within, as suggested by David Tracy's model of conversation and by the coalition work among our cases. Although Tracy advocates fully theological or particularlist engagement unlike the mediated philosophical versions to which Baxter objects, he advocates more of a two-way street engagement than the unidirectional influence Baxter (or George Lindbeck) favors.[30] Tracy rightly fears that if theology does not engage critically and self-critically in the global, interdisciplinary conversation it will not escape ideological distortion from within.[31] He warns that to refuse to take seriously various hermeneutics of suspicion (feminist, Darwinian, Marxist, or otherwise)—as a self-enclosed model risks doing—is to fail to regard "religion's own suspicions on the existence of those fundamental distortions named sin, ignorance, or illusion."[32]

Baxter is influenced by a Lindbeckian approach in which the biblical text absorbs the world rather than this model of conversation, yet an approach that joins Christian formation to fully theological, mutual engagement should not diminish biblical literacy and will help guard against distortion from within. As Hollenbach writes, "being schooled in the biblical story and simply repeating what we have already learned of the Bible's meaning are two different things. Rather, the pilgrim nature of Christian life has an intellectual counterpart. Having learned from both Bible and past tradition, we then will be ready to recognize new moral insights through inquiry into new dimensions of experience and from traditions outside that of the Christian community. These new moral insights, in turn, can lead to a new understanding of the biblical story itself."[33] Furthermore, a focus such as Baxter's on the purity or uniqueness of Christian doctrine alone does not attend to the ways in which Christianity is and always has been shaped by culture.[34]

The internal practices of the organizations that compose our case studies provide some examples of efforts to safeguard against distortion from within by means of self-critique. For example, PCUSA and NETWORK continually reexamine how they as organizations might be complicit in the injustices they are attempting to oppose in wider society, and how they might continue to evolve, purify, and expand to embody the change they want to see. Each group's anti-racism efforts provide a key example of such efforts: PCUSA is undertaking a major new initiative to counter racism and NETWORK has hired new staff to help recruit a wider and more diverse membership and has strived to make its board more multicultural.[35] Furthermore, part of PCUSA's very mission entails bringing to bear Christian norms of peace and justice on the church itself, not just wider society. Similarly NETWORK's feminist perspective constitutes a similar prophetic edge with potential for self-critique and protection against distortion from within, perhaps more readily available to such smaller groups than the bishops.[36]

Although critique of the church is more central to PCUSA's mission, NETWORK's very presence as a feminist Catholic voice serves to implicitly critique or lift up a prophetic strain of the mainstream Catholic tradition. NETWORK's membership survey results indicate that it fills an important role as such, because "Christian feminism is a perspective too often absent from Catholic social teaching advocacy."[37] Other members note that it is important for the church and others to know that "'Catholic' and 'feminist' are not mutually exclusive."[38] In addition, NETWORK's commitment to democratic methods also involves an implicit critique of official church protocol. Staff members note that the priority given to the consultation-affirmation process for determining legislative priorities and shifting agenda items reflects NETWORK's commitment to full participation and democracy that grows out of the unique experience of women religious and their struggles.

Coalition work among lobbying groups holds potential for serving this directive to guard against distortion from within and enable learning from outsiders alongside teaching. NETWORK more than the other organizations seems to value collaborative work in and of itself, with its theological commitment to learning from others rather than merely strategic alliances or coalition work; NETWORK perceives God at work in other human rights movements and within other peace and justice organizations. Veteran NETWORK lobbyist Catherine Pinkerton, C.S.J., notes that NETWORK staffers continually ask themselves how they can find God at work amid pluralism and open themselves to what may appear as strange or other, but oftentimes resonates with Catholic beliefs. As she puts it, "How do we find God at work and cooperate with that work of God dancing across the world?"[39] Thus, theirs is not a unidirectional or triumphalistic imposition of Catholic beliefs—although these staffers do understand their work as deeply grounded in Catholic social teaching—but rather a mutual engagement with an active openness to the presence of God outside of the church and to learning from the other.

The distinct motivations of each organization for its coalition work raises the question of what mechanisms the USCCB and PCUSA have in place for learning from outsiders or allowing public activity to enrich its own stance. Although PCUSA polled its membership as it expanded its areas of concern following the fall of the Berlin Wall, it does not seem to share NETWORK's commitment to openness to others and mutual exchange toward right relationship and dialogue. Rather, PCUSA prioritizes sustaining a dramatic and prophetic voice for peacemaking, and it collaborates with others strategically when it can merge similar efforts, but not in efforts to inform its own vision per se. Although USCCB collaborates less frequently than the other organizations, it typically cuts across partisan divisions in the collaboration work it does engage in to a greater degree than the other two organizations. In line with attentiveness to the fullness of the tradition, Catholics should seek to collaborate and learn as a value in and of itself; in line with the comprehensiveness of the Christian ethic, collaboration that cuts across typical divides will also contribute to mechanisms of learning and self-critique. Again, much as the clergy abuse scandal highlights ways in which the church might learn from wider society, it also highlights the dangers of insulation from self-critique.

Although conversation and mutual engagement with outsiders can provide important ways of safeguarding risks like distortion from within, this is certainly not to imply a relativistic understanding of different norms and practices. As Baxter emphasizes, there do exist risks to Christian engagement amid pluralism that we might term "distortion from without." Just as we must guard against internal distortion, it is equally important for us to deliberately install mechanisms to prevent such external distortion. Although Baxter's concerns about accommodation and the complete lack of harmony between church and culture might be overdrawn, as Hehir rightly suggests, Baxter's warnings about the dangers of some parts of culture to Christian identity and the need for constant discernment are well taken.[40] His stance instructs that a public church must install mechanisms to prevent overly optimistic participation or accommodation and to remain attentive to sin and to the gospel's countercultural demands, particularly amid the violence and consumerism that pervade American culture.

Our methodological analysis suggests the fundamental significance of discernment of social context in determining one's proper response in light of different circumstances—in understanding whether we are called to resistance or mutual cooperation. An understanding of liturgy that aids in the formation of conscience and educates to action for justice and peace offers important resources for guarding against these external risks. Hence, beyond bridging the typological divides noted in chapter 3, sacramental formation that assists in discerning when and how to engage the wider world can help to guard against distortion from without.

Any public church model must install mechanisms for preventing accommodation and for constantly testing (in Hehir's own words) "on what issues, with what stance, by what justification" Christians engage.[41] Although Hehir alludes to this need, his own optimism about public engagement and inattention to sin and external risks suggests that responsible political engagement requires more than just good intentions, but also requires concrete mechanisms to guard against co-optation. This will help ensure that proper formation continually purifies engagement efforts and allows practitioners to discriminate among activities that promote or diminish human flourishing. In this way, Baxter's emphases can inform Hehir's, further bridging the two poles explored, and allowing for the interactive testing of each's emphasis in light of the underrepresented strand or strategy.

Ideally, proper formation for discernment and mechanisms for guarding against distortion will enable us to better call both church *and* world to account, and to purify our efforts from distortion from within and without. As Mark Searle puts the task in terms of the role of liturgy, "Celebrating the liturgy should train us to recognize justice and injustice when we see it. It serves as a basis for social criticism by giving us a criterion by which to evaluate the events and structures of the world. But it is not just the world 'out there' that stands under the judgment of God's justice, sacramentally realized in the liturgy. The first accused is the Church itself, which, to the degree that it fails to recognize what it is about, eats and drinks condemnation to itself (1 Cor. 11:29)."[42]

The wider church's serious attention to quality liturgy, preaching and ongoing adult faith formation will help the faithful continue to understand their faith more deeply and to cultivate discernment of its social implications.[43] On the whole, the case studies lack this type of mechanism to guard against distortion from without. For example, NETWORK's openness to other traditions is laudable and prevents against other risks, but its lack of reference to Christian theological symbols during its thirtieth anniversary reflection suggests that the thickness of the tradition is not adequately informing its own discernment.

### *Related Issue: Participation*

An issue connected to such mechanisms is that of prioritizing internal participation among an organization's members. In addition to their processes of
membership consultation, both NETWORK and PCUSA identify empowering
grassroots public participation as one of their measures of success. PCUSA's
people's peace pastoral process serves as another example of promoting participation in working to reform existing church social teaching. The USCCB
has been praised for the processes of consultation it undertook when drafting
the economic and peace pastorals of the 1980s, and has been criticized for its
lack of consultation on other issues (such as its teachings on sexual ethics) in
ways that compromise its credibility on those teachings.[44] Prior to drafting the
"Economic Justice for All" and "The Challenge of Peace," the bishops con-
sulted widely and substantially among ethicists and public policy experts;
laity, priests, and religious; and others, and then revised subsequent versions
in light of comments received from ordinary Catholics when drafts were
widely circulated in dioceses across the nation.[45] At the 1986 NCCB meeting,
Bishop James Malone called the consultative critical process "a new and collegial method of teaching. . . . For the first time the people of God have been involved in [the pastorals'] formation."[46] The process of public consultation
and revision means that although the letters are bishops' statements, they are
"the work of a listening hierarchy."[47]

Whereas the bishops do not solicit feedback or participation on every social issue on which they teach, such efforts do represent the church performa-
tively learning and teaching and a commitment to consultative processes not
generally associated with the Catholic hierarchy. As Judge John T. Noonan has
written, "The [consultative] process itself can be seen as living demonstration
of the organic, interactive, reciprocally dependent character of policy formation in the Catholic Church."[48] Reintroducing and expanding such participative processes in the realm of social teaching may be viewed, then, as another
strategy for avoiding distortion and approximating a responsible and credible public ethic.[49] Renewed attention to sustaining effective structures of consultation and lay participation more broadly conceived will also contribute to
the health of the church's public witness.[50]

### 3. Address a Comprehensive Range of Issues

*Catholic political engagement should be guided by a commitment to
addressing a comprehensive range of social issues.*

Finally, mutual clarification of theory by praxis suggests that the Catholic
Church as a whole should strive to address a comprehensive range of social

issues and avoid single-issue politics. No single issue should serve as a lit-mus test for voting or political behavior, but rather the larger texture of many issues rightly constitutes the context for political discernment and participa-tion. Accordingly, our final guidepost indicates that, amid the fullness and uni-versality of the Catholic tradition and insights from our cases, a comprehen-sive range of social issues should constitute an important goal of the church's social mission as a whole, and such breadth should also inform discrete ad-vocacy groups within the church. Although more specialized advocacy groups will appropriately persist, such groups should attend to comprehensiveness by challenging their own agendas in light of the values and priorities of the issues that they exclude.

Expansion beyond a narrow range or single-issue politics is, again, a les-son that the USCC learned in the 1980s, and Cardinal Bernardin's subsequent consistent ethic of life framework provides moral and ecclesiological reasons for retaining a broad range. Moreover, a narrow issue agenda is unlikely to remain sufficiently attentive to the fullness of tradition, nor sufficiently help counter distortion. The consistent ethic's emphasis on the interrelatedness of social issues further underscores the connection between breadth and credi-bility.[51] Although PCUSA does not primarily focus on a wide range of issues, its emphasis on the interrelatedness of social issues (such as violence and poverty) is noteworthy and should inform this directive. For example, more explicitly linking opposition to abortion to issues of poverty (concrete policy issues regarding prenatal care, infant feeding programs, health care, educa-tion) than is typically embraced by either political party would help Catholics guard against partisanship and attend to the full range of issues on which the tradition touches.

In addition to Bernardin's stress on the consistency and interrelatedness of life issues, an emphasis on comprehensiveness of one's range of issues is crit-ical to guarding against partisanship and a narrow perspective. With a more restricted focus, it becomes harder to avoid interest group politics, the church's credibility is weakened, and it becomes more difficult to counter distortion from within, given the temptation to skew the rest of a particular agenda to en-sure allies' support on a single issue. This is perhaps a particularly dangerous temptation for U.S. Catholics, perhaps, because the comprehensive Catholic stance defies the typical partisan configurations.

Hehir's ecclesiological and moral analysis of Bernardin's consistent ethic is borne out in our comparative study and highlights this normative dimen-sion to a broad range of issues: "Ecclesiologically, there is the responsibility of the church to set a tone and an atmosphere in the civil life of society which it cannot do by focusing exclusively on a single-issue. Such a posture risks depicting the church as simply an interest group in a political struggle. The effect of single-issue voting strategies is to reduce the chance that parties and candidates will be judged by standards which test their vision of society and their capacity to address the basic needs of the common good. Morally, a single-issue strategy forfeits many of the resources of the moral teaching of the church. To highlight one question as the primary and exclusive objective in the policy process is to leave too many issues unattended and risks distortion of the single issue itself."[52] Theologians and activists across the spectrum can become equally vulnerable to single- or narrow-issue politics and the blindness or distortion that ensues. U.S. Catholics' prioritization of any one issue can blind them to the cause of others: Those who work with the poor can remain silent or even favor legalized abortion due to their progressive alliances on poverty issues. Those who prioritize antiabortion work can do so at the expense of addressing socioeconomic factors that contribute to unwanted pregnancies or can support the use of force when a pro-life administration goes to war.[53] Single-issue agendas of any stripe can blind Catholics to the fact that Catholic social doctrine is rooted in the dual reality of human life: humans are both sacred *and* social, so that we are called both protect human life and foster its development at every stage *and* ensure social institutions foster such development.

Although the U.S. bishops underscore this crucial link in "Faithful Citizenship" and their more recent task force statements on Catholics in political life, tensions do persist at the level of the church's public witness between understanding life issues in light of a house with foundations or a seamless garment metaphor.[54] These different perspectives, in part, contributed to the intra-Catholic political debates of 2004. In his postelection reflections, Cardinal Theodore McCarrick attempts to clarify Catholic responsibilities concerning human life and dignity:

> Surely, all of us must remember that the right to life is essential and that without it there is no subject to whom rights can be ascribed. *Primum est vivere* is the active and necessary phrase. Without life, we do not survive. And so we must begin always with great priority about the right to life, but we must not stop there. If someone says, "I believe in life and am opposed to any attacks against it," we must be in solidarity with that person; but you must go beyond that since Jesus himself came to preach "good news to the poor, liberty to captives and to set the downtrodden free." The church calls on all of us to embrace this preferential option for the poor and vulnerable, to embody it in our own lives and to work to have it shape public policies and priorities.[55]

Indeed, even as it gravely warns against supporting laws that attack human life, the Congregation for the Doctrine of Faith's doctrinal note reaffirms

"The Christian faith is an integral unity and thus it is incoherent to isolate some particular element to the detriment of the whole of Catholic doctrine. A political commitment to a single isolated aspect of the church's social doctrine does not exhaust one's responsibility to the common good."[56] Opposing life and dignity agendas weakens each cause and further divides the church, also compromising persuasive force. As Richard Doerflinger rightly points out, the pro-life message and pro-justice message deeply need one another: "Without a firm foundation in the radical value of each and every human life, efforts for justice are blind; without compassionate service to help those struggling to lead lives of dignity, the defense of life will be empty."[57] Hence, rather than opposing the two, emphasizing the interrelatedness of life and justice issues across a wide-ranging spectrum will enhance integrity and credibility.

A comprehensive array of issues can allow for the understanding that smaller or more focused groups will always exist and that not everyone can pursue every issue evenly. As Bernardin admits, "A consistent ethic does not say that everyone in the Church must do all things, but it does say that as individuals and groups pursue one issue . . . the *way* we oppose one threat should be related to support for a systemic vision of life. . . . And we can strive not to stand against each other when the protection *and* the promotion of life are at stake."[58]

Yet, beyond the manner with which discrete social programs are addressed, our comparative analysis cautions that to the extent that particular organizations avoid certain issues, they should regularly challenge their own agenda and values in light of the strand that particular issue represents or the challenges its exclusion poses. For example, NETWORK avoids the issue of abortion for some reasons related to its size and focus, the coherence of its staff and membership, its credibility, and questions about women's voices in the church. Yet NETWORK also seems to be the organization least explicitly informed by the evangelical strand of the tradition, as evidenced by the critiques Gudorf raised in the absence of thick theological symbols and language in its mission and advocacy. Baxter, however, holds up abortion as a pivotal issue for U.S. Catholics, whose genuine opposition should be cause for distancing from a liberal democracy that accepts it as one position among others. Although partial agendas within the church will appropriately persist, the tendencies borne out in theory and praxis indicate that a normative framework for public theology should include this norm of a comprehensive range of issues. Within smaller organizations, the norm implies that to the extent that one's agenda falls short of the full range of issues our Catholic faith impacts, the organization must continue to challenge its omissions by the values and priorities those exceptions represent.[59]

More stark issues such as abortion and pacifism continue to divide Catholic groups and individuals on the left and right, and the elevation of a single issue often risks blindness to its interrelatedness to other issues of life and justice as well as partisan tendencies in efforts to support the chosen issue at all costs. For example, in the bishops' conference's work on FMLA, Daly notes conservative Catholics criticized the bishops for being on the same side of an issue as the National Organization of Women (NOW), but she dismisses those as McCarthyite critiques based on who else is allied with your particular position. Daly notes that both the extreme left and right are guilty of this tendency.[60] A Catholic public theology must be careful to judge political issues in light of a comprehensive theological and ethical framework rather than partisan allegiances or single-issue litmus tests. Again, considered attention to the dynamics within our framework for mutual clarification will help guard against such tendencies. For in Bernardin's words, although there are limits to both competency and energy that point to the wisdom of defining distinct functions, the church "must be credible across a wide range of issues; the very scope of our moral vision requires a commitment to a multiplicity of questions."[61]

### Related Issues: Abortion and Pacifism

The issues of abortion and pacifism, in particular, have emerged as limit questions or issues particularly indicative of unacceptable compromise. Although the scope of this study did not allow for an in-depth investigation of any anti-abortion groups in particular, the stances reflected by Baxter and Stanley Hauerwas in chapter 3 make clear that for many Christians, opposition to abortion should put Americans unequivocally at odds with liberal institutions and ethos. Analogously, for others, the opposition to any use of force serves as a litmus test for fidelity to the gospel's hard sayings and trumps other sociopolitical issues. Certainly, as Daly noted, some issues of life and death have a starkness that other issues do not. Also, Hehir's admission that some issues divide precisely along the lines of religious beliefs (e.g., about where life begins and ends, such as abortion and assisted suicide) raises a more precise challenge about religious advocacy amid pluralism.

There are no easy answers to these particularly stark issues, yet our study suggests several implications for these matters. The advocacy efforts of the USCCB challenge Baxter's notion that any structural advocacy entails co-optation and suggest that such efforts may do more to oppose abortion ultimately than nonparticipation (e.g., witness the 2003 partial birth abortion ban). Furthermore, Hehir's acknowledgement of the specifically theological bases of public disagreements on such issues suggests that a more fully theological public engagement than the engagement that he advocates would at least bring the foundations of such sticking points into the debate. A more theological approach than Hehir favors may more adequately approximate an authentic and responsible social ethic—perhaps particularly with respect to such intractable issues. Baxter's warnings about the nature of issues like abortion or war that dramatically oppose Christian norms also serve to highlight the very ambiguity of American context and the need for continual discernment.

Finally, the consistent ethic's emphasis on the interrelatedness of issues can and does apply to these stark issues as well. Although the organization does not actively advocate against abortion, PCUSA grounds its official anti-abortion stance to unwavering respect for human life, rejecting any claims to the right to destroy life, whether individually or entire populations, and connects its opposition to a concern for the well-being of children, social conditions that limit women's options, and its stance on other life issues such as the death penalty, war, and nuclear arms race. The fullness of the Catholic tradition demands a universal concern that leads, on the whole, to sensitivity to the broad range of social and political issues our faith affects, as well as on the interconnectedness of those issues. Only commitment to a full range of issues—and continual testing or clarification of one's more narrow range by those issues excluded—will ensure fidelity to the fullness of the tradition and responsiveness to the signs of the times. The principle of attending to a comprehensive range of issues will likewise ensure attentiveness to both the evangelical and public church strands within the tradition. For as Bernardin has noted, "a Church standing forth on the entire range of issues which the logic of our moral vision bids us to confront will be a Church in the style of both Vatican II's *Gaudium et spes* and in the style of Pope John Paul II's consistent witness to life."[62] A commitment to a full range of interrelated issues will help encompass both strands within the tradition and enhance the church's integrity and credibility.

## THEORETICAL IMPLICATIONS

These particularly stark issues or limit questions that often divide precisely along the lines of religious belief suggest that a more fully theological approach than Hehir advocates is demanded for adequate religiopolitical engagement. Likewise, these directives of participation, mechanisms for self-critique, and learning from outsiders suggest that a more public engagement than Baxter advocates will better advance the dynamic between fidelity to the tradition and responsibility to our wider environment. A public theology that is more theological than Hehir's approach and more public than Baxter's serves to critique and round out the stance of each and build on the norms deduced from Catholic theory and praxis. Hehir's natural law approach risks relinquishing

Christian distinctiveness, whereas Baxter's stance risks irresponsibility to the range of social problems in a globalized, pluralistic environment.

We turn now to ways in which the book's conclusions reveal and surpass the false choice between the theological approaches Baxter and Hehir represent in order to approximate a faithful and responsible social ethic.

## Hehir and Baxter on Public Theology

Hehir and Baxter depart from mainstream public theology, as we have seen. Hehir favors a philosophical method as more responsive to the reality of pluralism and better suited to the complexity of the policy matters addressed. For his part, Baxter finds public theology insufficiently radical and unable to disrupt the dominant secular paradigms that privatize religion or resist a culture primarily marked by violence.[63]

In his contribution to a recent *Festschrift* for Charles Curran, Hehir distances his own preference for public philosophy from Curran's advocacy of public theology.[64] Hehir's method departs from others typically classified as operating from a public church model and who use theological categories and symbols in the service of ends similar to Hehir's philosophical approach. Hehir's approach also departs somewhat from Pope John Paul II's method. For example, Hehir writes that there exists a tension between John Paul's call in *Evangelium vitae* to enter scriptural discourse to find moral direction and "the secular pluralistic culture which the encyclical never acknowledges." It seems that Hehir might understand public theology as approaching an evangelical approach, because he judges that it insufficiently struggles with the world on its own terms, rather than associating it more closely with a public church approach as Baxter undoubtedly does. Writing on John Paul II's efforts to distinguish political institutions of democracy from the cultural context of democracies in *Centesimus annus, Veritatis splendor* and *Evangelium vitae*, Hehir notes that his proposals for civil law and policy to reflect moral law "do not struggle with the conditions which Catholic politicians, administrators, and professionals face even if they are wholly convinced of the moral vision of The Gospel of Life. . . . There is much to criticize in the cultural presuppositions of post-industrial society, but the dynamic of politics and culture requires more attention than even this long, welcome encyclical [*Evangelium vitae*] provides."[65]

Hehir asserts that the explicit use of public theology is more prominent in Protestant than Catholic circles, in large part because John Courtney Murray has been the foremost Catholic American voice on political issues and he advocated public philosophy rather than public theology. Hehir does not believe the difference to be merely terminological: as he puts it, "Murray, I believe, would have serious doubts about public theology."[66] Nevertheless, Hehir's own recent admission of the inadequacy of public philosophy for addressing premoral questions at the heart of numerous contemporary policy issues points to an advantage religious traditions can bring to public witness and advocacy.

Baxter challenges what he calls the state-centered understanding public theology promotes, that is, "a constellation of ideas that legitimate the dominant power relations of capitalist order by depicting particular forms of social and political life as natural or universal."[67] In line with his critique of Hehir's public church model, Baxter characterizes public theology's attempt to provide an ethic for wider society as undertaking a Constantinian agenda that "militates against the genuine catholicity of the church."[68] He calls the very notions of public theology and public church category mistakes, in view of the church's mission as *lumen gentium*; in his view such models understand the church as a subset of the nation, rather than as the more universal and genuinely public formation that the church already constitutes. Theologically, the reverse of that is true. He writes, "From this genuinely catholic perspective it becomes apparent that the beliefs and practices of the church do not need to be translated into public terms. They already are public. From this genuinely catholic perspective, it also becomes apparent that the public church and public theology are not very public at all. Indeed, they appear as aspects of a kind of false universalism that is endemic to the ideology of all earthly cities."[69]

Baxter would likely find even these efforts to allow different stances to mutually inform one another questionable; for he argues that mainstream efforts that rely on the typical paradigm of understanding "public" as accessible to and engaging national-level political discourse will necessarily privilege a public church model and fail to grant a radicalist approach normative status. Yet some of Baxter's more recent statements suggest that he may be more open to forms of public theology than his rhetoric implies. For in his affinity for a narrative approach, Baxter admits that particularity does not necessarily render Christian claims incommunicable beyond their community of origin, because we never know what will get through to someone else and we cannot determine in advance what mode (e.g., natural law, empirical, fully theological, radical) will convey Christian norms or commitments to another.[70] He admits that Christian ethicists frequently say particularly Christian things that will influence people beyond our community, but that his concern lies with theological literacy in forming Christians.[71]

## The Promise of Public Theology: Beyond Hehir vs. Baxter

Despite their respective reservations about the concept, public theology can serve to critique and complement Baxter's and Hehir's divergent approaches.

For on its own, each strategy is insufficient; a fully theological and fully public approach will facilitate our strategies for mutually clarifying and moving beyond the methodology of each: avoiding a false opposition between charity and structural justice and between embodiment and advocacy; utilizing liturgical resources for formation and discernment as well as education for justice and social outreach; ensuring mechanisms of self-critique to safeguard against distortion; engaging participation within and interaction without. A public theological approach like Tracy's models of classic and conversation, Hollenbach's intellectual solidarity, or Michael and Kenneth Himes' method in *Fullness of Faith* in some ways both unites and moves beyond Baxter and Hehir. Such tactics help ensure that Catholic public engagement remains firmly grounded in Catholic identity and takes seriously the empirical or worldly on its own terms. Thus, we might term a public theology like that promoted by Tracy, Hollenbach, and the Himes brothers the wide center within the possibilities and limits I have circumscribed, as it holds the most promise for the task of mutual clarification articulated above.

In the end, this public theological approach is the most adequate given the relative shortcomings of either approach on its own. Michael Barnes has similarly called for the distinctiveness and separateness of positions such as Baxter's to be counterbalanced by a greater openness to the world and cooperation in a larger common good, arguably called for by the Christian narrative itself.[72] Although many political theologians applaud postliberal theology's defense of an evangelical form of ecclesial resistance to individualistic, bourgeois academic interpretations of Christianity, they also challenge the postliberal inclination to separate the spiritual and the political, lack of attention to justice issues, to critiques of ideology, and to action for ecclesial and social reforms.[73] A fully theological and fully public approach will also help ensure attentiveness to the activity of the Spirit in the church *and* the world. In the words of Hollenbach, "The claim that there is an analogy between the inner sacramental life of the Church and the public life of society is not an argument for the re-establishment of Christendom. It is simply a claim that though neither Church nor secular society is the Kingdom, both can be *loci* in which the reality of the Kingdom becomes visible and actual in human experience. It is to maintain that the Church and secular society can both be the partial realization in history of the Kingdom of God. Whether this realization occurs in the ecclesiastical or political spheres it will have the same imaginative contours. These contours are expressed in the sacramental symbols which give form to the Church's life of worship."[74] Public theology along these lines will also aid our efforts to work together with outsiders in pursuit of such partial realizations and in light of our religious obligations to work for a more just society.

On this model, thick theological particularism and cooperative peace and justice efforts are not mutually exclusive. Reformed ethicist Richard Mouw joins a more evangelical sense of Christians as aliens or exiles with a sense of responsibility to the shared good, along similar lines to the mutual clarification our conclusions suggest. Describing Jeremiah's prophecy amid exile in Babylon, Mouw states, "Jeremiah comes to [the Israelites] and says there is a . . . new word. 'Build houses and live in them. Plant vineyards and eat the fruit thereof. Marry off your sons and daughters and multiply in the land.' And then this: 'And seek the welfare of the city in which I have placed you in exile, for in its welfare you will find your welfare. Seek the shalom of the city in which I have placed you in exile, for in its shalom you will find your shalom.' [Jer. 29: 4–9] That's a powerful word for Christians in North America today. What does it mean for us to seek the shalom of the United States with the conviction that in its shalom we will experience our shalom?"[75]

Mouw goes on to assert that this same theme given Jewish definition in Jeremiah carries over into the New Testament. He cites 1 Peter: "Beloved, I beseech you as aliens in exile, to maintain good conduct among the Gentiles so that when they see your good works they will glorify God on the day of visitation." He adds, "We are to honor all human beings" [1 Peter 2: 11–17]. As noted, scripture indeed remains multivocal with respect to the proper church-society stance, yet Mouw's connection of the sense of Christians' status as exiled pilgrims with a call to work toward the common good from his evangelical perspective illustrates possibilities for convergence and counters the false opposition of more narrow approaches. Moreover, Mouw relies on biblical rather than natural law–principles to advance the idea that we will realize our own good with reference to the common good.

This support for fully theological discourse is not meant to exclude natural law or other mediated forms from public discourse. As noted at the outset, the integration of both theologically explicit language and symbols in public debate and philosophical or more accessible arguments will help to ensure that public theology is thick enough to evoke the loyalties and imagination required to address the contemporary American cultural inadequacies, but also retains resources to address public issues amid pluralism in accessible ways.[76] The thick dimension provides more compelling and theologically persuasive elements alongside the intellectually persuasive advantages a more mediated dimension offers. Both fidelity to the tradition and responsibility to the signs of the times call for a fully theological and fully public approach. Yet efforts to communicate in accessible ways—whether by Hehir's natural law approach or political advocacy organizations' reliance on the experiences of the poor and empirical data—also remain necessary for the genuine engagement of differences in service of the common good to ensue.

# CONCLUSIONS

Despite differences in approach or divisive rhetoric, at their best the approaches of Baxter and Hehir, as well as the three Catholic political advocacy organizations, involve bringing the consequences of our supernatural end to bear on our shared life together. In light of their cumulative insights and limitations, I have suggested that an authentic and responsible social ethic requires a framework for ongoing mutual clarification of individual practices by different emphases. Whereas there exists a certain moral attractiveness to a radicalist approach such as absolute pacifism, such a stance comes up short on the axis of social responsibility. Conversely, although it might be tempting to hastily dismiss a more enclosed posture out of hand as inherently irresponsible, a stance that focuses on embodiment has much to offer in terms of formation in the tradition and integrity of approach. Complementary insights emerge from each basic stance that reflect the tensions inherent in the church-world question between the times and that should serve to mutually critique divergent approaches. It is my hope that the two-step dynamic between (1) different strands within the fullness of our tradition and (2) between fidelity to that tradition and responsibility to the signs of the times provides a useful guide for public theology and political advocacy. At the least, I hope that this framework and its companion directives will help move discussions of social ethics and public engagement toward a more creative and dynamic tension between distinct emphases, rather than mere coexistence or the destructive tension that often characterizes the debate. Mutual clarification of diverse approaches along the lines this study suggests may allow for a move away from rigid typologies and toward prophetic, critical engagement that models gospel values and engages the wider world on issues that touch human life and dignity.

Finally, these theoretical and practical analyses make clear that the appropriate context for such engagement should be an approach that remains fully theological and fully public. This theoretical stance will allow Catholics to remain at once "vigorous in stating our own case and attentive in hearing others in public life."[77] As these theoretical and practical analyses demonstrate, bringing Christian values to bear on political life involves carefully navigating among various risks. It will be no easy task to creatively combine insights from divergent models in the manners I have suggested in practice. To begin, just embodiment suggests organizations implement effective structures of accountability, transparency, and participation that foster lay empowerment.[78] It demands that Christian groups serve as models of justice by the way that they care for those they employ. Formation for prudential discernment requires quality liturgy, prophetic preaching on the full range of issues on which the tradition bears, and ongoing adult faith formation. It will also be nourished by ongoing exchanges among Catholics engaged in parish leadership, political advocacy, and social ethics.

The comprehensive and interrelated nature of the Catholic social vision invites open and sustained intraecclesial dialogue to counter ideological polarization and the distortion resulting from narrow or single-issue agendas. This might entail collaborative efforts among just-war proponents and pacifists or antiabortion and child welfare specialists. Ecumenical and interreligious dialogue will help ensure we remain attentive to the fullness of our tradition, insights from others, and our own blind spots. The dynamic of politics (including the complexity of issues and the fact that people of goodwill may disagree over specific strategies for realizing moral principles in public life) also suggests that active participation in broader public discourse will engender better applications of constant principles to the signs of the ever-changing times. John Allen identifies elements at the core of a spirituality of dialogue that provide particularly relevant parameters for each of these levels of exchange: epistemological humility; solid formation in Catholic tradition as a means of creating a common language; patience; global perspective; and full-bodied expression of Catholic identity.[79] Such discourse often ensues within academic confines alone, yet there is a demonstrated need for structuring such exchanges among and between bishops, theologians, activists, coalition partners, elected officials, and Christians themselves. Listening sessions should become the norm rather than the exception, in order to hear from our laity and citizenry as well as our ecclesial and political leadership. Deliberative dialogue in such veins will help us move beyond agreeing to disagree and toward authentic and responsible public theology.

Whatever concrete forms they take, efforts in service of Christian public witness must heartily embrace the challenge of remaining at once prophetic and public, light and leaven, pilgrim and citizen.

## NOTES

1. J. Bryan Hehir, "From Church-State to Religion and Politics: The Case of the U.S. Catholic Bishops," in Joseph F. Kelly, ed., *American Catholics* (Wilmington, DE: Michael Glazier Inc., 1989), 51–72 at 67–68.

2. Hehir drafted much of Cardinal Bernardin's material, and the presidential addresses of Bishops Malone, Roach, and Quinn between 1982 and 1988. Hehir is quick to point out that "drafting never means ownership," but his influence and language can be detected in these collaborative efforts, as well as in the peace pastoral, consistent ethic of life arguments, and the direction and rhetoric of the office of the Social Development and World Peace (SDWP) and its leadership since Hehir's time there. Interview with J. Bryan Hehir, July 13, 2002, Alexandria, Virginia.

3. Speaking about "The Challenge of Peace," Bernardin notes, "Despite the radical moral skepticism of the pastoral letter about ever containing the use of nuclear weapons within justifiable limits, the bishops were not persuaded that this moral judgment should lead to an ecclesial posture of withdrawal from dialogue or participation in the public life of the nation. Rather, in accord with the traditional Catholic conception, they affirmed a posture of dialogue with the secular world. I am the first to say—after the past three years—that it is a precarious posture, but one I find more adequate than either total silence within society or absolute separation from society." See Joseph Cardinal Bernardin, "Church Impact on Public Policy," *Origins* 13, no. 34 (February 2, 1984): 566–69 at 567.

4. Telephone interview with Johnny Zokovitch, PCUSA communications director, April 7, 2003.

5. Hehir might argue that its use generally is limited to its inner-ecclesial address, such as pastorals, such that it remains permissible, yet the USCCB uses scripture in its dual audience documents, as well.

6. Mary Hanna, "Bishops as Political Leaders," in Charles W. Dunn, ed., *Religion in American Politics* (Washington, DC: Congressional Quarterly Press, 1989), 75–86 at 85.

7. Thornton emphasizes the solidaristic aspect of Catholic anthropology and the fact that structural changes and priorities impact large numbers of people to whom we are all connected and for whom we are all responsible.

8. Interview with Kathy Thornton, R.S.M., Washington, D.C., July 26, 2002.

9. Telephone interview with John Carr, director, SDWP, USCCB, April 15, 2003.

10. Ibid.

11. Panel discussion on legislative office visits with Mark Gallagher (associate director, OGL, USCCB) and Kathy Curran (policy advisor, Office of Domestic Social Development, SDWP, USCCB) Annual Catholic Social Ministry Gathering, "Catholic Social Mission: Seeking Justice, Overcoming Poverty, Building Peace" (Washington, D.C.: February 9–12, 2003). Dave Robinson similarly notes that to compartmentalize Christ so that his teachings and life only impact that narrow area of life often characterized as "religious," or defined in terms of personal piety, is to be less than authentic in our discipleship to Christ. "Christ demands a say over all aspects of our lives—from the work we do to the way we raise our children to the way we engage politically" (telephone interview with Dave Robinson, May 5, 2005).

12. For an analysis of how just-war and pacifist responses to the events of September 11th similarly challenge typical theoretical distinctions, see Kristin Heyer, "U.S. Catholic Discipleship and Citizenship: Patriotism or Dissent?" *Political Theology* 4, no. 2 (June 2003): 149–77, esp. 165–74.

13. John A. Coleman, S.J., "Under the Cross and the Flag: Reflections on Discipleship and Citizenship in America," *America* (May 11, 1996): 6–14 at 13.

14. Coleman, "Under the Cross and Flag," 13.

15. Interview with Anne Curtis, RSM, Washington, D.C., July 25, 2003.

16. Ibid.

17. Ibid.

18. USCCB, *A Place at the Table: A Catholic Recommitment to Overcome Poverty and to Respect the Dignity of All God's Children* (Washington, D.C.: USCC, 2002). Carr notes that in contrast to this Catholic outlook, "the problem with Washington is that everyone is in love with one leg of the table!" Carr interview.

19. Bishop Ramón Torella Cascante, former auxiliary bishop in Barcelona and vice president of the Pontifical Commission Justice and Peace (head of drafting committee and special secretary of the 1971 synod for the theme of justice) makes this same point in an analogous way. Alluding to how work for justice is related to preaching the gospel and the difficulty of preaching the gospel in isolation from witness of action for peace and justice, Bishop Cascante emphasizes that "the dual dangers of dichotomy and identification must be avoided." Seeking to avoid a "fatal dualism between faith and justice," he said, "the synod should provide integration and synthesis." See Charles M. Murphy, "Action for Justice as Constitutive of the Preaching of the Gospel: What Did the 1971 Synod Mean?" *Theological Studies* 44, no. 2 (2001): 298–311 at 303.

20. Interview with NETWORK staff member, July 2002, and confirmed with Gudorf via email correspondence, May 25, 2005.

21. See Hollenbach, *Nuclear Ethics: A Christian Moral Argument* (New York/ Ramsey, NJ: Paulist Press, 1983), 31–32.

22. Baxter accuses a public church approach of falsely separating faith and reason or theology and politics, as we have seen, but Hehir might say that a stance that denounces efforts to communicate the public significance of faith (such as Baxter's) also leads to privatization.

23. See Lisa Sowle Cahill, *Love Your Enemies: Discipleship, Pacifism and Just War Theory* (Minneapolis: Fortress Press, 1994), 83.

24. Ibid., 82.

25. Thomas Massaro, S.J., *Catholic Social Teaching and United States Welfare Reform* (Collegeville: MN: Liturgical Press, 1998), 57–58. Massaro writes, "the future credibility and influence of Catholic social teaching within the American context is inextricably intertwined with the endeavor of ongoing ecclesiastical renewal. Until Church reform addresses these concerns, Catholic social teaching will remain not only a flawed instrument for public policy analysis, but also something of a stumbling block on the path which American Catholicism is following in its effort to become truly a 'public church,'" 58.

26. See Bishop Raymond A. Lucker, "Justice in the Church: The Church as Example," in John A. Coleman, S.J., ed., *One Hundred Years of Catholic Social Thought* (Maryknoll, NY: Orbis, 1991), 88–102.

27. Synod of Bishops, *Justitia in mundo* (1971), esp. chapter 3, in David O'Brien and Thomas A. Shannon, eds., *Catholic Social Thought: The Documentary Heritage* (Maryknoll, NY: Orbis Books, 1998), 288–300, esp. 294–95.

28. In *Dignitatis humanae* the Council admits ways in which it has learned from the wider experience of human beings (no. 1), and a string of papal apologies indicate that the contemporary church is somewhat conscious of its pilgrim nature, although further steps are necessary. See Charles E. Curran, *Catholic Social Teaching, 1891–Present: A Historical, Theological and Ethical Analysis*, (Washington, D.C.: Georgetown University Press, 2002), 104–5. Reflecting on Pope John Paul II's acknowledgement of Christian wrongs against non-Catholics throughout its history

and prayers for forgiveness in March of 2000 (Lent of the Jubilee year), Margaret Farley has written, "Embodying vulnerability in the expression of truth, never was the church more strong. Acknowledging not only mistakes but real evil, never was the church more prophetic in its commitment to justice. Respecting those who differ from the church—not only in belief but in policy—never were the church's own hopes for peace more clear." See Margaret Farley, "The Church in the Public Forum: Scandal or Prophetic Witness?" in Curran and Leslie Griffin, eds., *The Catholic Church, Morality and Politics* (New York/Mahwah, NJ: Paulist Press, 2001) 205–23 at 220. The piece originally appeared in the *Proceedings of the Catholic Theological Society of America* 55 (2000): 87–101.

29. Telephone interview with Sharon Daly, Catholic Charities vice president for social policy (former director, Domestic Social Development Office), April 1, 2003. She adds that, regrettably, diocesan Catholic school teachers' wages are "abysmally low" compared with public school teachers' wages.

30. Tracy writes, "Each of us contributes more to the common good when we dare to undertake a journey into our own particularity . . . than when we attempt to homogenize all differences in favor of some lowest common denominator . . . [or] are tempted to root out all particularity and call it publicness." See David Tracy, "Defending the Public Character of Theology," *The Christian Century* 98 (April 1981): 350–56 at 355. For a discussion of some of the underlying similarities between Lindbeck's and Baxter's work, see Michael Barnes, "Community, Clannishness and the Common Good," in James Donahue and M. Theresa Moser, R.S.C.J., eds., *Religion, Ethics and the Common Good*, Annual Publication of the College Theology Society 41 (Mystic, CT: Twenty-third Publications, 1996), 27–52.

31. Werner Jeanrond, "Theology in the Context of Pluralism and Postmodernity: David Tracy's Theological Method," in David Jasper, ed., *Postmodernism, Literature and Theology* (London: Macmillan Press, 1993), 143–63 at 145.

32. David Tracy, *Plurality and Ambiguity: Hermeneutics, Religion, Hope* (Chicago: University of Chicago Press, 1987), 112. It is interesting to note that although postliberal theologians such as Lindbeck (or arguably Baxter) contrast their own approach with those that seek to learn from secular society and other disciplines, postliberals use the analyses of individuals such as Thomas Kuhn, Peter Berger, Richard Rorty and others to justify their reliance on the Christian community alone. As Barnes ("Community, Clannishness and the Common Good," 35) puts it, "The irony is obvious: it is not just the community's narratives and practices but the largely secular and rational analyses of contemporary philosophy, sociology, and history that tell postliberal theologians they must rely on community narratives and practices alone."

33. David Hollenbach, "Tradition, Historicity and Truth in Theological Ethics," in Lisa Sowle Cahill and James F. Childress, eds., *Christian Ethics: Problems and Prospects* (Cleveland, OH: Pilgrim Press, 1996), 60–75 at 72–73.

34. See Kathryn Tanner, *Theories of Culture: A New Agenda for Theology* (Minneapolis: Fortress Press, 1997) for her argument that theological models of sectarian impermeability are practically impossible and that theology and religion always consist of "borrowed materials."

35. Thornton refers to the makeup of its board (two Native American women, two Asian American women, one Hispanic woman, one African American woman—

one-half of the board consists of women of color) as another effort to model in its leadership what it wants to see in the world.

36. As we noted in chapter 4, NETWORK "takes seriously the dialogic nature of the church and so we understand our responsibility as individuals and a group to reflect on the gospel and our life experience and offer our interpretation to the church," in Thornton's words. (Thornton interview.)

37. 1998 NETWORK membership survey. This comment was taken from the summary of responses from coalition members. In comments taken from the summary of responses from NETWORK founders, former and adjunct staff, respondents wrote "historically it was very unusual to have women lobbying and claiming the Catholic identity. We were an alternative to the clerics. However it defined a perspective and not an issue focus so it has been confusing and sometimes not clear. Others may not view us as feminist as it is defined by most as 'pro-choice.'"

38. 1998 NETWORK membership survey.

39. Interview with Catherine Pinkerton, C.S.J., Washington, D.C., July 23, 2002.

40. Stanley Hauerwas echoes this need for discernment, disputing stark alternatives between complete withdrawal and complete involvement: "The issue is how the church can provide the interpretive categories to help Christians better understand the positive and negative aspects of their societies and guide their subsequent selective participation. . . . What is required for Christians is not withdrawal but a sense of selective service and the ability to set priorities . . . such determinations can only be made by developing the skills of discrimination fostered in and through the church." Stanley Hauerwas, *Christian Existence Today: Essays on Church, World, and Living in Between*, (Grand Rapids, MI: Brazos, 1988), 11, 15–16.

41. Hehir interview, July 13, 2002.

42. Mark Searle, "Serving the Lord with Justice," in Searle, ed., *Liturgy and Social Justice* (Collegeville, MN: Liturgical Press, 1980), 13–35 at 29.

43. The USCCB refers to lifelong adult faith formation as "the chief form of catechesis." See USCCB, "Our Hearts Were Burning Within Us," (Washington, D.C.: USCC, 1999), 3. As Thomas Groome puts it, "Reaching beyond what the *GDC* [*General Directory for Catechesis*] calls 'mere information,' catechesis should enable participants to comprehend and embrace Christian teachings with conviction, to allow such convictions to shape their identity and holiness of life, and their commitment to forge God's reign in the world." See Thomas Groome, "The Purpose of Christian Catechesis," in Thomas Groome and Michael Corso, eds., *Empowering Catechetical Leaders*, (Washington, D.C.: National Catholic Educational Association, 1999). The bishops' "Pastoral Plan for Adult Formation in the U.S." enumerates moral formation among its six dimensions of adult faith formation, specifying, "Learn how to acquire and follow a well-formed conscience in personal and social life, clarifying current religious and moral questions in the light of faith, and cultivating a Christian discernment of the ethical implications of developments in the socio-cultural order." See USCCB, "Our Hearts Were Burning Within Us," 31.

44. "The peace and economic pastorals were written only after consultation with specialists who in many cases opposed church views, whereas the development of policy recommendations on abortion has not involved formal consultation with demographers, family planners, feminists, and legal and medical pro-

fessionals who do not accept the church's moral teachings on abortion." See Mary C. Segers, "The American Catholic Church in Contemporary American Politics," introduction to her edited volume, *Church Polity and American Politics: Issues in Contemporary American Catholicism* (New York: Garland Publishing, 1990), 3–26 at 11–12.

45. Hehir calls this method "democratic," but distinguishes it from the church conducting an opinion poll: "The core of these pastoral letters is a normative doctrine which is in place; the commentary relates much more to the persuasive quality with which the moral doctrine is conveyed, the quality of the empirical analysis in the letters and the wisdom of the policy recommendations." See Hehir, "From Church-State to Religion and Politics," 69.

46. Bishop James Malone, "The Church: Its Strength and Its Questions," *Origins* 16, no. 23 (November 20, 1986): 393–98 at 395.

47. Phillip Berryman, *Our Unfinished Business: The U.S. Catholic Bishops' Letters on Peace and the Economy* (New York: Pantheon Books, 1989), 11.

48. John T. Noonan, Jr., "The Bishops and the Ruling Class: The Moral Formation of Public Policy," Charles Curran and Leslie Griffin, eds., *The Catholic Church, Morality and Politics, Readings in Moral Theology* No. 12, (Mahwah, NJ: Paulist Press, 2001) 224–38 at 233. Noonan refers here to the process that produced the peace pastoral.

49. Mary Jo Bane argues "a process of deliberative democracy and discernment, both in creating policy documents and disseminating them, could make for a much more effective public voice." She contrasts that possibility to her perception that the effectiveness of the USCCB and Catholic Charities USA is currently limited by the fact that they are not perceived as speaking for a sixty-million-member church and its voters. See Mary Jo Bane, "Voice and Loyalty in the Church: The People of God, Politics, and Management," in Stephen J. Pope, ed., *Common Calling: The Laity and Governance of the Catholic Church* (Washington, D.C.: Georgetown University Press, 2004), 181–94 at 186.

50. For a recent theological discussion of how structures of participation, consultation, and accountability can revitalize the church, see Canon Law Society of America President Sharon Euart, R.S.M., "Structures for Participation in the Church," *Origins* 35, no. 2 (May 26, 2005): 17–25.

51. Whereas a comparative study undertaken several decades ago might have ranked the bishops' conference as most partisan resulting from its more narrow focus (at least at the level of electoral politics with respect to the abortion issue), in this more contemporary analysis with the USCCB's expansion to prioritize a full range of interrelated social issues, it ranks as least partisan among our case studies (up through 2003).

52. J. Bryan Hehir, "The Consistent Ethic: Public Policy Implications," in Thomas G. Fuechtmann, ed., *Consistent Ethic of Life* (Kansas City, MO: Sheed & Ward, 1988), 218–36 at 233.

53. For example, John Carr believes that "Catholic progressives should be measured by how we stand up for human life, how consistently, how courageously, how persistently. And Catholic conservatives should be measured by how often, how consistently, how persistently, how courageously we stand up for human dignity. The consistent life ethic doesn't give anyone a free pass. It challenges all of us."

John Carr, "The Church in the Modern World: Learning Lessons, Making a Difference and Keeping Hope," address to Catholic Social Ministry Gathering, February 21, 2005.

54. In "Living the Gospel of Life," the bishops refer to direct attacks on human life such as abortion and euthanasia as strikes at the house's foundation and neglect of these issues as equivalent to building a house on sand. USCCB, "Living the Gospel of Life: A Challenge to American Catholics," (Washington, D.C.: USCC, 1998), no. 23.

55. Theodore Cardinal McCarrick, "The Call to Serve in a Divided Society," *Origins* 34, no. 40 (March 24, 2005), 638.

56. CDF, "Doctrinal Note on Some Questions Regarding the Participation of Catholics in Public Life," *Origins* 32, no. 4.

57. Richard Doerflinger, "The Pro-Life Message and Catholic Social Teaching: Problems of Reception," in Margaret O'Brien Steinfels, ed., *American Catholics, American Cultures: Tradition & Resistance* (Lanham, MD: Rowman & Littlefield, 2004), 49–58 at 49–50.

58. Joseph Cardinal Bernardin, "A Consistent Ethic of Life: Continuing the Dialogue," in Thomas G. Fuechtmann, *Consistent Ethic of Life* (Kansas City, MO: Sheed & Ward, 1988), 12–19 at 15.

59. In his discussion of Bernardin's "Consistent Ethic of Life," James Walter argues that "one of the hallmarks of an *adequate* vision of moral experience is its ability to tie together attitude and doing, commitment and application. It seems to me that this is the adequacy Bernardin hopes to achieve in his emphasis on consistency." See Walter, "Response to John Finnis: A Theological Critique," in Fuechtmann, *Consistent Ethic of Life*, (182–95). This suggests a norm of comprehensiveness and consistency also supports my norm that unites embodiment and advocacy.

60. Daly interview.

61. Bernardin, "A Consistent Ethic of Life: Continuing the Dialogue," 15.

62. Ibid., 18.

63. "Given the present field of Catholic social ethics, [critiquing bourgeois religion] requires distinguishing the radicalist perspective of the Catholic Worker from the bourgeois perspective of public theology and unmasking public theology as a discourse that legitimates the nation-state. It requires a demolition of public theology using the 'dynamite of the church.'" Baxter uses "bourgeois religion" to refer to religion that "conforms to norms established by the social relations of capitalist production, religion that is designed to legitimate the workings of the state and market." See Michael J. Baxter, "'Blowing the Dynamite of the Church': Catholic Radicalism from a Catholic Radicalist Perspective," Michael L. Budde and Robert W. Brimlow, eds., *The Church as Counterculture* (Albany: State University of New York Press, 2000), 195–212 at 208.

64. J. Bryan Hehir, "A Catholic Troeltsch? Curran on the Social Ministry of the Church," in James J. Walter, Timothy E. O'Connell, and Thomas A. Shannon, eds., *A Call to Fidelity: On the Moral Theology of Charles E. Curran* (Washington, D.C.: Georgetown University Press, 2002), 191–207 at 203.

65. J. Bryan Hehir, "Get a (Culture of) Life: The Pope's Moral Vision," *Commonweal* 122, no. 10 (May 19, 1995): 8–9, at 9.

66. J. Bryan Hehir, "Public Theology in Contemporary America: Editor's Forum," *Religion and American Culture* 10, no. 1 (Winter 2000): 1–27, at 21.

67. Baxter, "Blowing the Dynamite of the Church," 207.

68. Baxter, "Review Essay: The Non-Catholic Character of the 'Public Church,'" *Modern Theology* 11, no. 2 (April 1995): 243–58 at 257. My conclusions throughout previous chapters challenge Baxter's generalization that public theology by nature advances a Constantinian agenda.

69. Baxter, "Review Essay," 257.

70. We cannot determine in advance what will best convey our faith by adhering to either an approach such as George Lindbeck's or David Tracy's, he notes (Baxter interview, July 18, 2002, Notre Dame, IN). We might add that one cannot determine in advance whether an evangelical or public church approach or a philosophical or theological argument will be accessible and compelling beyond the Christian community. Baxter's sentiment recalls Ronald Thiemann's claim in chapter 1 (in response to postmodern critiques) that "we cannot by philosophical or political fiat decide in advance which arguments we will accept in the public square. Rather, we must learn to understand and evaluate all arguments that seek a public hearing" (Thiemann, *Religion in Public Life*, 156).

71. Baxter conveys an analogy from theologian William Cavanaugh (also trained under Hauerwas) who likens the choice to a phenomenon prevalent in bilingual homes. Members of immigrant families who speak Spanish at home and English in public eventually lose their Spanish; likewise, if the religious language goes (as he argues that it does so not only when we use natural law approaches but also when public theology mediates gospel claims via social ethics or Catholic social principles), then we "lose all bearings" and we "lose our whole solar system" and he has himself encountered such theological illiteracy as a teacher even in a Catholic college (Baxter interview). We have treated the importance of formation in an integrated approach above.

72. Barnes, "Community, Clannishness and the Common Good," 30, 33.

73. Bradford Hinze and George Schner, "Postliberal Theology and Roman Catholic Theology," *Religious Studies Review* 21, no. 4 (October 1995): 299–304 at 302.

74. David Hollenbach, "A Prophetic Church and the Catholic Sacramental Imagination," in John C. Haughey, S.J., ed., *The Faith that Does Justice: Examining the Christian Sources for Social Change* (New York: Paulist Press, 1977), 234–63 at 251–52.

75. Richard Mouw, "Evangelical Protestants in the Public Square: Drawbacks and Opportunities," Annual Lecture on Prophetic Voices of the Church, Boisi Center for Religion and American Public Life, Boston College, Chestnut Hills, MA. April 10, 2003). Transcript available at www.bc.edu/bc_org/research/rapl/word/mouw_april2003.doc (accessed May 27, 2005).

76. By cultural inadequacies, I simply mean the lack of community, identity, purpose; eviscerated public discourse; and prevalent individualism referred to in chapter 1.

77. Bernardin, "A Consistent Ethic of Life,"1–11 at 10. Bernardin summarizes well the style with which Catholics should engage in public and political life: "The style should be persuasive, not preachy. We should use the model of the Second

Vatican Council's *Pastoral Constitution on the Church in the Modern World*. We should be convinced that we have much to learn from the world and much to teach it. We should be confident but collegial with others who seek similar goals but may differ on means and methods. A confident church will speak its mind, seek as a community to live its convictions, but leave space for others to speak to us, help us to grow from their perspective, and to collaborate with them." See Joseph Cardinal Bernardin, "The Consistent Ethic after 'Webster': Opportunities and Dangers," *Commonweal* 117 (April 20, 1990): 248. Interestingly, Richard Mouw has argued for a quite similar style, inspired by Martin Marty's "convicted civility." Mouw writes, "Marty has also influenced the ways in which I think about social ethics. For example, I was struck by a provocative comment he made in a 1981 autobiographical book, *By Way of Response* [Nashville: Abingdon Press]. A problem in contemporary life, he said, is that the folks who are good at being civil often don't have very strong convictions, and the people who have strong convictions usually aren't very civil. We need to find a way of combining a civil spirit with a 'passionate intensity' about what we believe." Mouw writes that Marty's call for a "convicted civility" inspired Richard Mouw's book *Uncommon Decency: Christian Civility in an Uncivil World* (Downers Grove, IL: Intervarsity Press, 1992). See Richard Mouw, "Public Religion: Through Thick and Thin," *The Christian Century* (June 7–14, 2000): 648–51 at 648.

78. For a timely collection of essays on these topics as related to ecclesial governance, see Stephen J. Pope, ed., *Common Calling: The Laity and Governance of the Catholic Church*, Washington, D.C.: Georgetown University Press, 2004.

79. These elements by the Vatican correspondent well reflect the methodological directives and broader efforts to combine distinctive identity with openness to others outlined herein. John Allen, Jr., "A Spirituality of Dialogue for Catholics," (Sixth Annual Catholic Common Ground Initiative Lecture, Catholic University of America, Washington, D.C., June 25, 2004) *Origins* 34, no. 8 (July 15, 2004): 122–26. The Catholic Common Ground Initiative's Principles of Dialogue are also relevant; see www.nplc.org/commonground/dialogue.htm (accessed May 24, 2005).

# Bibliography of Primary Sources

**MICHAEL BAXTER, C.S.C.**

"Review Essay: The Non-Catholic Character of the 'Public Church.'" *Modern Theology* 11, no. 2 (April 1995): 243–58.

"Writing History in a World without Ends: An Evangelical Catholic Critique of United States Catholic History." *Pro Ecclesia* 5 (Fall 1996): 440–69

"Reintroducing Virgil Michel: Towards a Counter-Tradition of Catholic Social Ethics in the United States." *Communio* 24 (Fall 1997): 499–528.

"Catholicism and Liberalism: Kudos and Questions for Communion Ecclesiology." *The Review of Politics* 60, no. 4 (Fall 1998): 734–64.

"Blowing the Dynamite of the Church: Catholic Radicalism from a Catholic Radicalist Perspective." Talk delivered at Creighton University on January 26, 1999. In John P. O'Callaghan, "Fr. Michael Baxter on 'Catholic Radicalism.' *Center for the Study of Religion and Society* newsletter, 11, no. 1 (Fall 1999). Available at http://puffin.creighton.edu/human/CSRS/news/F992.html. (Accessed on November 5, 2002.)

"In the World But Not of It." Interview with the editors of *U.S. Catholic*. *U.S. Catholic* 66, no. 8 (August 2001): 24–28.

"'Blowing the Dynamite of the Church': Catholic Radicalism from a Catholic Radicalist Perspective." In Michael L. Budde and Robert W. Brimlow, eds., *The Church as Counterculture*. Albany: State University of New York Press, 2000.

"Is this Just War? Two Catholic perspectives on the war in Afghanistan." Interview by editors with Baxter and Lisa Sowle Cahill. *U.S. Catholic* 66, no. 12 (December 2001): 12–16.

"Rekindling the Spiritual Revolution: Merton and Company on Faith and Reason." Address delivered to "New Wine, New Wineskins" conference, Notre Dame, IN (July 22, 2002).

"Dispelling the 'We' Fallacy from the Body of Christ: The Task of Catholics in a Time of War." *The South Atlantic Quarterly* 101, no. 2 (Spring 2002): 361–73.

"A Sign of Peace: The Mission of the Church to the Nations," *Catholic Theological Society of America, Proceedings* 59 (2004): 19–41.

## J. BRYAN HEHIR

"The Perennial Need for Philosophical Discourse." In David Hollenbach, S.J., ed., "Current Theology: Theology and Philosophy in Public: A Symposium on John Courtney Murray's Unfinished Agenda." *Theological Studies* 40 (1979): 710–13.

"Continuity and Change in the Social Teaching of the Church." In John W. Houck and Oliver F. Williams, C.S.C., eds., *Co-creation and Capitalism: John Paul II's* Laborem Exercens. Washington, D.C.: University Press of America, 1983.

"From the Pastoral Constitution of Vatican II to *The Challenge of Peace.*" In Philip J. Murnion, ed., *Catholics and Nuclear War: A Commentary on* The Challenge of Peace, *The U.S. Catholic Bishops' Pastoral Letter on War and Peace.* New York: Crossroad, 1983.

"The Implications of Structured Pluralism: A Public Church," *Origins* 14, no. 3 (May 31, 1984): 40–43.

"Church-State and Church-World: The Ecclesiological Implications." *Catholic Theological Society of America Proceedings* 41 (1986): 54–74.

"Church-Type Reinvigorated: The Bishops' Letter." In Paul Peachey, ed., *Peace, Politics, and the People of God.* Philadelphia: Fortress Press, 1986, 47–70.

"The Consistent Ethic: Public Policy Implications." In Thomas G. Fuechtmann, ed., *Consistent Ethic of Life.* Kansas City, MO: Sheed & Ward, 1988.

"From Church-State to Religion and Politics: The Case of the U.S. Catholic Bishops." In Joseph F. Kelly, ed., *American Catholics.* Wilmington, Delaware: Michael Glazier Inc., 1989.

"Papal Foreign Policy." *Foreign Policy* 78 (Spring 1990): 26–48.

"Responsibilities and Temptations of Power: A Catholic View." *Journal of Law and Religion* 8, no. 1–2 (1990): 71–83.

"The Right and Competence of the Church." In John A. Coleman, S.J., ed., *One Hundred Years of Catholic Social Thought: Celebration and Challenge.* Maryknoll, NY: Orbis, 1991.

"The Social Role of the Church: Leo XIII, Vatican II and John Paul II." In Oliver F. Williams, C.S.C. and John W. Houck, eds., *Catholic Social Thought and the New World Order: Building on One Hundred Years.* Notre Dame, IN: University of Notre Dame Press, 1993.

"Get a (Culture of) Life: the Pope's Moral Vision." *Commonweal* 122, no. 10 (May 19, 1995): 8–9.

"The Church in the World: Responding to the Call of the Council." In James L. Heft, SM, ed., *Faith and the Intellectual Life: Marianist Award Lectures.* Notre Dame, IN: University of Notre Dame Press, 1996.

"Personal Faith, the Public Church, and the Role of Theology," Convocation Address at the Opening of the 180th Year. *Harvard Divinity Bulletin* 26, no. 1 (1996): 4–5.

"Catholic Theology at its Best." *Harvard Divinity Bulletin* 27, no. 2/3 (1998): 13–14.

"Public Theology in Contemporary America: Editor's Forum." *Religion and American Culture* 10, no. 1 (Winter 2000): 1–27.

"Response to Stephen Pope's 'Catholic Social Teaching and the American Experience.'" Spring 2000 Joint Consultation, *American Catholics in the Public Square* initiative, Commonweal Foundation and Faith and Reason Institute.

Annapolis, MD, June 2–4, 2000. Available online at www.catholicsinthepublic square.org/papers/spring2000joint/pope/popeprint.htm. (Accessed March 18, 2003.)

"The Prophetic Voice of the Church." Lecture given at Boston College sponsored by the Boisi Center for Religion and American Public Life, April 1, 2002. Transcript available at www.bc.edu/bc_org/research/rapl/index.htm. (Accessed June 15, 2003.)

"A Catholic Troeltsch? Curran on the Social Ministry of the Church." In James J. Walter, Timothy E. O'Connell and Thomas A. Shannon, eds., *A Call to Fidelity: On the Moral Theology of Charles E. Curran.* Washington, D.C.: Georgetown University Press, 2002.

## UNPUBLISHED INTERVIEWS

### Individuals Interviewed

Baxter, Michael, C.S.C. 2002. Interview by Kristin E. Heyer. Tape recording. July 18. University of Notre Dame, South Bend, IN.

Hehir, J. Bryan. 2002. Interview by Kristin E. Heyer. Tape recording. July 13. St. Mary's, Alexandria, VA.

### Organizations Interviewed

### NETWORK Social Justice Lobby

Borden, Stephanie Beck. 2002. Interview by Kristin E. Heyer. Tape recording. July 23. Washington, D.C.

Clark, Mary Elizabeth, S.S.J. 2002. Interview by Kristin E. Heyer. Tape recording. July 24. Washington, D.C.

Curtis, Anne, R.S.M. 2002. Interview by Kristin E. Heyer. Tape recording. July 23. Washington, D.C.

Lauterbach, Christine. 2002. Interview by Kristin E. Heyer. Tape recording. July 25. Washington, D.C.

Niedringhaus, Stephanie. 2002. Interview by Kristin E. Heyer. Tape recording. July 22. Washington, D.C.

Pinkerton, Catherine, C.S.J. 2002. Interview by Kristin E. Heyer. Tape recording. July 23. Washington, D.C.

Scanlon, Amy. 2002. Interview by Kristin E. Heyer. Tape recording. July 26. Washington, D.C.

Sotelo, Nicole. 2003. Interview by Kristin E. Heyer. E-mail interview. March 24.

Thornton, Kathy, R.S.M. 2002. Interview by Kristin E. Heyer. Tape recording. July 26. Washington, D.C.

### United States Conference of Catholic Bishops

Carr, John. 2003. Interview by Kristin E. Heyer. Telephone interview, notes. April 15.

Daly, Sharon. 2003. Interview by Kristin E. Heyer. Telephone interview, notes. April 1.

## Pax Christi USA

Robinson, Dave. 2005. Interview by Kristin E. Heyer. May 5. E-mail interview.
Stokan, Jean. 2003. Interview by Kristin E. Heyer. Telephone interview, notes. April 7.
Zokovitch, Johnny. 2003. Interview by Kristin E. Heyer. Telephone interview, notes. April 7.

# Index

Note: Page numbers followed by *n* plus a number refer to notes.